AMERICAN Headway

Proven success beyond the classroom

2

THIRD EDITION

John and Liz Soars

Scope and Sequence LANGUAGE INPUT

SKILLS DEVELOPMENT

READING	LISTENING	SPEAKING	WRITING
A blind date A newspaper sets up a date between two readers. How will they get along? (jigsaw) p. 6	**My oldest friend** Three people talk about their oldest friend p. 5 **A blind date** Sally and Dominic talk about their date p. 6	**Discussion** Talking about your friends p. 5 **Exchanging information** Talking about a couple on a blind date p. 6 **Social expressions** Acting out conversations p. 9	**Describing friends** Symbols for correcting mistakes *enjoing* Sp Writing about your best friend p. 100
The happiness quiz *How happy are you?* Find out how happy you are, and how to be happier p. 14	**Song** *Money* – the best things in life are free p. 14 **Getting along with your neighbors** Two neighbors gossip about each other. Do they see things in the same way? p. 16	**Discussion** What is most important to you – money, job, health …? p. 10 **Exchanging information** Ask and answer questions about three people p. 12 **Describing** My perfect day p. 13	**Writing a postcard** Synonyms *great, wonderful, amazing …* Writing a postcard about a vacation p. 101
The flight attendant who lost his cool *Steven Slater* Day-by-day newspaper articles as a story breaks, goes global, and then dies p. 22	**The news** Radio news items p. 21 **Dictation** Transcribing a news story p. 21	**Narrating** Retelling a news story p. 20 **Project** Research a news story that interests you – tell the class p. 21 **Discussion** Famous for 15 minutes p. 22	**Narrative writing** Building a story *… a burglar broke into a large, expensive house….* Picture story *A fishy tale* Comparing stories p. 102
Unusual places to eat *No ordinary place to eat!* Three extraordinary restaurants (jigsaw) p. 30	**Our diet** A couple talks about their diet p. 27 **Unusual places to eat** People talk about their experiences of eating in extraordinary restaurants p. 30	**Discussion** A good diet p. 27 **Exchanging information** Talking about a restaurant p. 30 **Role play** Acting out a conversation p. 32	**Writing an email** Linking words *but, although, however so, because* Writing an email to a friend p. 104
Hope for the future *The girl with two families* A girl from Belarus whose life changed when she visited Ireland p. 38	**How does it feel to be 20-something?** Three people talk about what it's like to be in their twenties p. 37	**Describing** Talking about someone in their twenties p. 37 **Discussion** Living at home/leaving home p. 37 **Role play** An interview with Palina p. 38	**Writing for talking** My dreams for the future *In five years I would like to …* *One day I hope to …* Writing about future plans – tell the class p. 105
Multicultural London *The world on one street* Four people from different cultures talk about living in the most cosmopolitan city in the world (jigsaw) p. 46	**My family** People talk about who they are like in their family p. 45 ***What's happening?*** Deciding what to do in Los Angeles p. 49	**Talking about you** Who are you like in your family? p. 45 **Exchanging information** Talking about a new country p. 46 **Project** Research the life of someone from a different country – tell the class p. 46	**Describing my hometown** Relative pronouns *who/that/which/where* Denver – the town where I was born Writing a description of your hometown p. 106

Scope and Sequence   LANGUAGE INPUT

SKILLS DEVELOPMENT

1 Getting to know you

Questions • Tense review • Right word, wrong word • Social expressions

▶ **STARTER**

1 Match the questions and answers.

Where were you born?	Two years ago.
What do you do?	Twice a week.
Are you married?	In Argentina.
Why are you studying English?	I'm a teacher.
When did you start studying English?	No, I'm not.
How often do you have English classes?	Because I need it for my job.

2 **CD1 2** Listen and check. Ask and answer them with a partner.

WHERE DO YOU COME FROM?
Tenses and questions

1 **CD1 3** Listen to **Anton Kristoff**. Where does he come from? Say one thing you can remember about his present, past, and future.

2 Complete the text about Anton with verbs from the boxes.

present	past	future
~~come~~	was born	'm going back
earn	arrived	'm going to study
have	had	
like	moved	
'm living	didn't speak	
'm working		
'm saving		

CD1 3 Listen again and check.

3 Work with a partner. Make sentences about him. Begin like this:

Anton comes from Canada, but now he's working in ...

4 Write one sentence each about your present, past, and future. Read them aloud to the class.

Anton Kristoff
from Toronto, Canada

present "Hi! I'm Anton. I ¹ __come__ from Canada, but right now I ² _____ here in New York. I ³ _____ as a bike messenger. I really ⁴ _____ New York. It's the center of the universe and it's very cosmopolitan. I ⁵ _____ friends from all over the world. I ⁶ _____ about $150 a day in this job. That's good money. I ⁷ _____ money for my education."

5 Look at the photo of **Rowenna Lee**. Where does she come from? What do you think her job is?

6 **CD1 4** Listen to Rowenna. What can you remember about her present, past, and future?

present	past	future

7 Complete the questions about Rowenna. Ask and answer them with a partner.

1 Where _**does she**_ live? With who?
2 What _____ do?
3 What _____ doing right now?
4 When and why _____ to the US?
5 How long _____ study law?
6 How much money _____ borrow from the bank?
7 How many children _____ have?
8 Why _____ excited?

CD1 5 Listen and check. Practice again.

past "I ⁸_____ in Toronto, but my parents are from Bulgaria. They ⁹_____ to Canada 30 years ago. When they first ¹⁰_____ , they ¹¹_____ any English. They always worry about me. Last month, I ¹²_____ a bad accident on my bike, but I'm fine now."

future "Next September, I ¹³_____ home to Toronto and I ¹⁴_____ for a master's degree, and then I hope to get a good job."

Rowenna Lee
from Melbourne, Australia

GRAMMAR SPOT

1 Find examples of present, past, and future tenses in **CD1 4** on p. 114.

2 Name the two tenses in these sentences. What is the difference between them?

He **lives** in Toronto.
He's **living** in New York right now.

3 Match the question words and answers.

What ...?	Because I wanted to.
Who ...?	Last night.
Where ...?	$10.
When ...?	A sandwich.
Why ...?	For two weeks.
How many ...?	In Mexico.
How much ...?	My brother.
How long ...?	The blue one.
Whose ...?	It's mine.
Which ...?	Four.

▶▶ **Grammar Reference 1.1–1.3 p. 132**

PRACTICE

Asking questions

1 Read the interview with Serkan, a Turkish student in the US. Complete the questions with question words from the box.

what	where	who	why	which
how often	how much	how many		

I Hi, Serkan. Nice to meet you. Can I ask you one or two questions?

S Yes, of course.

I First of all, ¹_____ do you come from?

S I'm from Istanbul in Turkey.

I And ²_____ are you here in the US?

S Well, I'm here mainly because I want to improve my English.

I ³_____ English did you know before you came?

S Not a lot. I studied English in school, but I didn't learn much. Now I'm studying in a language school here.

I ⁴_____ school?

S The A Plus School of English.

I That's a good name! Your English is very good now. ⁵____'s your teacher?

S Thank you very much. My teacher's name is David. He's great.

I ⁶_____ did you do back in Turkey?

S Well, actually, I was a teacher, a history teacher. I taught children from the ages of 14 to 18.

I ⁷_____ children were in your classes?

S Sometimes as many as 40.

I Wow! That's a lot. ⁸_____ do you go back home?

S Usually I go every year, but this year my brother is coming here. I'm very excited. I'm going to show him around.

I Well, I hope your brother has a great visit.

2 **CD1 6** Listen and check. Find examples of present, past, and future tenses in the interview. Role-play the interview with a partner.

Whose or Who's?

3 *Whose* and *Who's* sound the same.
CD1 7 Listen and repeat.

> *Whose* ... asks about possession.
> *Who's* = who is
> **1** "*Whose* phone is ringing?"
>   "It's mine."
> **2** "*Who's* calling?"
>   "It's my brother."

4 Work with a partner. Choose the correct word.

1 "*Who's / Whose* brother is coming to stay?"
   "Serkan's brother."

2 "*Who's / Whose* talking to Serkan?"
   "I think it's a reporter."

3 "*Who's / Whose* dictionary is this?"
   "It's Serkan's."

4 "*Who's / Whose* going to Ben's party?"
   "I'm not."

5 "*Who's / Whose* is that expensive car?'
   "It's my neighbor's."

6 "Do you know *who's / whose* bag this is?"
   "It's mine."

5 **CD1 8** Listen to the sentences.

> If the word is **Whose?** shout **1**!

> If the word is **Who's?** shout **2**!

Questions about you

6 Each of these questions has one word missing. Write it in.
1 What ʲ*do*ʲ you like doing in your free time?
2 Do you like listening music?
3 What kind music do you like?
4 What did you last weekend?
5 What you doing tonight?
6 What are you going do after this class?
7 How many languages your teacher speak?
8 What your teacher wearing today?

CD1 9 Listen, check, and repeat.

7 Ask and answer the questions with a partner.

CD1 10 Listen and compare.

Pete

Judy and Kenny

LISTENING AND SPEAKING
My oldest friend

1 Write down the names of some of your friends.
- Why do you like them?
- When did you first meet?
- Who is your oldest friend?

Discuss your list with a partner.

2 Three people are talking about their oldest friend. Look at the pictures. Who are they talking to? Who are they talking about?

3 **CD1 11** Listen to their conversations. When and where did they meet their oldest friend? What did they like about them? Make notes after each conversation.

Damian and Toby

Kenny _____
_____
_____ .

Damian _____
_____
_____ .

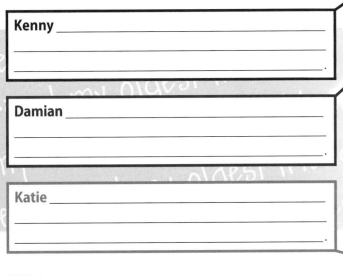
Zac

Katie _____
_____
_____ .

4 **CD1 11** Listen again. Answer the questions about the people.
1 Who has a lot of friends on Facebook? How many?
2 Whose moms met before they were born?
3 Who's going to travel around the world with a friend?
4 Whose friend lives in Canada?
5 Who's talking to their oldest friend?
6 Who doesn't have many friends?
7 Which friends don't see each other very often?
8 Who named his son after a friend?
9 Whose friend is like a sister?
10 Whose brother is boring?

Check your answers with a partner.

Katie and Beth

5 Put the words in the right order to make sentences about the people.

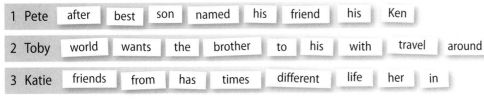

1 Pete	after	best	son	named	his	friend	his	Ken
2 Toby	world	wants	the	brother	to	his	with	travel	around
3 Katie	friends	from	has	times	different	life	her	in

Katie and Beth

▶▶ **WRITING** Describing friends *p. 100*

READING AND SPEAKING
A blind date

1 In a survey, 10,000 couples were asked how and where they first met. How do you think most couples meet? Look at the chart and match a phrase with a percentage.

How did they meet?	%
at school or college	12%
at work	
at a club	15% 20%
online	5%
through friends	8%
through family	13%
on a blind date	4%
while shopping	
none of these	22% 1%

CD1 12 Listen to the survey results. Did anything surprise you? Talk about couples you know. How did they meet?

2 Each week the *Guardian* newspaper sets up a blind date between two readers. Look at the pictures and read the introduction.
- Who are the people? How old are they?
- What are their jobs?
- Where did they meet?

3 Work in two groups.

Group A Read what **Sally** says about **Dominic**.
Group B Read what **Dominic** says about **Sally**.

Answer the questions in your group.
1 Were they both nervous when they met?
2 How does he/she describe her/him?
3 What did they talk about?
4 Why was he/she embarrassed?
5 What did they use to eat their food?
6 What were the best things about him/her?
7 What didn't he/she talk about?
8 How did the evening end?
9 How did he/she travel home?

4 Compare answers with someone from the other group. What do Sally and Dominic have in common? What don't they have in common?

What happened next?

5 Do you think Sally and Dominic will meet again? Take a class vote.

6 **CD1 13** Listen to Dominic and Sally. What did they do? What are they doing now? What are they going to do?

A blind date

This week

Sally Fox, 25, tennis coach meets Dominic Evo, 29, actor.

They met in a Chinese restaurant called Ping Pong. Will they ever meet again?

Sally
talking about Dominic

Dominic
talking about Sally

First impressions? He was friendly, tall, and attractive. We laughed in the beginning, I think because we were both a little bit nervous.

What did you talk about? So many things – places we want to travel to, such as South America. Sports, of course. Unfortunately, Dom doesn't play many sports, but he's going to run a marathon this year. His acting – I don't go to the theater often, so I didn't have a lot to say.

Any difficult moments? I couldn't decide how to greet him when we first met. I shook his hand and he tried to kiss my cheek. That was embarrassing, but we laughed about it.

Good table manners? Yes, very. He couldn't use chopsticks, but he tried.

Best thing about him? He was talkative and funny. He didn't just talk about himself, he asked me questions. It was nice to meet a guy who wasn't crazy about soccer.

Did you go somewhere else? Just to the square next to the restaurant. There was a piano with a sign that said "Please play me" – so Dom did. He can play the piano really well. It was a great way to end the evening. He lives out of town, so he took the train.

Score out of 10? I liked him more and more as the evening progressed. 8.

Would you like to meet again? Maybe. We exchanged numbers, so we'll see.

First impressions? She smiled a lot. She has a beautiful smile and amazing green eyes. I think she was a little bit nervous. I loved her dress – it was very red.

What did you talk about? Everything – travel, we both want to visit Chile; cooking, I love it, Sally hates it; sports, I hate them, Sally loves them, but I am training to run a marathon for charity; the theater, I have a small part in a small theater right now.

Any difficult moments? Not really. Oh, yes, I could see that the waiter knew it was a blind date. That was embarrassing.

Good table manners? Very good. I like a woman who enjoys her food and she could use chopsticks. I was impressed with that.

Best thing about her? Her green eyes! And she was really easy to talk to. She was interested and interesting. She didn't just talk about sports.

Did you go somewhere else? Well, we didn't go far. We found a piano – they are all over the city right now with signs saying "Please play me." I played, but I'm not very good. Sally sang, but she can't sing at all. We made a terrible noise! It was a lot of fun. Then she took the bus home.

Score out of 10? She can't sing, but I like her. 9.

Would you like to meet again? Definitely. She left in a hurry, but she has my number.

Vocabulary

7 Match the lines about Sally.

| Sally was interest**ed** | because she was funny and made him laugh. |
| Sally was interest**ing** | so she asked him a lot of questions. |

8 Complete the adjectives with *-ed* or *-ing*.

1 Thank you. That class was really interest_____ .

2 It's my birthday tomorrow so I'm very excit_____ .

3 Look at the view! It's amaz_____ .

4 I didn't like her new boyfriend. He was very bor_____ .

5 Don't be embarrass_____ . Everybody cries sometimes.

VOCABULARY
Right word, wrong word

Work with a partner. These exercises will help you think about how you learn new vocabulary. Use a dictionary.

Verbs of similar meaning

1 Choose the correct verb for each line.

1 **play go**

Can you _____ the piano?

Do you _____ running every morning?

2 **do make**

I _____ too many mistakes in English.

I _____ my homework in the evening.

3 **speak talk**

She can _____ three languages.

He can _____ forever! He never shuts up!

4 **say tell**

Excuse me! What did you _____ ?

Can you _____ me the time, please?

5 **pay for buy**

How much did you _____ that meal?

Where can I _____ some sunscreen?

Adjectives and nouns that go together

2 Choose two nouns that go with the adjective.

1 **important**   person / meeting / price

2 **delicious**   vacation / cake / meal

3 **high**   price / mountain / man

4 **long**   tree / trip / time

5 **heavy**   bag / sunshine / rain

6 **busy**   street / day / traffic

Prepositions

3 Complete the sentences with the correct preposition. You can use some prepositions more than once.

to   from   at   about   of   on   in   with   for

1 He comes _**from**_ Istanbul _**in**_ Turkey.

2 He's crazy ____ soccer, but I'm not interested ____ it at all.

3 I am married ____ John. I met him ____ college ____ 2007.

4 I live ____ my parents ____ an apartment ____ the first floor.

5 He's very good ____ playing the piano.

6 I like going ____ walks ____ the park.

7 This is a picture ____ me ____ vacation ____ Thailand.

8 I got this sweater ____ my sister ____ my birthday.

Words with two meanings

4 Look at these sentences. What are the two meanings of *date*?

I met my husband on a blind **date**.
Dates and raisins are good for you.

5 Write two sentences that show two possible meanings for these words.

left		
train		
run		
rest		
kind		
light		
mean		

CD1 14 Listen to some sample answers.

Social expressions

1 In everyday situations we use a lot of social expressions. Read the expressions. Where are the people?

A "Hi, Anna. How are you?"
B "I'm fine, thanks. How are you?"

C "Thank you very much."
D "You're welcome."

E "Can I help you?"
F "No, thank you. I'm just looking."

G "Excuse me. Is this seat free?"
H "No, sorry, I'm afraid it isn't."

CD1 15 Listen and repeat. Pay attention to stress and intonation.

2 Match a phrase in **A** with a phrase in **B**.

A	B
1 Good morning!	___ Bye! See you later!
2 See you tomorrow!	___ Sure. What's the problem?
3 How do you do?	___ That's OK. Maybe another time.
4 Thank you very much.	___ Thanks! Same to you.
5 I'm sorry. I can't come tonight.	___ Good morning! Nice day today!
6 Can you help me with this exercise?	___ Yeah! About nine, in the coffee shop.
7 Bye!	___ Don't worry. You're here now.
8 Bye! Have a good weekend!	___ You're welcome.
9 Sorry I'm late.	___ Fine, thanks. Nice to meet you.
10 Cheers!	___ Cheers! Here's to your new job!

CD1 16 Listen, check, and practice.

3 Choose a line to continue the conversations.

a I don't know what this word means.
b Yes, it's really warm for this time of year.
c Nice to meet you, too.
d Thanks a lot. I'm excited, but a little bit nervous.
e It was nice of you to pay.
f I'm free tomorrow night. How about then?
g OK. Nine is good for me, too.
h Yes. Let's meet after class.
i Thanks. Are you doing anything special?
j Yeah, I missed the bus.

CD1 17 Listen and check.

4 With a partner, choose two of the conversations.
Continue them if you can and act them out for the class.

> Good morning!
>
> Good morning! Nice day today!
>
> Yes, it's really warm for this time of year.
>
> They say it's going to rain again tomorrow! Enjoy it while it lasts.

Bye! See you later!

Sure. What's the problem?

How do you do?

Good morning!

Thank you very much.

Oxford Online Skills Program
Log in for additional online learning

Whatever makes you happy

Present tenses • *have* • Things I like doing • Making conversation

.ant to you?
. 6 = least important.

☐ money
☐ having fun
.thy ☐ family

.ur ideas as a class.

.e most important thing is having a good job.

I LOVE WHAT I DO

Present tenses and *have*

1 Look at the pictures of Lee Strong and Moziah Bridges.
  What's remarkable about them? Who likes telling jokes?
  Who likes making bow ties?

2 **CD1 18** Read and listen to the article about Lee.
  How old is she? What does she do?
  What does her family think of her?

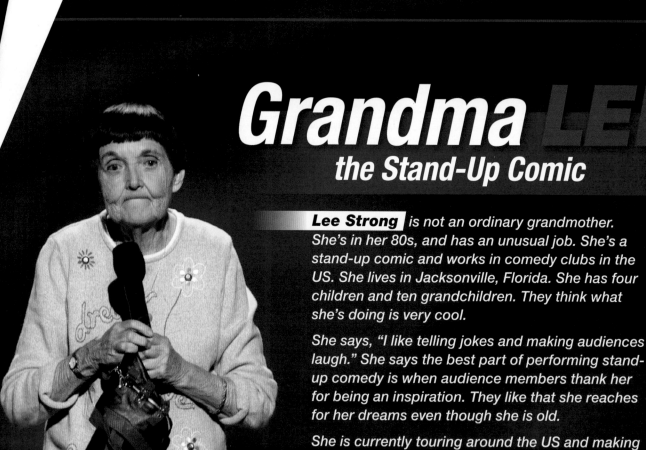

Grandma *LEE*
the Stand-Up Comic

Lee Strong is not an ordinary grandmother.
She's in her 80s, and has an unusual job. She's a
stand-up comic and works in comedy clubs in the
US. She lives in Jacksonville, Florida. She has four
children and ten grandchildren. They think what
she's doing is very cool.

She says, "I like telling jokes and making audiences
laugh." She says the best part of performing stand-
up comedy is when audience members thank her
for being an inspiration. They like that she reaches
for her dreams even though she is old.

She is currently touring around the US and making
audiences laugh.

Grandma Lee has a great life. She says, "I can't go
anywhere without being recognized. It's awesome."

3 **CD1 19** Read and listen to the article about Moziah. What is his company? How old was he when he started it?

The Bow Tie Businessman

MOZIAH BRIDGES is an extraordinary young man. He has his own company, Mo's Bows, which he started when he was just nine. "I love dressing up," he says. "I look and feel so much better in nice clothes." He makes bow ties using sewing tips from his great-grandmother.

Mo's bow ties are online and in stores throughout the US. The business is growing fast with $30,000 from online sales alone in 2013. And he has a charity that sends kids to summer camp.

Mo is a busy boy – designing bow ties, going to school, and playing football – but he has his family to help him make his colorful bow ties.

4 Work with a partner. Ask and answer questions a Lee and Mo.

LEE	MOZIAH
1 What/do? **What does Lee do?** **She's a stand-up comic.**	1 What/do?
2 Where/work?	2 Why/like nice clothes?
3 How many children/have?	3 Whose/sewing tips/ use?
4 What/like doing?	4 Where/you buy his bow ties?
5 Why/like her audience?	5 What/growing fast?
6 What/doing right now?	6 What/like playing?

CD1 20 Listen and check.

5 **CD1 21** Listen to an interview with Lee. Does she like being famous? What do her friends think of her job? Complete the sentences.

1 I'm just an old lady _____ .

2 I _____ an old woman in a retirement home…

3 Because it _____ me happy!

4 It _____ how old you are.

6 **CD1 22** Listen to Moziah. What does he like about his work? What does he say about friends and family? Complete the interviewer's lines.

1 It _____ to me you really love what _____!

2 _____ any free time?

3 _____ you _____ a girlfriend?

4 _____ do _____ live with?

7 Lee and Moziah both use the expression *"It's none of your business!"* What does this mean? What are they talking about?

...h *have* in the question, ...ow are the forms different?

Do you have a car? Yes, I do. No, I don't.

Do you have a bike? Yes, I do. No, I don't.

I don't have a camera.

I don't have an iPhone.

...k and answer questions about these things.

Do you have any pets? Yes, I do.

What ...?

...find

...hich

...mpany ...d time.

...bout

...d sisters
...asses
.../a vacation home

– exchanging information

...at the photos of Alicia, and Bill ...Christina. With a partner, take turns ...ing and answering questions about ...e people.

Student A Look at p. 147.
Student B Look at p. 149.

Alicia

Bill and Christina

Where does Alicia come from? She comes from ...

Where do Bill and Christina come from? They come from ...

Stative verbs

4 Some verbs don't usually take the Present Continuous. Complete the sentences with a verb in the Simple Present in the correct form.

think	~~not know~~	not believe	look	not agree	love
mean	not matter	need	own	not understand	

1 "What time is it?" "I ___don't know___ . Sorry."
2 I'm thirsty! I _____ a drink.
3 I _____ your bag! Where did you get it?
4 "I _____ Thomas is stupid." "I _____. I think he's smart."
5 Her English isn't very good. I _____ her.
6 He's very rich. He _____ a house in Malibu.
7 You _____ sad! What's the matter?
8 "Sorry I forgot your birthday!" "Don't worry. It _____."
9 "I'm 74 years old."
  "I _____ you! You don't look a day over 60."
10 I don't understand *none of your business*. What _____
  it _____?

Check it

5 Choose the correct sentence.

1 ☐ Angela live with her parents.
  ☐ Angela lives with her parents.

2 ☐ Where do you go on vacation?
  ☐ Where you go on vacation?

3 ☐ She doesn't work here anymore.
  ☐ She no works here anymore.

4 ☐ He's at the bus stop. He waits for a bus.
  ☐ He's at the bus stop. He's waiting for a bus.

5 ☐ I'm liking black coffee.
  ☐ I like black coffee.

6 ☐ I don't got a phone.
  ☐ I don't have a phone.

▶▶ **WRITING** Writing a postcard *p. 101*

VOCABULARY AND SPEAKING

Things I like doing

1 Work with a partner. Match a **Verb** with a **Phrase**.

Verb	Phrase
play	emails and texts
go out	games on my smartphone
download	music and movies
send	with my friends

Verb	Phrase
shop	in front of the TV
take	friends for coffee
relax	for clothes online
meet	a nap

Verb	Phrase
listen to	music
go out	nothing
get	for a meal
do	take-out food

Verb	Phrase
read	basketball on TV
chat	to the gym
go	magazines
watch	with friends online

CD1 24 Listen, check, and practice.

2 When and where do you do some of these things?

> I like playing games on my smartphone at home after school.

> I just love taking a nap on Saturday afternoon.

3 Complete the sentences with words from Exercise 1.

1 I like shopping at the mall, but mainly I ____shop online____ .

2 When I hear a band I like, I _____ their _____ from the Internet.

3 I _____ on my phone when I go jogging.

4 I spend hours _____ , even though I'm with them all day at school!

5 Sometimes I like to chill out at home and _____ .

6 I'm always so tired after work that I just want to _____ .

7 On Saturdays, I _____ , and I sleep all afternoon.

8 Do you want to cook tonight, or should we _____ ?

9 It's Pete's birthday tonight, so we'll _____ . Indian, I think.

10 I like staying in shape. I _____ three times a week.

CD1 25 Listen, check, and practice.

My perfect day

4 What is your idea of a perfect day? Make notes.

take a nap, go to a café, meet friends

5 Work in groups. Talk about your perfect day.

> For me, a perfect day is when I go to a café for breakfast. Then, I meet my friends. And then I take a nap.

READING AND SPEAKING
The happiness quiz

1 Look at the pictures. What are the people doing? Why are they happy?

2 Read the introduction to the quiz and answer the questions.

   1 What does happiness depend on?
   2 What do you need to know about yourself?
   3 How can you learn to be happier?

3 Take the quiz and add up your score to see how happy you are. Do you agree?

4 The quiz is in four sections. Write one of these headings above each section.

Your enjoyment of life

Your health

Your relationships

Happiness with yourself

5 In which sections of the quiz did you score a high number? What can you do to be happier?

How happy are you?

What do you think?

6 Here are the results of a recent survey about happiness. Work in groups. Do you agree?

- $50,000 per year is all we need to make us happy.
- Buying things doesn't make us happy.
- Experiences such as vacations and living abroad make us happier.
- Be happy with what you have. Stop wanting what you don't have.
- Enjoy what you're doing.

7 **CD1 26** Listen to the beginning of the song *Money*.

   1 According to the song, what is more important, love or money?
   2 "The best things in life are free."
     Does the singer agree? Do *you* agree?

Project

Research the life of someone rich and famous in the news right now. Have fame and fortune brought them happiness? Bring information and pictures to class. Tell the others about your person.

Your happiness depends on how you see yourself, what you want from life, and how well you get along with other people.

But you need to know yourself. What kind of person are you? What makes you happy? Do you know how to make yourself happier? If you can answer these questions, you can learn to change the way you think and behave. And you *can* actually be happier. It just takes practice.

Take the quiz and find out how happy you are. Write 1–5 for each statement.

1 = very true   4 = not very true
2 = mainly true   5 = not true at all
3 = about 50/50

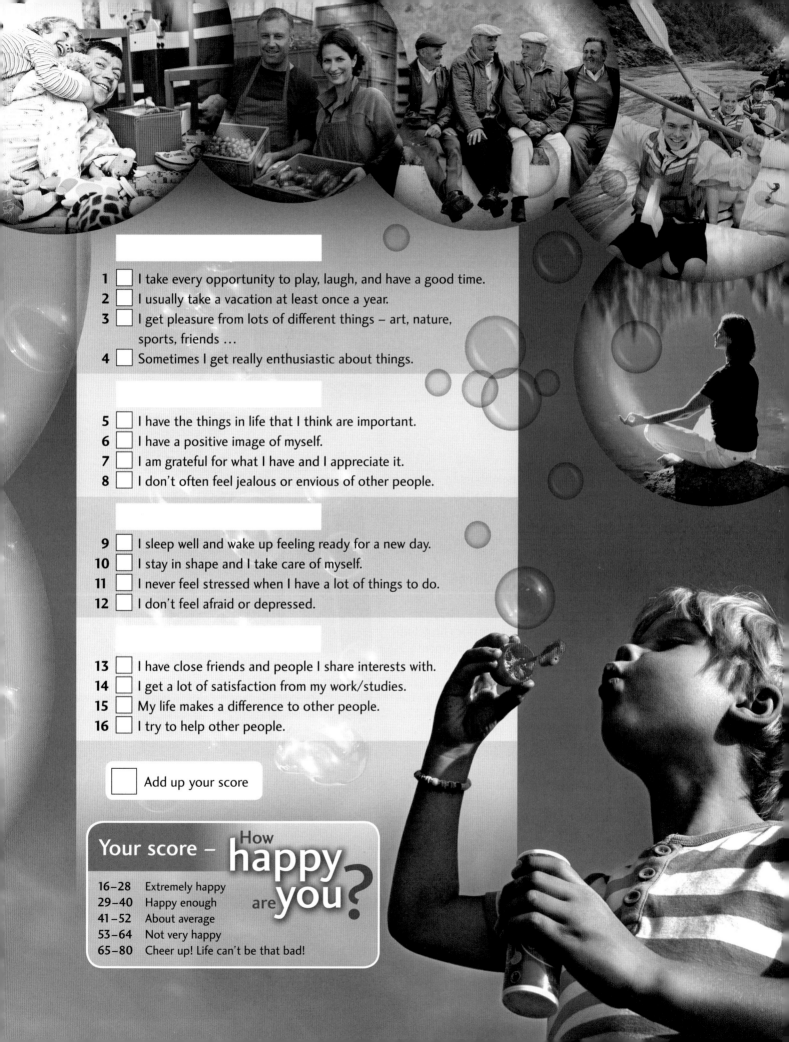

1. ☐ I take every opportunity to play, laugh, and have a good time.
2. ☐ I usually take a vacation at least once a year.
3. ☐ I get pleasure from lots of different things – art, nature, sports, friends …
4. ☐ Sometimes I get really enthusiastic about things.

5. ☐ I have the things in life that I think are important.
6. ☐ I have a positive image of myself.
7. ☐ I am grateful for what I have and I appreciate it.
8. ☐ I don't often feel jealous or envious of other people.

9. ☐ I sleep well and wake up feeling ready for a new day.
10. ☐ I stay in shape and I take care of myself.
11. ☐ I never feel stressed when I have a lot of things to do.
12. ☐ I don't feel afraid or depressed.

13. ☐ I have close friends and people I share interests with.
14. ☐ I get a lot of satisfaction from my work/studies.
15. ☐ My life makes a difference to other people.
16. ☐ I try to help other people.

☐ Add up your score

Your score – How **happy** are **you?**

16–28	Extremely happy
29–40	Happy enough
41–52	About average
53–64	Not very happy
65–80	Cheer up! Life can't be that bad!

LISTENING AND SPEAKING
Getting along with your neighbors

1 What do you know about your neighbors?

Their names are ...   He's a ...   They have ...   She's a ...

How well do you know them?

Really well/not at all/just to say hello to ...

2 What makes a good neighbor? Read the ideas.
Do you agree or disagree?

> ### A good neighbor is someone who . . .
> * always says hello.
> * doesn't make too much noise.
> * I never see.
> * minds his/her own business.
> * invites me to parties.
> * feels at home in my house.
> * sometimes comes over for coffee.

Discuss your ideas in small groups.

Two neighbors

3 **CD1 27** You are going to listen to two neighbors,
Mrs. Boyle and Nathan, talking about each other.
Read the questions.

First, listen to Mrs. Boyle. Answer the questions.

1 Where is Nathan's apartment?
2 Do Nathan and Mrs. Boyle speak to each other?
3 What does he wear? What *doesn't* he wear?
4 Does he have a job?
5 What time does he go to bed? What time does he get up?
6 How many people are staying in Nathan's apartment?
7 Does he have a girlfriend? Where does she live?
8 Why does he make so much noise? What's he doing now?
9 What does Nathan think about Mrs. Boyle?

Check your answers in small groups.

4 **CD1 28** Now listen to Nathan. How does he answer
questions 1–9? What differences are there?

5 In your groups, discuss who you think is telling the truth.

Role play

Work with a partner. Role-play a conversation between Nathan
and Mrs. Boyle where they actually get to know each other.

> **A** Hello. I'm Nathan, your neighbor. You're Mrs. Boyle,
> aren't you?
> **B** Oh, Nathan, hello. I don't usually see you in the
> mornings ...

💬 EVERYDAY ENGLISH

Making conversation

1 **CD1 29** It is the first day of a new school semester. Listen to the conversations between two students and two teachers. The teachers are trying to be friendly. Which conversation is more successful? Why?

2 When you are having a conversation, it helps if you …
- add a comment
- don't just answer *yes* or *no*
- ask questions
- express interest

Find examples of these in **CD1 29** conversation 2 on p. 117.

3 Match a line in **A** with a reply in **B**.

A	B
1 What a nice day it is today!	☐ a No, I didn't. I missed it.
2 Are you having a good time in Los Angeles?	1 b Yes, beautiful, isn't it?
3 Have a good weekend!	☐ c Nothing special.
4 Did you have a nice weekend?	☐ d Thank you! They're new.
5 What are you doing tonight?	☐ e She's OK, thanks.
6 How's your mother these days?	☐ f Yes, I am. It's a very interesting city.
7 Did you watch the game last night?	☐ g Yes, I did. It was really good.
8 I like your shoes.	☐ h Thanks. Same to you.
9 If you have a problem, just ask me.	☐ i Thank you very much.

1 John and Maria

2 Maggie and Jean-Jacques

CD1 30 Listen and check. How does **B** keep the conversation going?

4 Practice the conversations with a partner. Cover **B**, and then **A**. Remember the extra lines.

Keeping a conversation going

5 Work with a partner. Begin a conversation with one of these lines. Keep the conversation going as long as possible.

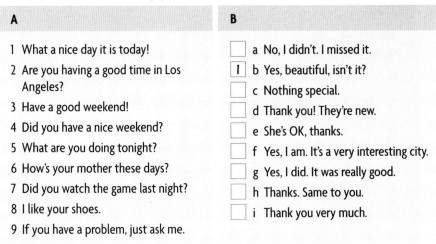

    I went on vacation last month.

    I have a new boyfriend/girlfriend.

    I go to Hong Kong a lot on business.

    I met the president yesterday.

    I went shopping over the weekend.

    Skiing is my favorite sport.

CD1 31 Listen to an example and compare.

3 What's in the news?

Simple Past and Past Continuous • Adverbs • Saying when

▶ STARTER

1 What is the Simple Past of these verbs?
Which are regular? Which are irregular?

leave	take	become	begin
go	do	think	meet
walk	arrive	explain	end
want	decide		

2 Practice saying them around the class.

leave, left   take, took

HE WALKED 6,000 MILES!
Simple Past and Past Continuous

1 Look at Ed Stafford's web page.
What was he the first to do?

2 Read and complete the text with verbs
from the box in *Starter* in the
Simple Past.

CD1 32 Listen and check.

3 Work with a partner. Write the questions.

1   How far/Ed walk?

   How far did Ed walk?

2   When/journey begin?
3   Where/journey end?
4   Which countries/go through?
5   How long/journey take?
6   Why/do it?

Now look at the map and read the text
again. Answer the questions.

4 CD1 33 Listen and check. Practice
the questions and answers with
your partner.

Walking the Amazon

Home | Map | Videos | Photos | Team | FAQs

Amazing journey ends after 6,000 miles

Ed Stafford [1]____**became**____ the first man in history to walk the length of the Amazon River from the source to the ocean. He [2]_____ for 860 days.

The journey [3]_____ in April 2008 when Ed [4]_____ the town of Camana on the Pacific coast of Peru. It [5]_____ in August 2010 when he [6]_____ in Maruda, on the Atlantic coast of Brazil.

He [7]_____ through three countries, Peru, Colombia, and Brazil. The journey [8]_____ nearly two and a half years. "I [9]_____ it for the adventure," says Ed.

Ed's journey

Atlantic Ocean
Maruda
COLOMBIA
Amazon River
PERU
BRAZIL
(BRASIL)
South America
Pacific Ocean
Camana
0   500 miles
0   500 km

5 Read **Cho's story**. Who is Cho?

6 Which tense are the verbs in **bold** in Cho's story?
Complete these sentences.
1 Cho was working in the forest when he …
2 They were walking in a dangerous part of the forest when they …
3 The tribe didn't understand what Ed …

7 Write the questions. Ask and answer them with your partner.
1 What/Cho doing/when/met Ed?
2 Where/walking when/saw/tribe?
3 Why/tribe think/Ed/crazy?

CD1 34 Listen and check.

Cho's story

Home | Map | Videos | Photos | Team | FAQs

Ed didn't take the trip alone. His companion was Gadiel "Cho" Sanchez Rivera, a forestry worker from Peru.

Cho said, "When I first met Ed, I **was working** in the forest. I thought he was crazy, but I wanted to help him and be his guide."

"One day we **were walking** in a very dangerous part of the forest when we saw a hostile tribe. They didn't understand what Ed **was doing** there. I explained he was an adventurer and he **was walking** along the Amazon. They decided he was crazy, too."

GRAMMAR SPOT

1 The Simple Past expresses a completed action in the past.
  Ed **walked** along the Amazon. He **began** his journey in 2008.

2 Complete the question and negative.
  When _____ the journey begin?
  They _____ finish the journey until 2010.

3 The Past Continuous expresses an activity in progress in the past.
  Cho **was working** in the forest when he met Ed.
  Compare these sentences.
    I **took** a shower last night. (= simple, completed action)
    I **was taking** a shower when the phone rang. (= interrupted activity)

▶▶ **Grammar Reference 3.1–3.3** p. 134   ▶▶ **Irregular verbs** p. 154

8 Read Ed's blog. Put the verb in parentheses in the Simple Past or the Past Continuous.

Popular | Latest | Comments | Tags

Ed's blog

July 12
The day I nearly died

Today I ¹_____ (walk) next to the river when I nearly ²_____ (stand) on a snake. I ³_____ (stop) immediately. The snake's fangs ⁴_____ (go) in and out. I was terrified. I ⁵_____ (not move). One bite and you're dead in three hours.

September 10
Knives and guns!

Early this morning we ⁶_____ (cross) the river by boat when we ⁷_____ (see) five canoes. The tribesmen ⁸_____ (carry) knives and guns. They were angry because we ⁹_____ (not have) permission to be on their land. We ¹⁰_____ (leave) as fast as we could.

November 24
The jungle at night

I ¹¹_____ (lie) in my hammock last night trying to sleep, but it was impossible because the noise of the jungle was so loud. Monkeys ¹²_____ (scream) in the trees, and millions of mosquitos ¹³_____ (buzz) around my head. I ¹⁴_____ (take) a sleeping pill and finally ¹⁵_____ (fall) asleep at 3:00 a.m.

CD1 35 Listen and check.

9 Think of more questions to ask about Ed and Cho.
• What did they eat?   • How did they navigate?

Go online and find out more about Ed. Were your questions answered? What else did you learn? Tell the class.

PRACTICE

Pronunciation

1 Write the past tense in the chart.

		/d/	/t/	/ɪd/
stop	decide	stay**ed**	stop**ped**	decid**ed**
stay	work			
end	play			
laugh	call			
want	visit			
look	answer			

CD1 36 Listen and check.

2 **CD1 37** Listen and repeat the sentences you hear.

We stayed in a hotel.   They stopped at lunchtime.

3 **CD1 38** Listen and practice the sentences. Notice the pronunciation of *was* and *were*.

/wəz/
I was having dinner.

/wəz/
What was she wearing?

/wər/
They were playing baseball.

/wər/
Where were you going?

/wʌznt/
He wasn't listening.

/wərnt/
They weren't enjoying the party.

Discussing grammar

4 What's the difference between these pairs of sentences?

When we arrived, she **was making** some coffee.
When we arrived, she **made** some coffee.

I **read** a good book in bed last night.
I **was reading** a good book in bed last night.

5 Choose the correct verb form.

1 I *saw / was seeing* a good movie yesterday.

2 While I *shopped / was shopping* this morning, I *lost / was losing* my wallet.

3 The police *stopped / were stopping* me on the freeway because I *drove / was driving* at 90 miles per hour.

4 "What *did you do / were you doing* when you saw the accident?"
"I *walked / was walking* down the street."

5 "What *did you do / were you doing* when you saw the accident?"
"I *called / was calling* the police."

6 "How *did you break / were you breaking* your leg?"
"I *was skiing / skied* and I *hit / was hitting* a tree."

7 I *was cutting / cut* my finger while I *was cooking / cooked*.

8 *Did you have / Were you having* a good vacation?

Game – Truth or Lies

6 Write one true and two false sentences about where you were, and what you were doing. Tell a partner. Use three of these examples.

- at 7:15 this morning
- at 1:00 p.m. yesterday
- at 10:00 p.m. last night
- at 10:00 a.m. last Sunday

Can your partner guess which sentence is true?

At 7:15 …

I was jogging in the park.

I was at home. I was getting ready for work.

I was coming home in a taxi after a party.

Talking about the news

7 Look at these newspaper headings. What do you think the stories are about?

Texting woman falls into fountain

Chinese vase sells for $69 million

The app that saved an iPad

Choose one of the stories. Read the article on p. 151.

8 Work in small groups. Tell your story to the others. DON'T read it! The other students can ask questions.

⚇⚇ LISTENING AND SPEAKING

The news

1 How do you keep up to date with what's happening in the world?

Which of these news topics interests you most?

politics … celebrities … sports … fashion … culture … the arts …
crime … international news … national news … local news …

Do you listen to the radio? Which station(s)?

2 **CD1 39** Listen to five radio news headlines. What is the first story about? The second? Write a number 1–5.

☐ a strike ☐ a crime ☐ a death
☐ an explosion ☐ a hockey game

3 Which words do you think are from each story?

cameras	thieves	guard	ex-wife
Picasso	cancer	goals	theft
half-time	higher pay	beat	protesting
injured	closed		

4 Write the question words.

_____ was injured?

_____ paintings did they steal?

_____ were they on strike?

_____ times was he married?

_____ was the score?

Work in groups. Choose one of the news stories.
What else do you want to know? Think of more questions.
Write the questions on the board.

5 **CD1 40** Listen to the news stories. Which questions were answered?

Dictation

6 **CD1 41** You will hear the story about the art theft at dictation speed. One student should write the exact words on the board. The other students help.

> You missed a word.

> That isn't how you spell **thieves**.

> She didn't say that. She said …

Project

7 Find a news story that interests you. Do some research. For the next class, bring in pictures and articles. Tell the class about the story. Be prepared to answer questions.

💬 READING AND SPEAKING

The flight attendant who lost his cool

1 Talk as a class. What makes you lose your cool?

Bad drivers.   My little brother.

2 Look at the picture story about the flight attendant, Steven Slater. What made him lose his cool? In groups, write some sentences about the story. Compare ideas.

3 Read each article. After each one, answer the questions and have a class discussion.

4 Look at the pictures above again. Retell the story in more detail.

What do you think?

1 After August 16, this story "died." Why was it such big news for a week?

2 Steven Slater appeared in court two months later. Do you think he paid a fine or went to prison? Look at the article on p. 151 for the answer. Do you think this was fair?

3 The artist Andy Warhol once said, "In the future everyone will be world-famous for 15 minutes." How does the Steven Slater story illustrate this?

Steven Slater

1 August 10

Emergency exit for flight attendant who lost his cool

Flight attendant Steven Slater made an emergency exit from an Airbus after he had an argument with a passenger.

The incident happened at New York's JFK Airport soon after the JetBlue flight from Pittsburgh landed.

As the Airbus A320 was taxiing slowly on the runway, a passenger stood up to get her luggage. Mr. Slater told her to sit down, but she refused. The businesswoman was taking her suitcase out of the overhead bin when it hit Mr. Slater on the head.

He started bleeding, and it was then that the flight attendant lost his temper. He marched to the front of the cabin and spoke furiously over the plane's PA system, saying, "That's enough! After 28 years in this business, I quit!"

He then took two drinks from a refrigerator, opened the door, activated the plane's emergency chute, and jumped onto it. Mr. Slater then ran to his car and drove home.

Police arrested Mr. Slater at his home a short time later.

1 When and where did the incident happen?
2 What did the female passenger do?
3 What did the Steven Slater say to her?
4 What did she do to him? How did he react?
5 How did Steven Slater leave the plane?

Discussion

• Was this a very important story?
• Why do you think it was in the newspapers?

2 August 11

Angry flight attendant becomes Facebook hero

The flight attendant Steven Slater, who left his plane via the emergency exit, is becoming a folk hero in the US.

Last night a "Free Steven Slater" page on Facebook had 170,000 fans. People wrote how much they admired him. "I would really love to quit my job like you did!" is the message from many.

Tens of thousands of people, including other cabin crew members, left messages of support.

"You only did what everyone else feels like doing," wrote one.

Slater appeared in court in New York yesterday and pleaded not guilty to charges of criminal damage and endangering life. He could face up to seven years in prison.

1 What did people think of Steven the next day?
2 How did they show their support?
3 Why did the public admire him?
4 What did other cabin crew members say?

Discussion

- Why did people think he was a hero?

3 August 12

Steven Slater thanks public

Flight attendant Steven Slater, 39, who left his job after an attack by a passenger, said he was amazed by the public sympathy he received.

Slater has messages from millions of people all over the world.

He said, "I really appreciate this enormous support."

As he was leaving a Bronx police station, people were shouting "You're a hero!" T-shirts that read FREE STEVEN SLATER are on sale.

JetBlue confirmed that Slater was still an employee, but suspended from duty.

1 How did Steven feel?
2 How did people show their support?
3 Where was he?

Discussion

- How is it possible that this story went around the world in two days?

4 August 15

Folk hero Slater relaxes on the beach

Ex-flight attendant Steven Slater spent the weekend relaxing on the beach. He was having a few drinks and enjoying his new worldwide fame as the latest American folk hero.

The 39-year-old was wearing a gray T-shirt, white shorts, and a baseball cap as he talked to excited fans on the beach near his home in New York.

Yesterday supporters shouted, "Good for you, Steve!" and "We love you!" as he sat down on a chair, took off his shirt, and put on his sunglasses.

1 What is Steven called in the headline?
2 What actually happened on the beach?

Discussion

- Why was this day's story in the papers?
- What did Steven Slater do to deserve being called a folk hero?

5 August 16

Ex-flight attendant to get TV Show

Steven Slater is in talks to get his own reality show. TV production company Stone Entertainment wants to give the flight attendant the chance to star in a program that shows unhappy workers how to leave their job.

1 How is Steven going to become more famous?
2 What will the program be about?

Discussion

- Why did a TV production company want to give him a show?

VOCABULARY
Adverbs

1 Look at these sentences from the articles on pages 22 and 23. Underline the adverbs.

… he spoke furiously …

… the Airbus A320 was taxiing slowly on the runway…

"I would really love to quit my job . . ."

2 Many regular adverbs end in *-ly*. Match each verb in **A** with an adverb in **B**.

A	B
1 drive	fluently
2 love	carefully
3 speak	patiently
4 rain	bravely
5 wait	heavily
6 fight	passionately

CD1 42 Listen and check. Try to remember the sentences.

3 What do you notice about the adjectives and adverbs in these sentences?

Wow! This is a **fast** car.
Slow down! You drive too **fast**!

I work **hard** and play **hard**.
She's a very **hard** worker.

I got up **late** this morning.
We had a **late** breakfast.

4 What is the adverb form of these adjectives? Complete the lines with the adverbs.

clear	quiet	slow	honest	perfect
complete	good	bad	easy	

1 play a game **well** and win
2 play a game … and lose
3 explain the rules …
4 shut the door …
5 forget something …
6 get out of bed …
7 play the piano …
8 pass an exam …
9 answer the questions …

NO CHILD ON BOARD
DON'T DRIVE CAREFULLY

CALIFORNIA
CKU 4972

Word order

5 Correct the word order in these sentences.
1 She speaks very well English.
   She speaks English very well.
2 He started last week a new job.
3 Please read carefully the instructions.
4 Do you work still for the same company?
5 Never I can remember her name.
6 We took last year in Thailand a vacation.

6 Put the adverbs in the correct place in the sentences.
1 My grandma is 75, and she goes swimming.
   (**nearly still regularly**)
2 "Do you love me?" "I do. I'll love you."
   (**really of course always**)
3 I was relaxing with a good book when someone knocked on the door. (**just really loudly**)
4 My sister is three, but she can read, and she can write.
   (**only already too**)
5 Break the eggs into a bowl with some milk and butter. Heat it gently. When it's ready, serve the scrambled eggs with toast. (**first then immediately**)
6 All my friends have a smartphone. They're on Facebook. My dad's on Facebook. (**almost as well even**)

CD1 43 Listen and check.

▶▶ **WRITING CD1 44 Narrative writing** *p. 102*

Saying when

1 Answer the questions. Tell a partner.

1 What's the date today/tomorrow/the day after tomorrow?
2 When's your birthday?
3 What's your date of birth?
4 What year were you born?

CD1 45 Listen and compare.

2 Look at the two ways of saying the date.

A What's the date today?
B It's the twenty-second of June.

A What's the date today?
B It's June twenty-second.

Practice saying these dates in two ways.

CD1 46 Listen and check.

3 **CD1 47** Listen to how the British say the dates. What's the difference between American and British English?

4 Practice saying the years.

**2012 2002 2015
2010 1980 1969
1994 1848**

5 **CD1 48** Write the dates you hear.

1 _____ 3 _____ 5 _____
2 _____ 4 _____

6 What days are national holidays in your country?

7 Write down three dates that are important to you. Tell a partner.

July 25 – it's my wedding anniversary.

Time expressions

8 Complete the time expressions with *in/at/on*, or no preposition.

____ six o'clock	____ Saturday
____ 2004	____ Monday morning
____ last night	____ April
____ the weekend	____ yesterday evening
____ the evening	____ summer
____ January 18	____ two weeks ago
____ the 1960s	____ this morning
____ the other day	____ midnight

▶▶ **Grammar Reference 3.4 p. 134**

9 Work in small groups. When did you last …?

• go to the movies

I went to the movies last Friday/on Monday evening/ two weeks ago.

• play a sport   • get a present
• go to a party   • buy some clothes
• take an exam   • go online
• take a vacation   • make a meal

4 Eat, drink, and be merry!

Expressing quantity • *something/no one …* • Articles • *A piece of …*
Can you come over for dinner?

STARTER

1 What did you eat and drink yesterday? Make a list.

2 Compare your list with the class.
Who ate the healthiest?

For breakfast I had a cup of coffee, some cereal, and …

HOW TO LIVE TO BE 120!
Expressions of quantity

1 Read about Claus and Elvira Bonrich.
1 What is their extraordinary ambition?
2 What are their jobs?
3 What kind of food do they eat? Do they cook their food?

An extraordinary ambition!

Claus Bonrich (33) and his wife **Elvira** (28) are a successful young couple. Claus is a software programmer and Elvira works in a health food store. In many ways their life is ordinary, but they have an extraordinary ambition. They want to live until they are 120. And they believe they can do this by following a health plan called the "Calorie Restriction Diet." Claus and Elvira eat a lot of raw food. They steam some food, but they don't fry, grill, or roast anything, and there are many things they don't eat at all.

"We want to live to be 120!"

2 Look at the nouns in the boxes. Which group can you count? Which can't you count? Label the boxes *Count* or *Noncount*.

apples	grapes
carrots	clams
vegetables	calories

meat	fish
orange juice	coffee
tea	fruit
broccoli	soda

3 Work with a partner. Read and complete the questions and answers about the diet with the nouns from Exercise 2.

1 Q Do you eat any __meat__?
  A No, we don't eat **any** _____ at all, but we eat **some** _____.

2 Q **How much** _____ do you eat?
  A We eat **a little** _____ like cod or salmon, but we love shellfish so we eat **a lot of** _____.

3 Q Do you eat **much** _____?
  A Oh, yes, we eat **a lot of** fresh _____ – _____ and _____, everything.

4 Q And do you eat **many** _____?
  A Yes, of course, we eat **lots of** raw _____.

5 Q You don't cook **any** vegetables at all?
  A We cook **some**. Sometimes we steam **a few** _____ and **a little** _____.

6 Q And what do you drink?
  A Well, we don't drink **any** _____ or _____, and of course, there's **no** _____ in our diet, but we do drink **a lot of** _____.

7 Q **How many** _____ do you have every day?
  A About 1,500. That's about 1,000 fewer than most people.

4 **CD1 49** Listen and check. Practice the questions and answers with your partner.

GRAMMAR SPOT

1 Look at the expressions of quantity in **A**, **B**, and **C**. Which group is used with plural, count nouns? Which group with noncount nouns? Which is used with both?

A	B	C
How much …?	How many …?	some/any
not much	not many	not any/no
a little	a few	a lot of/lots of

Find examples in the interview in Exercise 3.

2 *Much* and *many* are not usually used in affirmative statements. When do we use them? Correct the sentences.

There are ~~many~~ books in my bag. ✗
There's ~~much~~ homework tonight. ✗

3 Look at these sentences. Which is a request?

Is there *any* orange juice? Can I have *some* orange juice?

▶▶ **Grammar Reference 4.1 p. 135**

5 Work in small groups. Do you think the Bonrichs eat and drink the things in the box? Discuss with your partner and complete the lists.

cereal	~~bread~~	milk	cheese	butter
tomatoes	peppers	olive oil	nuts	rice
pasta	sugar	bananas	mangoes	cookies
fresh juice	potatoes	French fries	potato chips	diet soda
tap water	bottled water			

Do you think they eat any cereal?

Yes, I think so. Maybe just a little, not much.

What about …?

✓ cereal

✗ bread

Compare your list with the class.

6 **CD1 50** Listen and find out if your ideas were correct.

7 What do you think of the diet? Will the Bonrichs live to be 120? Why/Why not?

PRACTICE

Discussing grammar

Work with a partner. Complete the sentences.

1 some / any

1 Do they have _____ children?
2 We don't need _____ olive oil.
3 Can I borrow _____ money?
4 Is there _____ gas in the car?
5 Can I have _____ cake?

2 much / many

1 Do you have _____ homework?
2 We don't need _____ eggs. Just half a dozen.
3 Is there _____ traffic in your town?
4 I don't know _____ students in this class.
5 How _____ time do you have?

3 a little / a few / a lot of

1 I have _____ very close friends. Two or three.
2 He has _____ money. He's a billionaire.
3 "Do you take sugar in your coffee?" "Just _____."
4 I'll be ready in _____ minutes.
5 She speaks good Spanish, but only _____ French.

something/someone/somewhere ...

4 Complete the lines with the correct word.

some	every		thing	where
any	no	**+**	one/body	

1 "Did you meet _____ nice at the party?"
  "Yes. I met _____ who knows you!"
2 "Ouch! There's _____ in my eye!"
  "Let me look. No, I can't see _____."
3 "Let's go _____ hot for our vacation."
  "But we can't go _____ that's too expensive."
4 "Where are my glasses? I can't find them _____."
  "What's on the top of your head?"
5 "It was a great party. _____ loved it."
  "They did. _____ wanted to go home."
6 "Did you get _____ nice at the sale?"
  "No, _____. I couldn't find _____ I liked."

CD1 51 Listen and check. Practice them with a partner.

5 **CD1 52** Listen. There is a word missing in each sentence. Call out what it is. Say the complete sentence.

Do you know ... famous?   ANYONE!

THE SECRET TO A LONG LIFE
Articles – *a/an, the*

1 Do you know anybody who lived to an old age? How old were they? Why do you think they lived so long?

2 **CD1 53** Read and listen to the text. Answer the questions.

1 How long did the grandfather live?
2 Where did he live?
3 What kind of farm did he have?
4 How many children did he have?
5 Why did everyone love him?
6 When did he stop working?
7 What was his secret to a long life?

My Grandfather's

My grandfather lived until he was 92 years old. He was a farmer with a cattle farm in a small town near a river in the southeastern part of New York State. He had two sons. The family lived in an old farmhouse. The oldest son, my uncle, owns the farm now.

In those days, people often bought beef directly from local farmers. My grandfather raised some of the best beef in the area. People came to his farm by car and truck to buy it.

Everybody loved my grandfather because he was such an honest and friendly man. He never went out to have dinner at restaurants, but every now and then he invited his family and friends to the farm for a picnic. He served hamburgers made from his beef. He didn't retire until he was 80. He said the secret to a long life was a happy marriage and a glass of warm milk before going to bed.

GRAMMAR SPOT

Articles

1 Find examples of the definite article (*the*) and the indefinite article (*a/an*) in the text.

2 What do you notice about these phrases?

...**traveled by car**.
...never went out to **have dinner**.
...before going **to bed**.

3 Read the rules in **Grammar Reference 4.2 p. 135**. Find some examples of these rules in the text.

PRACTICE

Reading aloud

1 Join the lines about the grandfather with *the, a, an,* or no article.

	the a an no article	
My grandfather was		farmer.
He lived in		small town.
He had a cattle farm in		southeastern part of New York State.
His family lived in		old farmhouse.
He raised some of		best beef in the area.
Some people came by		car to buy his beef.
He was such		honest man.
He never went out to have		dinner at restaurants.
He liked to have		little warm milk before bed.

CD1 54 Listen and check. Read the lines aloud to a partner.

Discussing grammar

Work with a partner.

2 Complete the sentences with *a/an, the,* or no article.

1 He has _____ boy and _____ girl. _____ boy is 22 and _____ girl is 17.

2 His son is _____ engineer and his daughter is _____ student.

3 He always has _____ cheese sandwiches for _____ lunch.

4 _____ whole family stayed at _____ Grand Hotel.

5 _____ few people came by _____ taxi to _____ party.

6 It was such _____ wonderful vacation. We had _____ best time ever.

7 I don't leave my house to go to _____ work. I work at _____ home on my computer.

8 I do all my shopping on _____ Internet. What _____ great way to shop!

Check it

3 Find *one* mistake in each sentence and correct it.

1 He's mail carrier, so he has breakfast at 4:00 a.m.
2 The love is more important than money.
3 I go to school by the bike.
4 I'm reading one good book right now.
5 "Where are the children?" "In a kitchen."
6 I live in middle of town, near the hospital.
7 My parents recently bought the nice house in the country.
8 I don't eat the bread because I don't like it.

READING AND LISTENING
Unusual places to eat

1 Are there lots of places to eat and drink in your town? Where are they? What do they serve?

2 Read the introduction. Look at the pictures and the Fact Files. What's unusual about the three restaurants?

3 Work in three groups.

> **Group A** Read about *Dinner in the Sky*.
>
> **Group B** Read about *Ithaa Undersea Restaurant*.
>
> **Group C** Read about *'s Baggers Restaurant*.

Answer the questions about your restaurant.

1 Where is the restaurant?
2 In what ways is it unusual?
3 When did it open?
4 How's the food?
5 How expensive is it?
6 Are there any problems?

4 Find a partner from the other two groups and compare the restaurants.

Listening

5 **CD1 55** Listen to people who visited the restaurants. Answer these questions after each person.

- Which restaurant did they visit? Who with?
- What was good about it?
- What wasn't so good?
- What were the other guests like?

Alexander	Tomo	Lucy

What do you think?

- Which do you think is the *most* unusual restaurant?
- Which would you like to visit? Why?
- Do you eat out? How often? What's your favorite resturant?
- Do you know any unusual restaurants? Tell the class.

No ordinary
place to eat!

Dinner in the Sky

FACT FILE
- 160 feet up in the air
- a table 30 feet x 16 feet
- diners hang from a crane
- no bathroom

Dinner in the Sky is for people who want more than a little excitement when they go out to eat. They sit at a huge table that hangs from a crane 160 feet in the air. It's not a good idea for people who are afraid of heights or for those who don't have much money. It costs $6,000. The twenty-two diners wear seat belts and relax and enjoy the views while the chefs prepare the finest food in front of them. The restaurant opened in Belgium in 2006, but now has branches in Paris, Dubai, Florida, and Las Vegas.

David Ghysels, the Belgian organizer says, "We realized that people were bored with going to the same old restaurants. They wanted to try something different. The sky's the limit with us!"

The crane is checked carefully before every sitting. The table is 30 feet x 16 feet and weighs 13,000 pounds. In the center there is a sunken platform for the chef and two servers. The food is delicious, but most guests don't feel like eating until they get used to being up so high. They then get the courage to look down at the ground where tiny people are looking up in amazement and waving.

Dinner in the Sky is exciting with good food, but there are problems. For example, even in quiet weather conversation is difficult because of the wind. Guests shout to each other across the table. Also, the bathroom. You can't go to the bathroom until the table descends again. Difficult for some! But later, back on earth, after a visit to the bathroom, the guests have a great experience to talk about.

For hundreds of years when tired travelers stopped on their journeys, there were only a few places to eat and drink. These days, streets are lined with restaurants, cafés, and snack bars, but some people want something more unusual.

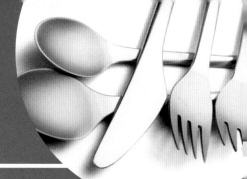

Ithaa Undersea Restaurant

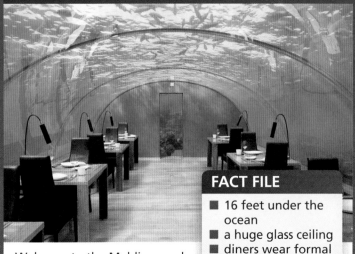

FACT FILE
- 16 feet under the ocean
- a huge glass ceiling
- diners wear formal clothes
- they eat face-to-face with sharks

Welcome to the Maldives and the first underwater restaurant in the world. The *Ithaa Undersea Restaurant* on Rangali Island sits 16 feet below the Indian Ocean. *Ithaa* means "pearl" in the Maldivian language and guests are like pearls in a glass oyster.

It's not cheap – about $265 for dinner – and there aren't many seats, only a dozen, so it's not easy to get a reservation even if you have enough money. However, it is easy to get to. You don't need to be a swimmer or a scuba diver, but you do have to wear formal clothes. You simply go down the spiral stairs to the restaurant.

The manager, Carlton Schieck says, "We have used aquarium technology to put diners face-to-face with the fish. Our guests are speechless at the color and beauty of the underwater world. They can enjoy the views and the fine food and not get their feet wet."

The views are spectacular. In the crystal-blue ocean, a few feet from your head, there are sharks, sting rays, turtles, and thousands of tropical fish looking at you as you eat. There is also a fabulous coral garden to add to the color. The experience is both romantic and magical – and you can guess what's on the menu!

The restaurant opened in 2004 and cost almost $5 million to build. In April 2010 it also became a hotel. If you want more excitement and would like to sleep underwater with the fish, you can do this for just $12,000 a night!

However, an underwater building can't last forever. It is thought that it will have a life of about twenty years.

's Baggers Restaurant

FACT FILE
- no servers
- food sent from above
- email as you eat
- eat now, pay later
- no tips

Germany likes to call itself The Land of Ideas and *'s Baggers Restaurant* in Nuremberg is certainly an amazing idea. It's a restaurant with no servers. You do everything for yourself with touch-screen TVs and computers. It opened in 2007 and is the first automated restaurant in the world.

When you arrive, you pick up an *'s Baggers* credit card and go to sit at a big, round table with three or four computer screens. You put your card into the computer and order your meal by touching the pictures on the screen. You don't see the chefs. They are in the kitchen high above you. They're real people, not machines (at least not yet). The food is all freshly cooked and when it is ready, it is put in a pot and sent down a spiral tube where it lands on the table in front of you. This gives a new meaning to fast food! The TVs are connected to the Internet, so if you get bored while waiting, you can send and receive emails and text messages.

A businessman named Michael Mack had the idea for *'s Baggers*. He decided that servers were unnecessary and expensive. "You don't need servers running to and from customers taking orders to the kitchen and back." Mack is planning to open more restaurants and now has the patent for the idea.

The meals are not expensive – about €8 ($11) a serving. And if you want, you can pay by debit card at the end of the month. And something else that saves money – there is, of course, no need to leave a tip!

VOCABULARY AND LISTENING
A piece of …

1 Work in small groups. Match amounts in **A** with nouns in **B**. How many can you make?

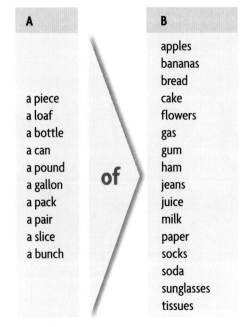

A		B
		apples
		bananas
		bread
a piece		cake
a loaf		flowers
a bottle		gas
a can		gum
a pound	**of**	ham
a gallon		jeans
a pack		juice
a pair		milk
a slice		paper
a bunch		socks
		soda
		sunglasses
		tissues

2 **CD1 56** Listen and repeat the expressions. How much are some of these things in your country?

I think a large loaf of white bread costs about $4.00.

3 **CD1 57** Listen to six conversations.

1 Where is the conversation taking place?
  • a newsstand • a clothing store • a pharmacy
  • a convenience store • a café • a supermarket

2 What does the customer want to buy?
3 Are there any numbers or prices that you hear? Write them down.

4 Who says these lines – the customer or the clerk? What is each line about?

1 "No problem. I have change."
2 "Do you have any in blue?"
3 "I'm afraid there are only two slices left."
4 "Take these three times a day."
5 "Do you have any cold soda?"
6 "They're in the first aisle, over there."

5 **CD1 57** Listen again and check. Work with a partner. Turn to p. 119 and choose one of the conversations. Learn it by heart and then act it out for the class.

▶▶ **WRITING** Writing an email *p. 104*

EVERYDAY ENGLISH

Can you come over for dinner?

1 What is happening in the picture? What are the people eating and drinking?

2 Match a question in **A** with a response in **B**.

A	B
1 Would you like some more rice?	___ a Black, no sugar. Do you have any decaf?
2 Could you pass the salt, please?	___ b No, not at all. I got it online. I'll give you the website.
3 Can I have some water, please?	___ c Do you want tap or bottled?
4 Please, just help yourselves to the dessert.	___ d No, thanks. But could I have another piece of bread?
5 Would anybody like some more ice cream?	___ e Yes, of course. Do you want the pepper, too?
6 How do you take your coffee?	___ f No, but I'd love some more fruit. Is there any left?
7 This is delicious! Would you mind giving me the recipe?	___ g No, of course not. You're our guests!
8 Do you want some help with the dishes?	___ h We will. It looks fantastic. Did you make it yourself?

CD1 58 Listen and check. What is the next line? Practice the conversations with a partner.

3 Complete the requests with *Can/Could I …?* or *Can/Could you …?*

1 _____ have some apple juice, please?
2 _____ tell me where Market Street is, please?
3 _____ see the menu, please?
4 _____ use your iPad for a few minutes, please?
5 _____ lend me $20, please?
6 _____ take me to school, please?
7 _____ help me with my homework, please?
8 _____ give me a ride to the train station, please?

Practice the requests with a partner. Give an answer for each request.

> Can I have some apple juice, please?

> Sorry, we …

> Yes, of course. Would you like …?

CD1 59 Listen and compare.

4 Make 5–8 in Exercise 3 more polite using *Would you mind + -ing?*

> Would you mind lending me $20?

> Not at all. Is 20 enough?

CD1 60 Listen and check. Practice saying them.

5 Request things from your teacher and other members of the class.

> Can I borrow your …?

> Could you lend me your …?

> Would you mind helping me with …?

Oxford Online Skills Program
Log in for additional online learning

5 Looking forward

Verb patterns • Future forms • Phrasal verbs • Expressing doubt and certainty

STARTER

Complete these sentences with ideas about you. Tell the class.

- *One day I want to …*
- *Tonight I'm …*
- *Right now, I'd like to …*
- *This weekend I'm going to …*

I'D LIKE TO …
Verb patterns

1 Read what the people say. What do they do? What are their problems? What do you think they want to do?

2 Work with a partner. Which sentences go with which person?

1 "I'm going to study hard for my final exams because I want to get a well-paid job." **Abby**

2 "I'd like to quit now and get a job, any job. I hope to earn some money."

3 "I'm thinking of applying for another job with a company in New York."

4 "Now I like sleeping late and planning vacations online for me and my wife."

5 "I'm looking forward to taking a break. We're going to the Caribbean this summer."

6 "I enjoy taking care of the kids, but I'd love to travel, too."

CD2 2 Listen and check. What else does each person say?

3 **CD2 2** Listen again. Complete the lines. Who says them?

1 I'd love __to work__ there.
2 I'm planning _____ nothing but read on the beach.
3 I _____ owing so much money.
4 I get fed up with _____ home all day. I'm looking forward to _____ back to work.
5 I'm pretty good at _____ a computer.
6 My parents say that I _____ quit school.

TOM

I'm 16 and I'm fed up with school and exams …

ABBY

I'm a student in my last year of college. I have almost $50,000 of student loan debt …

KELLY

I'm a paramedic. I love my job, but it's very stressful …

ALISON

I have three kids under seven and my husband travels for work a lot of the time …

GRAMMAR SPOT

1 Find examples in Exercises 2 and 3 of:

    verb + infinitive   verb + -ing
    prepositions *at, of, with,* and *to* + -ing

2 What's the difference between these sentences?

    I **like working** in New York.
    I'**d like to work** in New York.

3 Complete the sentences with the phrase *work in New York.*
Put the verb *work* in the correct form.

    I want …   *to work in New York.*
    I'd love …
    I enjoy …
    I'm fed up with …
    I hope …
    I'm thinking of …
    I'm looking forward to …

▶▶ **Grammar Reference 5.1** *p. 136* ▶▶ **Verb patterns** *p. 154*

MARTIN

> I work in I.T. There's nothing I don't know about computers, but I need a change …

BILL

> I'm a retired newspaper delivery man, and I didn't have a day off for 40 years …

PRACTICE

Discussing grammar

1 In these sentences, one or two verbs are correct, but not all three. Work with a partner. Select the correct verbs.

  1 I ___ to work in Paris.
    a ☑ want   b ☐ enjoy   c ☑ 'd like

  2 We ___ going to Florida for our vacation.
    a ☐ 're hoping   b ☐ like   c ☐ 're thinking of

  3 She ___ leave work early tonight.
    a ☐ wants   b ☐ 'd like   c ☐ can't

  4 I ___ to see you again soon.
    a ☐ hope   b ☐ 'd like   c ☐ 'm looking forward

  5 He ___ playing sports games on the computer.
    a ☐ wants   b ☐ 's good at   c ☐ enjoys

  6 Are you ___ learning languages?
    a ☐ want   b ☐ like   c ☐ good at

  7 We ___ taking a few days off soon.
    a ☐ 're going   b ☐ 'd love   c ☐ 're looking forward to

  8 I ___ doing housework.
    a ☐ 'm fed up with   b ☐ hate   c ☐ don't want

  CD2 3 Listen and check.

2 Make sentences with the verbs that weren't correct in Exercise 1. Read them aloud.

  CD2 4 Listen and check.

> I enjoy working in Paris.

Making questions

3 Write questions.

  1 I hope to go to college. (*What/want/study?*)
  2 One of my favorite hobbies is baking. (*What/like/bake?*)
  3 I'm bored. (*What would/like/do?*)
  4 I'm looking forward to the party. (*Who/hoping/see/there?*)
  5 We're planning our summer vacation.
    (*Where/thinking/going?*)

  CD2 5 Listen and check. How do the conversations continue? Practice some of them with a partner.

Talking about you

4 Ask and answer the questions with a partner.

  • Where would you like to be right now?
  • Do you like learning English?
  • Would you like to learn any other languages? Which ones?
  • Would you like to take a break now?

▶▶ **WRITING** **CD2 6** **Writing for talking** *p. 105*

DO YOU HAVE ANY PLANS?

will, going to, and the Present Continuous for the future

1 Match questions 1–4 with an answer from Pete and an answer from Debbie. Who has definite future plans? Who doesn't have definite future plans?

1 What are you doing this evening?
2 Are you doing anything interesting this weekend?
3 Are you going to have a party for your birthday?
4 Where are you going on vacation?

Pete

a Of course! I'm going to invite all my friends.
b I'm going surfing in Costa Rica.
c Yes, I am. I'm going to stay with an old friend from school.
d I'm meeting my brother for dinner.

Debbie

e I haven't thought about it. Maybe I'll just celebrate at home with a few friends.
f I can't decide. Maybe I'll go bike riding in Colorado.
g No, I'm not. I'll call you and maybe we can do something together.
h Nothing much. I think I'll just watch a movie and order a pizza.

CD2 7 Listen and check.

2 Pete is talking to his friend, Ben. Debbie is talking to Ella. Answer the questions.

1 Why can't Ben go out with Pete and his brother?
2 Why is Pete going to visit his old school friend?
3 Where's Ben going on vacation?
4 Where's Ella going on vacation?
5 When's Debbie's birthday?
6 Why won't Ella stay late?

Talking about you

3 With your partner ask and answer the four questions in Exercise 1 about you.

GRAMMAR SPOT

Will, going to, and the Present Continuous can all refer to future time.

1 **Will** can express an intention decided *at* the time of speaking.
   I'll call you later.

2 **Going to** can express a plan decided *before* the time of speaking.
   I'm going to stay with a friend.

3 The **Present Continuous** can express an arrangement.
   I'm working late this evening.

▶▶ **Grammar Reference 5.2 p. 136**

PRACTICE

Discussing grammar

1 Work with a partner. Choose the correct verb form.

1 **A** Have you decided which college to apply to?
   B Yes. *I'll / I'm going to* apply to Reed College.

2 **A** I don't have your number.
   B Really? *I'll / I'm going to* text it to you right now.

3 **A** We don't have any fruit in the house.
   B *I'll go / I'm going* shopping this afternoon.
   I'll / I'm going to get some apples.

4 **A** My bag is really heavy.
   B Give it to me. *I'll / I'm going to* carry it for you.

5 **A** Tony's back from vacation.
   B Is he? *I'll / I'm going to* give him a call.

6 **A** What *will we have / are we having* for dinner?
   B *I'm going to / I'll* make spaghetti and meatballs.

CD2 8 Listen, check, and practice. What's the extra line?

What can you say?

2 CD2 9 Books closed, listen to the beginning of the conversations. Respond to each one.

> **Why are you looking forward to the weekend?**
>
> Because I'm ...

3 CD2 10 Listen and compare.

When can we meet?

4 With a partner, find a time to meet next week.
Student A Your calendar is on p. 147.
Student B Your calendar is on p. 149.

> **What are you doing on Monday afternoon?**
>
> I'm ...

Will you, won't you?

5 Use the words in **A** and make sentences with *I think … will …*. Match them with a line in **B**.

> I think you'll pass ...

A

1 you/pass your driver's test
2 my team/win
3 it/warm today
4 I/join a gym
5 they/get divorced
6 I/go by train

B

___ I won't go on a diet.
___ You won't fail again.
___ You won't need your sweater.
___ I won't fly.
___ They won't stay together.
___ They won't lose this time.

6 CD2 11 Listen and check. What is the extra line?

🗨 LISTENING AND SPEAKING

How does it feel to be 20-something?

1 Think of someone you know in their twenties. Tell a partner about them.
name • age • relationship to you • job • interests • ambitions

2 *The Times* newspaper asked people to find out how it feels to be a 20-something in the 21st century. What is a 20-something?

3 CD2 12 Listen to three 20-somethings, Leo, Elsa, and Dan. Who is happy? Who feels grown-up? Who knows what they want to do in the future?

I still can't believe I'm a grown-up!

Leo 28   Elsa 26   Dan 24

4 Complete the questions with the correct name.

1 How old is __Leo__'s nephew?
2 How much did _____ owe when he graduated from college?
3 Why did _____ give up studying law?
4 How much does _____ earn as a junior reporter?
5 How long did _____ travel?
6 What questions did _____'s nephew ask?

Ask and answer the questions with a partner.

5 CD2 12 Listen again. After each 20-something, answer the questions.

Leo
1 Why was he shocked by his nephew's questions?
2 Is he happy? Why?
3 What is he going to do next year?
4 When does he think get married?

Elsa
5 Where did she travel?
6 What is she doing now?
7 What does her father keep asking her?
8 How is her life different from her mother's at Elsa's age?

Dan
9 Why is he a *boomerang kid*?
10 Does he think that his situation is unusual?
11 When does he think he'll marry his girlfriend?
12 What happens when you're still at home with your parents?

What do you think?

- When do you think is the best time for children to leave home?
- What are the pros and cons for parents if their children move back home?
- What are the pros and cons for the children?

1 Do you know the name Chernobyl? Do you know where it is? Find out about it on the Internet. Discuss with the class.

2 Read the introduction to *Palina – the girl with two families*.

- Where does Palina come from?
- When was she born?
- Why didn't her future look good?

3 Read *Life in the village of Polessye*. Are the sentences true or false? Correct the false ones.

1 Palina was born the same year as the disaster.
2 She grew up in Ireland.
3 She was an only child.
4 Experts came to her school in Minsk.
5 The forest was dangerous.
6 The experts paid for the children to take vacations abroad.
7 Palina wanted to go to Ireland because she could speak English.

4 Read *Life in Ireland*. Answer the questions.

1 How did Palina communicate with the family at first?
2 Why was she so surprised in the shopping mall?
3 Was her English fluent at the end of the vacation?
4 How often did she visit her Irish family?

5 Read *Palina today*. Why is Palina lucky? What reasons can you find?

6 Read the sentences. Who do you think said each one?

1 "It's difficult to sell any of our produce these days."
2 "We aren't going to pick any more mushrooms."
3 "Would you like to go to Ireland?"
4 "I'm a little worried about going."
5 "Welcome to Ireland. We hope you'll be happy here."
6 "Let's play outside!"
7 "We'll pay for your education."
8 "One day I'm going to return as a doctor."

What do you think?

- "The disaster changed the lives of everybody in the village." What does this mean? How do you think life changed?
- Was Palina's family rich? How do you know?
- Do you think Palina was ever homesick?

Role play

Work in groups and think of questions to ask Palina about her life. In pairs, take the roles of Palina and the interviewer. Ask and answer questions.

Nice to meet you Palina. Can I ask you some questions?

Sure.

CD2 13 Listen and compare.

When and where were you born?

Palina

In the early hours of April 26, 1986, the worst nuclear accident in history occurred in the Ukrainian city of Chernobyl.

Two years later and two hundred miles away, Palina Yanachkina was born in the village of Polessye, in northern Belarus. Like many others in her village she had a lot of health problems and her future didn't look good. Then a vacation in Ireland changed everything.

— the girl with two families

Life in the village of Polessye

The nuclear disaster changed the lives of everybody in the village. It took away all hope for the future. However, when Palina was born in 1988 her parents did their best to give her and her brother a good life. They were farmers and before the accident, they sold meat, fruit, and vegetables to the international market. After the disaster, no one wanted to buy anything.

The villagers were often sick and depressed. When Palina was eight, experts from the capital, Minsk, came to her school and did health tests on the children. The experts told them to stop picking the mushrooms in the forest because they were badly contaminated. When she was ten, the experts returned with news of a charity that helped children like Palina take vacations abroad. They asked her if she would like to go to Limerick, Ireland and stay with a family. Palina felt a little nervous about leaving home and she didn't speak a word of English, but she decided to go.

Life in Ireland

When Palina met her Irish family, she liked them immediately. John and Fiona Quaid and their two children, Chloe and Evan gave Palina a warm welcome. At first the only way to communicate was with a phrase book, but soon she became good friends with the children. They didn't need language to play.

So many things in Ireland surprised Palina. They visited a shopping mall and she couldn't believe her eyes because there was so much to choose from. She only knew her little village store. She missed her family, but couldn't speak to them because they didn't have a phone.

By the time she went home, Palina could speak a few words of English and was very happy when the Quaids invited her back. After, she started to visit the family twice a year and often spent three months with them in summer.

Palina today: "I'm so lucky!"

When Palina was in her teens, the experts returned to Polessye and checked her again. They couldn't believe how healthy she was. Her time in Ireland was improving her health and her English.

In her free time Palina helped run the farm. However, she didn't want to continue doing this for the rest of her life. She dreamed of becoming a doctor, but had no money to study. John and Fiona understood her problem. They offered to pay for her to study in Ireland and said she could stay with them full-time. Palina was amazed and happy. It was hard for her parents to see her leave, but they wanted the best for their daughter.

Palina is now studying biochemistry at the University of Limerick. She hopes to study medicine one day and return to Belarus to help those who are not as lucky as she is.

VOCABULARY AND SPEAKING

Phrasal verbs – literal

Phrasal verbs consist of a verb + adverb/preposition. Some phrasal verbs are literal. Look at these examples.

> I wanted to **move back** home. (move + back)
> It **took away** all hope for the future. (take + away)
> She **grew up** in a small village. (grow + up)

1 Complete the sentences with a word from the box.

out   at   down   on   back   off

1 Come in and **take** _____ your coat!
2 **Put** _____ something warm. It's cold today.
3 There's some ice cream in the freezer. Can you **take it** _____ ?
4 If you don't feel well, go and **lie** _____ .
5 **Look** _____ the ocean. Isn't it beautiful?
6 I can lend you $20. **Pay** me _____ when you can.

2 Work with a partner. Take turns acting out one of these phrasal verbs. Can you guess what your partner is doing?

- throw something away
- try something on
- look for something
- turn something off
- turn around
- pick something up

3 Complete the sentences with a phrasal verb from Exercise 2. Read them aloud.

1 Help me _____ my glasses. I can't find them.
2 I like these shoes. Can I _____ them _____ ?
3 Those jeans look great. _____ _____ so I can see the back!
4 Don't throw it on the ground! _____ it _____ !
5 Don't _____ that newspaper _____ . I want to read it.
6 Why are all these lights on? _____ them _____ .

Phrasal verbs – idiomatic

Some phrasal verbs are idiomatic.

> I **gave up** my job because I was bored. (= stopped)
> She **picked up** English from the children. (= learned it little by little)
> The plane **took off** late. (= left the ground)

4 Match the phrases with the pictures.

look up a word   take care of a baby   run out of milk break up with someone   get along with somebody

5 Complete the sentences with a phrasal verb from Exercise 4 in the correct form. Read them aloud.

1 "What does this word mean?" "I don't know. I'll _____ it _____ ."
2 My boss is a great guy. I _____ very well _____ him.
3 Leave little Emma with me. I'll _____ her while you're out.
4 It was a horrible car ride – traffic jams all the way, and we almost _____ gas.
5 I feel miserable because I _____ my boyfriend last weekend.

Talking about you

Complete the questions with one of the phrasal verbs on this page in the correct form.

1 Where did you _____ ? Do you still live in the same house?
2 How do you _____ your parents?
3 Did you ever _____ a boyfriend or girlfriend?
4 Would you like to be a doctor or nurse and _____ people?
5 Are you good at _____ foreign languages?
6 Do you _____ a lot of words in your dictionary?

CD2 14 Listen and check. Ask and answer the questions about you with a partner.

1 Read the questions and the possible answers. Which are …?

- 100% certain
- 75% certain
- 50% certain

1 Q Do you think Tom will pass his final exams?

A – Of course he will.
– He might.
– Mmm … maybe.
– I doubt it.
– No chance.

2 Q Does Martin earn a lot of money?

A – Yes, absolutely.
– I think so.
– Mmm … I'm not sure.
– I don't think so.
– Definitely not.

3 Q Is the US going to win?

A – Definitely!
– Maybe.
– They might.
– Anything's possible.
– Not a chance.

2 **CD2 15** Listen to the conversations. Which answers above do the two people give? Do they agree with each other?

3 **CD2 15** Listen again. Pay attention to the stress and intonation. Practice in groups of three. Choose your own replies.

4 Complete these conversations with a word or phrase from Exercise 1.

1 A Kelly's job is stressful, isn't it?

B _____ . She's a paramedic.

A Is she going on vacation soon?

B I _____ so. She says she _____ go to the Caribbean.

2 A It's Rob's birthday next week, isn't it?

B Yes, _____ . It's on the 22nd.

A So he's a Capricorn.

B No, I _____ . I think he's an Aquarius.

3 A Do you think Anita and Paul are in love?

B _____ . They're getting married in Hawaii.

A How nice! Are you going to the wedding?

B _____ . I can't afford it.

CD2 16 Listen and compare.

5 Work in groups. Ask everyone in the group for their opinion.

1 Did Leo Tolstoy write *War and Peace*?
2 Is Nicole Kidman American?
3 Was Sherlock Holmes a real person?
4 Is the population of China more than two billion?
5 Do some vegetarians eat fish?
6 Is the weather going to be nice next weekend?
7 Are you going to be rich and famous one day?
8 Is your school the best in town?

CD2 17 Listen and compare.

6 The way I see it

What ... like? • Comparatives and superlatives • Synonyms and antonyms
What's happening?

STARTER

Look at the picture of Mia. Describe her. **She's in her 20s. She has ... She's very ...**

TELL ME ABOUT HER
What's she like?

1 **CD2 18** Listen to four conversations about Mia. Which question ...?

- asks about her health
- asks for a physical description
- uses *like* as a verb
- means *Tell me about her*.

1 **"Do you like Mia?"** "Yes, I do. I like her a lot."	**3** **"What's Mia like?"** "She's really nice. Very friendly."
2 **"How's Mia?"** "She's doing very well."	**4** **"What does Mia look like?"** "She's tall with brown eyes and black hair."

2 Think of more answers to the questions.

> Do you like Mia?

> Yes, she's my best friend.

> No, I can't stand her!

> She's all right.

3 Match a question in **A** with an answer in **B**.

A	B
1 What's your teacher like?	___ a Beautiful! Warm and sunny.
2 What sports do you like?	___ b She's great! She helps us a lot.
3 What does your brother look like?	___ c They're OK. Busy as usual.
4 Do you like pizza?	___ d He has blond hair and blue eyes.
5 What's the weather like today?	___ e Mmm, I love it!
6 How are your parents?	___ f Bike riding and skiing.

CD2 19 Listen and check. Ask and answer the questions about you.

PRACTICE
What's it like?

1 Mia often travels for her job. She's talking to her friend, Tom, about Shanghai. Complete Tom's questions.

T What *'s Shanghai* _____ like?
M It's very big and noisy, but it's very exciting.
T What _____ like?
M It's the best in the world! I just love Chinese food!
T What _____ like?
M They're very friendly, and they really want to do business.
T What _____ like?
M When I was there, it was hot and humid.
T What _____ like?
M There are new buildings everywhere, but if you look hard, you can still find some older ones, too.

2 **CD2 20** Listen and check. Practice the conversation with a partner.

3 Ask and answer the same questions about the town or city you are in now.

Shanghai

Singapore

Dubai

SINGAPORE, SHANGHAI, AND DUBAI
Comparatives and superlatives

1 **CD2 21** Mia also went to Singapore and Dubai. Listen and complete some of the things she says.

THE CITY   Singapore is older than Shanghai, but it's _____ smaller. Shanghai is _____ bigger than Singapore and _____ noisier, too.

BUSINESS   They're both top financial centers, but Singapore is _____ important. It's better for investment.

BUILDINGS AND PEOPLE   Shanghai is more _____ than Singapore, but it isn't as cosmopolitan. Dubai is _____ newest and _____ city, and it's the most _____ .

CLIMATE   Singapore is _____ than Shanghai. But it isn't _____ hot _____ Dubai. Dubai is the _____ place. Singapore is very humid, so it's _____ than Shanghai. But Dubai is the _____ . It only rains for a few days a year.

WHICH IS BEST?   For me Shanghai is the _____ because it's the _____ and the _____ exciting.

2 **CD2 21** Listen again and check. What extra information do you hear?

3 What questions did Tom ask about each topic in Exercise 1? Ask and answer them with a partner.

GRAMMAR SPOT

1 What are the comparative and superlative forms of these adjectives?

old	busy	big	important
small	noisy	wet	modern
new	dry	hot	exciting

When do we use -er and -est? When do we use *more* and *the most*?

2 These adjectives are irregular. What are the comparative and superlative forms?
   good   bad

3 Look at these patterns.
   It's **a little** bigger.   It's **a lot/much** smaller.
   It's **isn't as** hot as Dubai.

▶▶ Grammar Reference 6.1–6.2 p. 137

PRACTICE

Pronunciation

1 **CD2 22** Listen and practice the sentences.

/ə/ /ə/ /i/
I'm older than Jane. But I'm not as old as John. He's the oldest.

2 **CD2 23** Listen and practice the conversation with a partner.

> **Smart**
> **A** WHO's smarter, YOU or BEN?
> **B** ME, of course! He's smart, but he isn't NEARLY as smart as ME!

Practice again using these adjectives.

> | kind | funny | good-looking | ambitious |
> |---|---|---|---|

CD2 24 Listen and compare.

Comparing people

3 Read the profiles of the four people. Complete the sentences comparing them.

1 Agnes has the <u>largest</u> family. She has _____ children. Kevin doesn't have _____ children _____ Agnes. He has only has two.

2 Marilou is _____ . She's 41. Wilfredo is _____ . He's only 25. Agnes is a little _____ Kevin. She's 34, and he's 32.

3 Kevin works the _____ hours – 60 hours a week. Agnes doesn't work as _____ hours as Kevin, but she still works hard. She works _____ than Wilfredo, who only works 35 hours a week.

4 Kevin earns the _____ . He has the _____ salary. Marilou has the _____ salary. Wilfredo doesn't earn as _____ as Agnes. She earns almost twice _____ as him.

5 Agnes has _____ house than Marilou, but it isn't _____ Kevin's. He has a huge house – six bedrooms! Wilfredo has _____ house.

4 Compare the two women. Then compare the two men.
Agnes is younger than Marilou.

5 Make sentences about their personalities. Compare two or three of them.
Marilou isn't as ... , but she's more ...

6 Work in small groups. Who do you think ...?

- has the most important job
- is the most creative
- is the busiest

Why do you think Agnes is the happiest?
Why is Marilou the unhappiest?

AGNES
in Sweden

LIFE DATA

Age: 34

Family:
Married, 3 children

Job:
Interior designer

Works hours/week:
50

Salary:
$75,000 a year

House:
4 bedrooms

PERSONALITY

Intelligent:
★★★★★

Ambitious:
★★★

Happy:
☺☺☺☺☺

KEVIN
in Chicago

LIFE DATA

Age: 32

Family:
Married, two sons

Job:
Financial advisor

Works hours/week:
60

Salary:
$100,000 a year

House:
6 bedrooms

PERSONALITY

Intelligent:
★★

Ambitious:
★★★★★

Happy:
☺☺☺

WILFREDO
in Mexico

LIFE DATA

Age: 25

Family:
Single

Job:
Baker

Works hours/week:
35

Salary:
$35,000 a year

House:
2 bedrooms

PERSONALITY

Intelligent:
★★★

Ambitious:
★★

Happy:
☺☺☺☺

MARILOU
in the Philippines

LIFE DATA

Age: 41

Family:
Married, 1 daughter

Job:
Nurse

Works hours/week:
55

Salary:
$25,000 a year

House:
3 bedrooms

PERSONALITY

Intelligent:
★★★★

Ambitious:
★

Happy:
☺☺

💬 LISTENING AND SPEAKING
My family

1 What are you like as a person?
Do any of these adjectives describe you?

messy	neat	lazy	moody	noisy
kind	selfish	shy	ambitious	happy

2 **CD2 25** Listen to three people talking about their family. Complete the chart.

Sally 20
Who is she like? _____
In what ways? _____
_____
_____

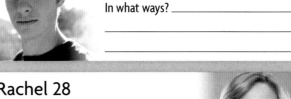

Jamie 16
Who is he like? _____
In what ways? _____
_____
_____

Rachel 28
Who is she like? _____
In what ways? _____
_____
_____

3 How are these people different from each other?
• Sally and her sister, Lena
• Jamie and his twin brother, Rob
• Rachel and her father
• Rachel and her sister, Jenny

4 **CD2 25** Listen again. Complete the sentences.

Sally
1 We _____ movies …
2 And she's _____ size as me.

Jamie
3 We _____ interests.
4 We _____ art.

Rachel
5 I hope I'm _____ him.

5 Who are *you* like in *your* family? Who do you look like?

1 What do you want from the country you live in? Put these qualities in order of importance for you (1 = most important).

- ☐ a safe and honest society
- ☐ a good education for children and adults
- ☐ the opportunity to find work and have a career
- ☐ a good place to raise your children
- ☐ a society where people are free to say and do what they want

Talk with a partner, and then in small groups. Discuss your answers as a class.

2 Read the introduction to the article. What is special about London? What is special about Stroud Green Road?

3 Look at the pictures and profiles of the people in the article. Where are they from? What are they doing in London?

4 Work in small groups. Choose two of the people. Read about them and answer the questions.

1 When and why did he/she move to England?
2 How did he/she find it at first?
3 What does he/she say about her/his business?
4 How does England compare to his/her own country?
5 What family does he/she talk about?
6 How does he/she feel about living in England?
7 Does he/she want to stay or go back home?

5 Find a student from another group. Compare and exchange information.

6 Which of the qualities of a country in Exercise 1 are important to these four people? Did they find these qualities in England?

What do you think?

- When people move to a foreign country, they can experience "culture shock." What do you think this phrase means?
- Why do people leave their own country? What are they looking for? What are they escaping from?

Project

Find someone living in your country who is from a different country. What do they do? How do they feel about living in your country? Bring the information to class and tell the other students.

▶▶ **WRITING Describing my hometown** *p. 106*

The world on one street

STROUD GREEN ROAD N4

London is one of the most multicultural cities in the world. On an ordinary street in north London, people from across the globe live and work side by side. Here on **Stroud Green Road** there are people from Turkey, China, Afghanistan, Pakistan, Vietnam, Colombia, Poland, Kenya, and France.

What are the thoughts of the people who live here? How do they feel about the land they now call home?

Profile

Name	Burkan Mehmet, 41
Born	Istanbul, **Turkey**
Business	The Sunflower Gallery

This area is very cosmopolitan, and that's why I love it. When I first came to England in 1986, I thought it would be like New York, but it was much quieter. I didn't know anybody, and I wanted to go home.

I came here to study business in college. First, I had a restaurant. Now I run this florist shop. My customers come from so many different cultures – I learn something new every day.

What I like about England is that there's a system that works. Things are more organized here. I'm a British citizen now. When I go back to Turkey, I see how I've changed. Life in Turkey is faster and more hectic than here.

I would like to go back to Istanbul one day. But for now, I love London. I'm married, and I have a daughter, Ceren. I wouldn't think of living anywhere else.

My parents divorced, and my mother came to England to make a new start. I was 19.

For me it was an enormous shock. When you are in Colombia, you think everything in Europe is wonderful. I arrived in September, the weather was awful and the skies were gray. London wasn't nearly as exciting as I thought.

I spent a year studying English and then I then fell in love. The marriage didn't work, but I had two children, Jennifer and Julian.

I bought this restaurant. It's becoming more and more popular, especially with Europeans. I love my work. It's the most interesting job in the world. I'm not just serving food, I'm giving people an experience of my culture.

I'm so thankful now that I came here. There is more opportunity. I go to Colombia every year, but when I'm there I miss England. I really love being here.

Profile

Name	Luz-Elena Lamprea, 41
Born	Tuluá, **Colombia**
Business	Los Guadales Restaurant

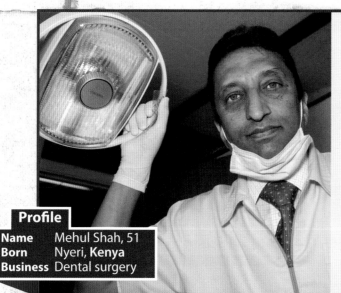

I always wanted to study medicine. I had an uncle in London, so when I was 16, I came here.

It was very hard. I remember the drive from the airport. The roads were so much bigger and busier than in Kenya. It was summer, and the weather was beautiful. But then of course the first winter came. It was the coldest winter for years!

My patients are of all nationalities, all religions, all colors. I love it. I'm seeing the third generation of the same families.

This is a democratic country. You're free here, you can say, and think, and do what you like.

England is a welcoming society. My children were born here. All their friends are English. I feel British now. I became a British citizen 24 years ago. Britain gave me an education and the opportunity to better myself. This is my country, my home.

Profile

Name	Mehul Shah, 51
Born	Nyeri, **Kenya**
Business	Dental surgery

I was a doctor in China. My daughter wanted to study in England, so we moved here in 2000.

Life for us here was impossible for the first few years. It was hard to find work. It was also difficult to talk to people. But things got easier as my English improved. People in the West are now more interested in herbal medicine.

My daughter is married and has a son and lives here. I see her every day. That is Chinese culture – children and parents stay together.

This is the big difference for us. In China we are surrounded by family. Here I feel like a foreigner. I miss my friends and colleagues, and my wife is very close to her family back home.

My daughter is settled here, but I think my wife and I will return to China one day. We'll see.

Profile

Name	Ming Liang Chen, 50
Born	Qingdao, **China**
Business	The Chinese Medical Center

VOCABULARY
Synonyms and antonyms

1 Look at the extract from the text on p. 47.

> ❝ It was hard to find work. It was also difficult to talk to people. But things got easier … ❞

Which words are synonyms?
Which words are antonyms (opposites)?

2 We use synonyms and antonyms because we don't want to repeat words. What's wrong with this conversation?

A It's a nice day, isn't it?
B Yes, it's *nice*!
A But it wasn't *nice* yesterday, was it?
B No, it wasn't.

With a partner, practice the conversation using the words *beautiful* and *great*.

Synonyms

3 Complete the conversations with a synonym in the box.

tiny	smart	annoyed	wealthy	fed up	satisfied

1 "Maria comes from a very rich family."
   "Really? I knew her uncle was very _____."

2 "Was Sophie angry when you were late?"
   "Yeah. She was pretty _____, that's for sure."

3 "Jack's such an intelligent boy!"
   "Mm. He's very _____ for a ten-year-old."

4 "I've had enough of this long, cold winter."
   "I know. I'm _____ with the dark nights."

5 "Dave and Sarah's apartment is small, isn't it?"
   "It's _____. I don't know how they live there."

6 "Are you happy with your new car?"
   "Yes, I'm very _____ with it. It runs well."

CD2|26 Listen and check. What's the extra line of each conversation?

4 Think of another word for these adjectives.

good-looking	amazing	crazy	big
new	old	awful	cold

5 Work in pairs. Write sentences using an adjective in Exercise 4. Read them to another group. They reply using a synonym.

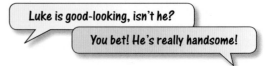

Luke is good-looking, isn't he?

You bet! He's really handsome!

Antonyms

6 We can agree with people by using *not very* + an antonym.

A Tom's so messy!
B Yes, teenagers aren't very neat, are they?

7 Think of a word that means the opposite of these adjectives.

easy	_difficult_	loud	_____
noisy	_____	exciting	_____
miserable	_____	generous	_____
polite	_____	clean	_____

8 Agree with these sentences using antonyms.

1 That man was so rude to me!

Yes, he wasn't very polite, was he?

2 Some people are so generous!
3 Dave's apartment is always so dirty!
4 His wife always looks so miserable!
5 Their children are so loud!
6 This class is boring!

CD2|27 Listen and compare. Practice the conversations.

💬 EVERYDAY ENGLISH
What's happening?

1 Read the listings and find the answers to these questions.
- How much is it to go to The Getty Center?
- Is the Pollock exhibition open on Sunday?
- How many nights is the concert on at the Walt Disney Concert Hall?
- Is the movie at the Regent Theatre suitable for young children?
- Is *Cats* popular? How do you know?

2 **CD2 28** Listen and complete the conversations.

1 A What do you want to do today?
 B I'm not sure. How about _____ ?
 A Mmm ... I don't really feel like _____ .

2 B OK. Would you like to go to an exhibition?
 A That sounds interesting! _____ ?
 B Well, there's a Jackson Pollock exhibition.
 A Is it _____ ?
 B I think it _____ good!

3 A _____ ?
 B It's on at the The Getty Center.
 A How much is it?
 B It's _____ .
 A What time is it open?
 B From 10:00 till 5:30.
 A Great! _____ !

3 **CD2 28** Listen again. Practice the conversations in pairs.

4 Work with a partner. Have similar conversations about other things to do.

5 Imagine you are in Los Angeles for a weekend. You and your partner have $250 each to spend on going out. Talk together and decide what you want to do.

Listings
Time Out — Los Angeles

Natural History Museum
Exposition Park
900 Exposition Boulevard
Los Angeles, CA
9:30 a.m. – 5:00 p.m.
$12; $9 SENIORS/ COLLEGE STUDENTS WITH ID;
$8 CHILDREN 13–17;
$5 CHILDREN 5–12;
FREE CHILDREN UNDER 5
Exhibitions
Shells
Rare, endangered, and extinct seashells from around the world
Insect Zoo
The interesting world of bugs
Gems and Minerals
More than 2,000 valuable specimens to examine

The Getty Center
1200 Getty Center Drive
Los Angeles, CA
Tues – Fri and Sun
10:00 a.m. – 5:30 p.m.
Sat 10:00 a.m.– 9:00 p.m.
Closed Mondays
FREE
Exhibition
Jackson Pollock's Mural
Pollock's transition from a more traditional artist to an experimental artist.

Walt Disney Concert Hall
111 South Grand Avenue
Los Angeles, CA
(323) 850-2000
Concert
Mozart & Brahms
Thurs 3rd, 8:00;
Fri 4th, 11:00;
Sat 5th, 2:00
$23.50–$191.00
The Los Angeles Philharmonic performs Mozart's Piano Concerto No. 21 and Brahms' Symphony No. 1.

Regent Theatre
1045 Broxton Avenue
Los Angeles, CA
(310) 208-3250
GENERAL ADMISSION $10.50; BARGAIN ADMISSION $8.00
Movie
The Survivors (R)
10:40am, 1:50, 4:00, 6:10, 8:20, 10:30
Family fights to live after nuclear war destroys world. They bravely fight the challenges they face without losing one another.

La Mirada Theatre
14900 La Mirada Blvd
La Mirada, CA
(562) 944-9801
Musical
Cats
Wed – Thurs 7:30 p.m.;
Fri – Sat 8:00 p.m.; Sat – Sun matinee 2:00 p.m.
$20–$70. RUNS 2 HRS. ORDER TICKETS IN ADVANCE.
Based on a poem by T.S. Eliot, Andrew Lloyd Webber's award-winning musical is one of the longest running shows. For over 20 years, this musical tells the story of Jellicle cats and how they select one to go to the "the Heaviside layer."

7 Living history

Present Perfect • *for* and *since* • *ever* and *never*
Word formation • *Agree with me!*

 STARTER

What's the Simple Past and the past participle of these
verbs? Which are regular? Which are irregular?

live	have	be	give	go	eat
know	meet	move	work	write	

A HOUSE WITH HISTORY
Present Perfect, *for* and *since*

1 **CD2 29** Look at the pictures. Listen and read about **Max**.
Answer the questions.

1 Where does he live?   3 Where did he meet his wife?
2 What's his job?   4 Does he have any children?

2 Read about **Max's apartment**. Why is it famous? Who lived
there? When? What tense are the verbs in **bold**? Why?

3 Work with a partner. Read the questions.
Are they about **Max (M)** or **John Steinbeck (JS)**?

1 How long has he lived in the apartment?	M
2 How long did he live in the apartment?	___
3 Where does he work?	___
4 How long has he worked there?	___
5 What was his job in New York City?	___
6 Which newspaper did he write for?	___
7 How long has he been married?	___
8 How long was he married to his second wife?	___

Max

"Hi! I'm Max. I live in New York City in an apartment on
East 51st Street. I**'ve lived** here for three years. I'm a
press photographer. I**'ve worked** for *The Daily News*
since 2012. My wife's name is Meg. We**'ve been** married
for two years. We met in college. Meg's a receptionist at
Lennox Hill Hospital. I get around the city on a bicycle. I**'ve
done** this since I moved here. Meg goes by bus. We don't
have any children yet."

4 Ask and answer the questions in Exercise 3 with your partner.

CD2 30 Listen and check. Practice again.

GRAMMAR SPOT

1 What are the tenses in these sentences? Why are they used?

John Steinbeck **lived** there for one year.
Max **has lived** there for three years.

Find more examples in the texts.

2 How do we form the Present Perfect?

3 Look at the examples. When do we use *for*? When do we use *since*?

for three years/two hours/a long time
since 6:00/Monday/2009/July/I moved

▶▶ **Grammar Reference 7.1 p. 137**

---

5 Read the texts again. What differences and similarities are there between Max and John Steinbeck?

Max's apartment

Max's apartment is famous. John Steinbeck, the American writer and novelist, **lived** there for a year in the 1940s. He **moved** to New York City in 1943 and **worked** as a war correspondent for a newspaper. He **wrote** for the *New York Herald Tribune*. He **was** married three times. He and his second wife of five years, Gwyndolyn, **had** two sons.

PRACTICE

for or *since*?

1 Complete the time expressions with *for* or *since*.

_____ half an hour	_____ a long time	_____ October
_____ 2001	_____ ten o'clock	_____ last Tuesday
_____ I was 14	_____ three months	_____ a couple of weeks

2 Match the phrases in **A** and **B** with a sentence in **C**. There is more than one possible answer. Read them aloud to a partner.

A	**B**	**C**
1 I've known John	from 2005 to 2007.	We went to Brazil.
2 I last went to the movies	for over an hour.	We met in college.
3 I've had this watch	two weeks ago.	I really need some coffee.
4 I lived in New York	since 2008.	My grandpa gave it to me.
5 I've lived in this house	since I was a child.	I had a great time there.
6 We last took a vacation	for years.	What have you been up to?
7 I haven't seen you	for three years.	The movie was really boring.
8 We haven't had a break	two years ago.	It has a big backyard.

CD2 31 Listen, compare, and practice. Make similar sentences about you.

Asking questions

3 Complete the conversations. What tense is used in each question?

A Where ___*do you*___ live, Susan?
B In an apartment near the river.
A How long _____ there?
B For three years.
A Why _____ move there?
B Because we wanted to be in a nicer area.

CD2 32 Listen and check. Practice the conversation with a partner.

4 With your partner, make more conversations using these prompts.

1	**2**
A What ... do?	**A** ... know Dave Brown?
B I work ...	**B** Yes, I ...
A How long ...?	**A** How long ...?
B For ...	**B** For ...
A What ... do before that?	**A** Where ... meet him?
B I worked ...	**B** We ...

CD2 33 Listen and compare.

5 Work with a partner. Ask and answer questions with *How long ...?* Then ask for more information.

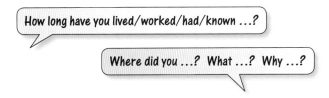

How long have you lived/worked/had/known ...?

Where did you ...? What ...? Why ...?

AN ARCHAEOLOGIST
Present Perfect – *ever* and *never*

1 Look at the pictures of Frieda Hoffmann and read the introduction. What's her nationality? Which countries has she been to? What are her passions?

2 Read the interview with Frieda and write the questions below on the correct line in the interview.

> Have you always been interested ...?
> ~~When did you first go abroad?~~
> Why did you move there?
> Have you ever discovered anything?
> How many times have you been to Egypt?
> ~~Which countries have you been to?~~
> How many books have you written?
> ... have you ever been in danger?
> How did you travel?

CD2 34 Listen and check.

3 Work with a partner. Ask and answer questions about Frieda.

- Which countries ... been to?

> Which countries has she been to?

> She's been to Egypt, Algeria, Kenya, South Africa, China, ...

- ... ever / South America?
- When / move / England?
- Where / her father get a job?
- When / see / the Tutankhamun Exhibition?
- How many times / to Egypt?
- How many books ...?

GRAMMAR SPOT

1 What are the tenses in these sentences?

> You**'ve traveled** a lot in your lifetime.
> Which countries **have** you **been** to?
> When I **was** six, my family **moved** to England.

Which tense refers to a definite time in the past? Which tense refers to an experience over time in your life?

2 The adverbs *ever* and *never* are often used with the Present Perfect.

> Have you **ever** been in danger?
> I've **never** been to South America.

▶▶ **Grammar Reference 7.2 p. 138**

Frieda Hoffmann – archaeologist and writer

Frieda Hoffmann was born in Germany, but she has lived most of her life abroad. She has a passion for history and ancient civilizations. Her greatest love is Africa, and she has written several books about ancient Egypt.

Driving in South Africa

Walking the Great Wall of China

Crossing the Sahara, Algeria

The Nile River, Kenya

Archaeological site, Egypt

I   Frieda, you've traveled a lot in your lifetime.
    ¹ **Which countries have you been to?**

F   Well, I've been to a lot of countries in Africa and Asia, but I've never been to South America.

I   ² **When did you first go abroad?**

F   When I was six, my family moved to England.

I   ³ _____?

F   Because my father got a job as a professor of history at Cambridge University.

I   ⁴ _____ in archaeology?

F   Yes, I have. When I was ten, there was an exhibition in London of Tutankhamun, the Egyptian king. My father took me to see it, and I was fascinated! After that I knew that I wanted to go to Egypt and be an archaeologist.

I   ⁵ _____?

F   At least twenty times! I go as often as I can.

I   ⁶ _____?

F   Yes, I've made some very important discoveries. I was the leader of a team that discovered some ancient tombs near Cairo.

I   You've written books about Egypt, haven't you?
    ⁷ _____?

F   I've written three about the pharaohs. And I've written a book about a journey I made from Cairo to Cape Town.

I   ⁸ _____? By train? By car?

F   In a Land Rover, of course!

I   In all of your travels, ⁹ _____?

F   Oh, my gosh, yes! Many times. But in situations like that you learn so much about yourself.

PRACTICE

Present Perfect or Simple Past?

1 **CD2 35** Listen and complete some lines from an interview with Frieda.

1 **Do you go back to Germany much?**
  ❝ No, I don't. I _____ back a few times, but I've _____ there again. ❞

2 **What _____ you _____ in college?**
  ❝ I _____ ancient history at Cambridge. ❞

3 **_____ you _____ an ordinary job?**
  ❝ Of course I _____! I _____ all kinds of things! After college I _____ any money. ❞
  So what _____ you _____?
  ❝ I _____ in a restaurant. I _____ it! ❞

4 **What's the most dangerous situation you _____ in?**
  ❝ Well, I _____ a very bad car accident in Cairo. I _____ seriously injured, and _____ several bones. ❞

What extra information did you hear? With a partner, practice the questions and answers.

2 Ask and answer more questions about Frieda. When did she do these things?

Has she ever ... Yes, she has. When did she do that?

1 ... cross/the Sahara? (in her early thirties)
2 ... walk/the Great Wall of China? (in 1995)
3 ... travel/up the Nile? (a student)
4 ... work/in a restaurant? (graduate from college)

Talking about you

3 Choose one of the questions in the box. Stand up and ask everyone in the class.

Have you ever ...	
done anything dangerous?	slept in a tent?
broken your arm or leg?	worked in a restaurant?
lost something important?	been to the hospital?
been to Africa?	written a story?

When you find someone who says *Yes*, ask more questions.

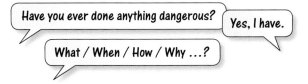

Have you ever done anything dangerous? Yes, I have.
What / When / How / Why ...?

VOCABULARY AND PRONUNCIATION
Word endings and word stress

1 What are the endings of the nouns in *italics*?

John Steinbeck, *writer* and *novelist*, worked with movie *directors*.

2 Use these endings to make jobs from words in the box.

-er -or -ist -ian -ant

'photograph	re'ception	'science	farm	art
'politics	'music	ac'count	'decorate	act
in'terpret	'library	e'lectric	law	

CD2 36 Listen, check, and repeat the jobs. Pay attention to changes in word stress.

3 Suffixes show the part of speech. Look at the suffixes in the box and complete the chart.

nouns	-tion -sion -ment -ness -ence/-ance -ility
adjectives	-y -ly -ous -ful -less -al

Noun	Verb	Noun	Adjective
_____	com'pete	fame	_____
_____	ex'plain	_____	'different
be'havior	_____	'critic	_____
_____	in'vite	_____	am'bitious
con'clusion	_____	suc'cess	_____
'student	_____	help	_____
_____	de'cide	_____	kind
di'scussion	_____	friend	_____
_____	em'ploy	'danger	_____
_____	in'herit	health	_____
co'llection		_____	re'sponsible

Word stress

4 **CD2 37** Listen and repeat the words. Where is the stress?

Two-syllabled nouns and adjectives

nouns	danger kindness critic artist difference
adjectives	dangerous healthy friendly famous different

Two-syllabled verbs

invite explain discuss employ decide compete

Nouns ending in *-tion* and *-sion*

invitation explanation competition ambition decision

READING
Living in a stately home

1 Look at the pictures and read the introduction. What is the house called? Who lives there? Who visits it? Where do you think the money comes from to run it?

2 You are going to read about the house and its owner. What do you want to know?

Write some questions on the board.

Where …?   How old …?   Who …?   When …?
How many …?   How much …?   Which …?

3 Read the article quickly. Which of your questions are answered?

4 Read the article again. Answer the questions.

1 Which family owns Biltmore House? For how long?
2 Who helps run Biltmore House now?
3 What do these numbers refer to?

115	255	65	8,000	$2.5b	1,000,000

4 How long has the house been open to the public?
5 How does the estate raise money?
6 What does the design of the estate reflect?
7 What was the estate used for during World War II?

Language work

Underline the correct tense.

1 Mr. Cecil *managed / has managed* Biltmore House since 1976.
2 His mother *died / has died* in 1976.
3 The Vanderbilt family *owned / has owned* the house for over 115 years.
4 In 2010 around one million people *visited / have visited* the house.
5 The original owner *didn't build / hasn't built* the estate.
6 An inn *was / has been* on the estate for 14 years.

What do you think?

• Are there houses like Biltmore House in your country? Who owns them? Are they open to the public?
• Is there an upper class in your country? What kinds of schools do they go to? What kinds of professions do they often have? What kinds of pastimes do they like?
• Is it fair that so much wealth can be inherited?

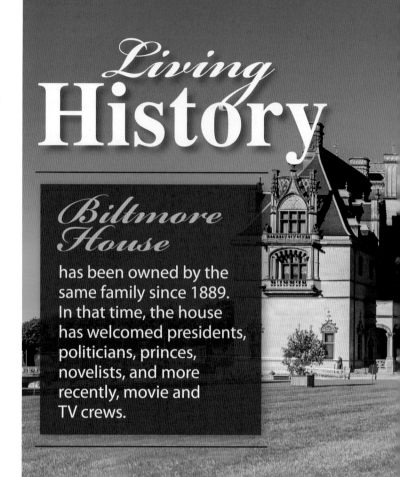

Living History

Biltmore House

has been owned by the same family since 1889. In that time, the house has welcomed presidents, politicians, princes, novelists, and more recently, movie and TV crews.

William A.V. Cecil, Senior and his son, Bill Jr., have managed the estate since 1976, when Mr. Cecil's mother died.

His family has owned the estate for over 115 years. Biltmore House has been passed down the Vanderbilt family for three generations. And the next generations, Mr. Cecil's son, daughter and grandchildren, are involved in the running of Biltmore House.

Mr. Cecil left a job in banking to manage the estate with his brother in 1960. He has worked hard to keep the estate financially independent by introducing new ways to make money and remain self-sufficient.

$126 millon a year to run

The largest private estate in the US

Biltmore House is situated in the Blue Ridge Mountains of Ashville, North Carolina. It is the largest privately owned house in the US. It has 255 rooms (with 65 fireplaces and 43 bathrooms) and is set on over 8,000 acres of land. Approximately 1,700 people work on the estate. The art collection includes paintings by Renoir and Sargent as well as many works by Tiffany. The whole estate is worth about $2.5 billion.

It costs approximately $126 million a year to run Biltmore House, so it has been open to the paying public since 1930, and now more than one million people visit each year. There are often flower shows, horseback riding events, and gardening seminars on the grounds.

The house also earns money from the movie and TV industry. It was used in the 1992 movie *Last of the Mohicans* with Daniel Day Lewis as well in the 1998 movie *Patch Adams* starring Robin Williams. In addition, it was featured in the TV series *One Tree Hill*.

A working estate

Many American estates were built during the late 19th century by wealthy families. George Washington Vanderbilt, the original owner, hired architect Richard Morris Hunt to design the estate to reflect a working French estate. In addition to the house, chicken, cow, and pig farms were set up. A furniture-making business was added as well. The idea was to make Biltmore House a self-supporting estate.

Over the years Biltmore House has evolved with the times. The opening of the estate to the public in the 1930s was to increase local tourism. During World War II, Biltmore House stored paintings for the National Gallery of Art to keep them safe. In the 1970s and 1980s the family started a winery. And in the 21st century, the construction of an inn, luxury shops, and restaurants help keep Biltmore House financially successful without the help of any government money.

■■■ LISTENING AND SPEAKING

A family history

The Bews family

1 What do you know about the lives of your grandparents? Talk about them in small groups.

2 **CD2 38** Listen to David Taylor Bews (33). He comes from England, but now lives in Perth, Australia. He has started to research his family history. Answer the questions.

1 How long has David lived in Perth?
2 Who are the two "Alices" in his life?
3 Where does his grandmother live?
4 Where were her brothers and sisters born?
5 What did her parents do for a living?
6 What happened in the 9th century?
7 Why do so many people in the family have blond hair?
8 Why did the family leave the Orkney Islands?

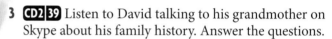

NORWAY
Orkney Islands
Newcastle

Alice Bews

3 **CD2 39** Listen to David talking to his grandmother on Skype about his family history. Answer the questions.

1 "… *she* married when she was just 17." Who is *she*?
2 "I can't remember *him* at all." Who is *him*?
3 "She had *two jobs* and a *big family*." What were her *two jobs*? How *big* was the *family*?
4 "*They* found work in the shipyards." Who are *they*?
5 "*It* wasn't unusual in those days." *What* wasn't unusual?
6 "*They* live all over the world." Who are *they*? Where do *they* live?
7 "*He* helps me keep in touch with you all." Who is *he*?
8 "*It's all* really wonderful, isn't it?" What is *it all*?

4 In your groups tell the story of David's family in chronological order. Use the maps to help.

David's ancestors came over to Scotland from …

What do you think?

- Is David's family history typical of many families?
- How far back can you go in your family history?
- You can explore your family history online. Has anyone in your family ever done that?

▶▶ **WRITING** A biography *p. 107*

Alice

David Taylor Bews

AUSTRALIA
Perth

Russell

EVERYDAY ENGLISH

Agree with me!

1 **CD2 40** Read and listen to the sentences.
Does the intonation go up or down at the end?

The <u>underlined</u> words are tag questions.
They aren't the same as questions.
When we use these tags, they mean ...*I want you to agree with me.*

> It's really wonderful, <u>isn't it?</u>

> You come from a small town, <u>don't you?</u>

> Life wasn't easy then, <u>was it?</u>

> You've lived here for years, <u>haven't you?</u>

2 **CD2 41** Read these conversations. How are the tag questions formed?
Listen and note the intonation. Practice with a partner after each one.

1 **A** It's a beautiful day, **isn't it?**
   B Yes, it is! Amazing!
   A We all love days like this, **don't we?**
   B We sure do!

2 **A** Mommy! Our cat isn't very big, **is she?**
   B No, she isn't. She's just a kitten.
   A And she loves fish, **doesn't she?**
   B She does! It's her favorite food.

3 **A** We had such a good vacation, **didn't we?**
   B We did. We had a great time.
   A And it wasn't too expensive, **was it?**
   B No, it wasn't. It wasn't expensive at all.

4 **A** The baby looks just like her mother, **doesn't she?**
   B Uh huh. Same brown eyes, same nose.
   A But she doesn't have her father's curly hair, **does she?**
   B No, she doesn't. Her hair is very straight.

3 Complete the sentences with a tag question.

1 It was a great party last night, _____ ?

2 Dave knows everything about computers, _____ ?

3 You went to school with my brother, _____ ?

4 Learning a language isn't easy, _____ ?

5 Our English has improved a lot, _____ ?

6 We haven't had a break for hours, _____ ?

4 We need to say more than just *Yes* or *No* when we answer
tag questions. Match these answers with a sentence in
Exercise 3.

a Yes, I did. We were really good friends.
b Yes, it was. I really enjoyed it.
c No, we haven't. It's time for one right now.
d No, it isn't. It takes a lot of practice and patience.
e Yes, it has. We're all much better now.
f Yes, he does. He can fix them and program them.

CD2 42 Listen and check. Practice the
conversations with your partner.

5 With your partner look at p. 152.
Choose two of the conversations and
decide where tag questions can be added.
Act them out for the class.

CD2 43 Listen and compare.

8 Girls and boys

have to/don't have to • *have to/should/must* • Things to wear • At the doctor's

STARTER

Which of these things do you think boys do better than girls, and vice versa?

> I think boys are better at ... than girls.

- cooking
- math
- sports
- driving
- making conversation
- learning foreign languages
- playing computer games
- talking about feelings

YOU HAVE TO HOLD ON!
have to/don't have to

1 Look at the picture. Can you find a tiny figure? Is it a man or a woman? What's happening?

2 **CD2 44** The tiny figure is **Tilly Parkins** from Sydney, Australia. She's one of the world's greatest climbers. Listen to the interview and answer the questions.

- Where does Tilly train during the week?
- What's her job?
- Was it difficult to climb Moon Hill Crag?
- Who is Adam Pretty?
- Why does Tilly go rock climbing?

Moon Hill Crag, Yangshuo Mountains, China

3 Work with a partner. Complete the lines from the interview with words in the box.

have to	don't have to	do you have to	had to	didn't have to	can't

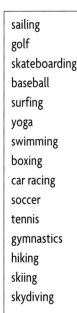

1 "I'm sure you ___have to___ be in great shape to go climbing."

2 "How often _____ train?"

3 "I _____ train every day, just two or three times a week, that's enough."

4 "Sometimes I _____ work at the hospital."

5 "I _____ climb very early in the morning."

6 "You _____ climb later in the day, it's too hot."

7 "He _____ climb with me. He took the picture from a nearby tourist spot."

CD2 44 Listen again and check.

4 Complete the questions and answers about Tilly.

1 "How often ___does___ she have to _____?"
  "Two or three times a week."

2 "_____ she _____ work on weekends?"
  "Yes, she does sometimes."

3 "Why _____ she _____ climb Moon Hill Crag just after dawn?"
  "Because later it gets too hot and you _____ climb in the heat."

4 "_____ Adam have to _____ the rock?"
  "No, he _____. He took the picture from a tourist spot."

CD2 45 Listen and check. Practice the questions and answers with your partner.

GRAMMAR SPOT

1 *have to* + base form expresses obligation.
  She **has to train** hard.
  Do you **have to work** on weekends?

2 Write the question, negative, and past tense of *have to*.
  _____ you _____ work late for your job?
  No, I _____ work late usually.
  But I _____ work late yesterday.

3 Write *have to*, *don't have to*, *can*, or *can't*.
  possible ___can___   not possible _____
  necessary _____   not necessary _____

▶▶ **Grammar Reference 8.1–8.2 pp. 138–139**

PRACTICE

Pronunciation

1 **CD2 46** Listen to these sentences. What are the different pronunciations of *have/has/had*?

  1 I have /hæv/ a good job.
    I have /hæf/ to work hard.

  2 He has /hæz/ a nice camera.
    She has /hæs/ to train a lot.

  3 We had /hæd/ a good time.
    We had /hæt/ to get up early.

  CD2 46 Listen again and repeat.

Talking about sports

2 Work with a partner. Choose a sport from the box, but don't tell your partner. Ask and answer *Yes/No* questions to find out what it is. Use these questions to help you.

sailing golf skateboarding baseball surfing yoga swimming boxing car racing soccer tennis gymnastics hiking skiing skydiving	**Do you …?** • do it inside/outside • play it with a ball • play on a team • do it in or on water **Do you have to …?** • wear special clothes • use special equipment • train hard for it • be very strong • run fast • have a special place to do it **Can you …?** • do it anywhere • do it with friends • do it on your own • earn a lot of money

Do you have to wear special clothes?

Yes, you do.

Can you …?

3 Which sports do both boys and girls play? Are there any sports where girls and boys compete against each other?

4 Which sports do you play? Describe one to a partner. Use the ideas in Exercise 2.

WHAT'S YOUR ADVICE?

should / must

1 Do you ever read advice columns? What kinds of things do people ask about?

2 Work with a partner. Read the problems in *Dear Annie*. Explain the headings. What advice would you give?

3 Read *Advice from Annie*. Match her advice with a problem. Write the names.

GRAMMAR SPOT

1 Look at these sentences. Which sentence expresses stronger advice?

He **must** get professional help.
You **should** show him this letter.

2 *Should* and *must* are modal verbs. Read the examples.

What **should** I do?
You **shouldn't** worry about this.
He **must** get help.

- How do we make the question and negative?
- Do we add *-s* with *he/she/it*?

▶▶ **Grammar Reference 8.3–8.4 p. 139**

---

4 Complete the sentences using the words in the box. Who is the advice for?

| shouldn't   should   must   don't think you should |

1 You _____ explain how you feel to your coach and your mother. However, in the end, the decision is yours and yours alone. You _____ decide your own future.

2 Tell him firmly that he _____ change his ways or he'll lose his wife and family. Talk to all your friends and family about the problem – you _____ suffer alone.

3 You _____ write your speech down, but I _____ read it aloud to the group. Just make notes to help you remember it. For more help, you _____ visit **speechtips.com**.

4 You _____ talk to your parents about how you feel. And you _____ feel jealous of your brother! He's older than you – that's all!

CD2 47 Listen and check.

Problems

Dear Annie!

annie@problemforum.com

1 No time for fun!

I'm 14 and I do gymnastics. I have to practice 30 hours a week because my mom and my coach want me to try out for the next Olympics. I like gymnastics, but I don't have time for anything else in my life. My school friends tell me that I'm missing all the fun. What should I do? **Tracy**

2 I've lost my husband to a game

My husband started playing online computer games last year. Since then he has lost all interest in everything else, even me and our baby. He starts playing as soon as he gets up, and begins again when he gets back from work. He gets angry if I talk to him about it. What should I do? **Paula**

3 I get so nervous

I'm in the army, and in my job I have to give talks to large groups of people. The last time was a disaster because I was so nervous. My hands shook and I spoke too fast. How can I control my nerves? What should I do? **Mark**

4 I hate him!

I'm 11 and my brother is 15. I think my mom and dad love him more than me. They just bought him the best computer – they say he has to have it for his final exams. I don't even have my own cell phone, and I have to wear all his old clothes! **Billy**

Advice from Annie!

a **Dear _____ ,**
Good preparation is the answer. You must prepare well and practice a lot. The first 30 seconds are the most important. You should begin with a personal story. It will relax you and the audience.

b **Dear _____ ,**
More and more people worldwide have become addicted to this. He must get professional help, but this is difficult because he won't accept that he has a problem. I think you should show him this letter, and tell him to visit the website **olganon.org**.

c **Dear _____ ,**
These feelings are very common between brothers and sisters. I'm sure your parents love you and your brother just the same, so you shouldn't worry about this. When you're older, you'll get your own phone – and your own clothes!

d **Dear _____ ,**
The fact is that to get to the top in sports, you do have to train very hard. You should talk to someone else about your doubts. I don't think you should listen to just your friends.

PRACTICE
Giving advice

1 Work in small groups. Give advice to people with these problems.

1 I can't sleep at night.

You must exercise more.
You shouldn't drink so much coffee.

2 I don't like my brother's new girlfriend.
3 I have an important exam tomorrow, and I'm really nervous.
4 A boy in my class is bullying me.
5 I'm horrible at all sports.
6 I fell and I think I twisted my ankle.
7 My computer's being really weird.
8 My car's making a funny noise.

CD2 48 Listen and compare your answers.

What do you think?

2 Make sentences from the chart to express your opinion.

If you want to …

| … learn English, |
| … be successful, |
| … stay in shape, |

| you have to |
| you don't have to |
| you should |
| you shouldn't |
| you must |

| … work hard. |
| … play some sports. |
| … learn the grammar. |
| … go to college. |
| … buy a dictionary. |
| … eat junk food. |
| … translate every word. |

Tell a partner.

▶▶ **WRITING** Letters and emails *p. 108*

🗨 LISTENING AND SPEAKING
Heptathlon champion

1 The word *Heptathlon* comes from the Greek *hepta* (seven) and *athlon* (contest). It is a track and field competition where there are seven events over two days. These are …

- 100-meter hurdles
- 800-meter race
- high jump
- shot put
- 200-meter race
- long jump
- javelin throw

Match the events with the pictures.

Jessica Ennis –
2012 Olympic heptathlon champion!

2 **CD2 49** Listen to an interview with Jessica Ennis. She is the 2012 Olympic women's heptathlon gold-medal winner. Choose the correct answer.

1 The 2012 Olympic Games were in *Los Angeles / London / Lima*.
2 Jessica missed the 2008 Olympics because she injured her *ankle / knee / wrist*.
3 She had to work with physical therapists for *five / nine / ten* months to recover.
4 Her mom works for a *pharmacy / non-profit organization / painter*.
5 Jessica's coach says that she has to be more *patient / determined / aggressive*.
6 He told her that she shouldn't *eat chocolate / get a dog / see her boyfriend*.
7 Her boyfriend is *always / sometimes / never* with her when she competes.
8 She keeps her *gold medal / dog / javelin* by her bed.

3 **CD2 49** Listen again. Answer the questions.
1 How did Jessica's mom describe her when Jessica was younger?
2 Why does her mother have to have a lot of patience?
3 What nationality is her father? What does he do?
4 What do Jessica and her coach fight about?
5 What are Jessica's interests other than track and field?
6 Which events does she have to improve?

What do you think?

Work in groups. Think of some successful people. What do they do? How and why did they become successful? Tell the class.

💬 READING AND SPEAKING
Families with all boys or all girls

1 Take a class survey. Which girls have sisters and no brothers? Which boys have brothers and no sisters? How does this affect their family?

2 Look at the adjectives in the box. Which do you think usually describe boys, and which usually describe girls? Use your dictionary if necessary.

athletic	gentle	boisterous	loud	quiet
talkative	messy	competitive	sensitive	polite

3 Read the introduction to *Sons and Daughters*. What was the aim of the TV show? Who were the two families? What did they have to do?

4 Work in two groups. Answer the questions.

Group A Read about the Cafearo family and the swap.
Group B Read about the Tibbett family and the swap.

THE FAMILY
1 What jobs do the parents have?
2 How long have they been married?
3 Why did they want a big family?
4 Why are the husbands happy with their families?
5 How do the children behave? Do they get along well?

THE SWAP
6 What were the parents' first impressions when they swapped families?
7 What differences did they find?
8 Do they think boys or girls are harder to raise?

5 Find a partner from the other group. Go through the questions together and compare your families.

What do you think?
• What are the pros and cons of all-girl or all-boy families?
• What is the ideal family? How many children is the ideal? Why?
• Are/Were there many house rules in your family? What do/did you have to do? Write a list of house rules for the ideal family.

Listening – Brothers and sisters

6 **CD2 50** Listen to three people talking about their families. After each one answer these questions. Who do you think is the happiest?
1 How many brothers and sisters do they have?
2 Where do they come in the family? First? Second?
3 What do they like about their situation?
4 What don't they like?
5 Do they think their parents have a favorite child?
6 How many children do they want?

SONS

THE CAFEARO FAMILY

THE TIBBETT FAMILY

AND DAUGHTERS

Is an all-boy family very different from having an all-girl family? What is it like to be totally outnumbered by the opposite sex in your own home? To find the answer, TV's Channel 4 asked Marianne and Jon Tibbett, the parents of four daughters to swap homes with Karen and Steve Cafearo, who have four sons.

Karen talks about her family

Karen Cafearo, 43, lives with husband, Steve, 49, a manager at Jaguar Cars, and their sons Francis (17), Alex (15), Joseph (11), and Samuel (9). Karen is an accountant. She says:

"I married Steve when I was 21. I'm the oldest of four children and I always wanted a big family. Also, I wanted a son for Steve; he's very athletic, loves his soccer, so he's delighted to have four sons. The boys love kicking balls and racing around on their bikes. They don't see danger. Steve says I shouldn't worry. He says boys will be boys. Sometimes I feel left out of all their sports, but I'm happy that I don't have to watch soccer in the pouring rain. The boys see everything in black and white. I should learn not to ask them about their lives and feelings. 'Dunno' is their usual answer. I have often wondered what a family of girls would be like."

THE SWAP
Karen and Steve Cafearo go to the TIBBETT HOME

When Karen and Steve arrived at the Tibbett family home, she had to laugh. There were piles of pink ballet shoes and riding boots all over the floor. Karen says:

"The four girls are as passionate about dancing and horseback riding as my boys are about soccer and rugby, but I was shocked by the mess. I have strict rules for my boys. They can't wear their shoes upstairs and they have to clean their rooms. The girls were so excited to see us, they wanted to talk and ask us questions. It was fantastic, but exhausting. They came to help me cook in the kitchen. They didn't want to play in the yard. I think girls need more attention than boys. Another shock for me was how nice the girls were to each other. The boys love each other, but they fight and argue endlessly.

The thing I loved most was shopping with the girls. We had so much fun. I miss that with boys. Poor Steve had to carry the bags. I saw a big change in him. With girls he was so sensitive and gentle.

I loved the talks with the girls, but I also like my own space. I think girls are harder work."

Marianne talks about her family

Marianne Tibbett, 38, lives with husband, Jon, 45, and their daughters Annabelle (14), Francesca (11), Genevieve (9), and Catherine (8). They run a road hauling business together. Marianne says:

"Jon and I met and married within 16 months. He was 29. People often ask us if we have so many children because we were trying for a boy. But this isn't true. I'm an only child and it was my dream to have a big family. We were excited when Annabelle arrived and equally excited when Francesca arrived three years later, followed by Genevieve and Catherine. Jon loves having four girls. He is their superhero dad! Our daughters are fabulous. Most of the time they get along really well together. They're a talkative group! But we were fascinated to try living with boys."

THE SWAP
Marianne and Jon Tibbett go to the CAFEARO HOME

Marianne expected the Cafearo boys to be loud and boisterous. In fact, on the first day they were very quiet and polite. Marianne says:

"They even took their shoes off before going upstairs. However, I soon realized why Karen and Steve had to have such strict house rules. The boys were constantly on the go and wildly competitive. They raced around the yard and dove into the pool. There was a fight between one of the little boys and his big brother. I tried to make them apologize, which is what I do with my girls, but it just made them more angry. The little one went off by himself, cried, then forgot all about it.

But the biggest shock for me was the change in my gentle husband. He became more and more competitive. We all went go-karting. We've never done this with our family. Jon joined in with the boys and it was clear he wanted to win as much as they did. He had a lot of fun and I loved seeing him so happy. I know he would love to have had a son to continue the business. But now we've seen the reality of having boys! They're exhausting. I honestly think they are much harder work than girls."

VOCABULARY AND SPEAKING

Things to wear

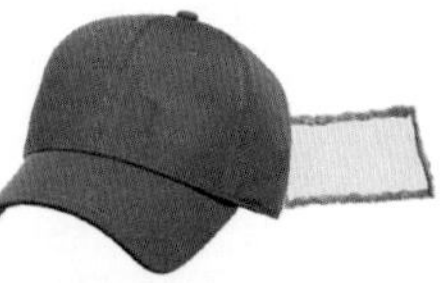

1 What things to wear can you see on this page?

2 Work with a partner. Read the words in **Things to wear**. Where do they go on Person X? Label the parts of the body you mention as you work.

Things to wear

a belt
a sweater
shorts
a skirt
a hat
makeup
socks
boots
pajamas
a blouse
a suit
a watch
a ring
a dress
aftershave
sunglasses
earrings
tights
sandals
a jacket
sneakers
a scarf
jeans
bikini
a shirt and tie
a T-shirt

3 Answer the questions.
  1 Which are usually for boys? Which are for girls? Which are for both?
  2 Which are *not* clothes?
  3 Which are for casual wear? Which are for business? Which are for both?
  4 Which do you usually wear in the winter? Which do you wear in the summer?
  5 What can they be made of? Match these materials with them.

  | leather wool denim cotton silk gold silver |

Dress Person X

4 Choose the clothes to dress Person X for one of the situations below. Describe the outfit to the class. Can they guess the gender and the situation?

  • a job interview
  • a beach vacation
  • a party
  • going to school
  • a skiing vacation

Person X

MANLY

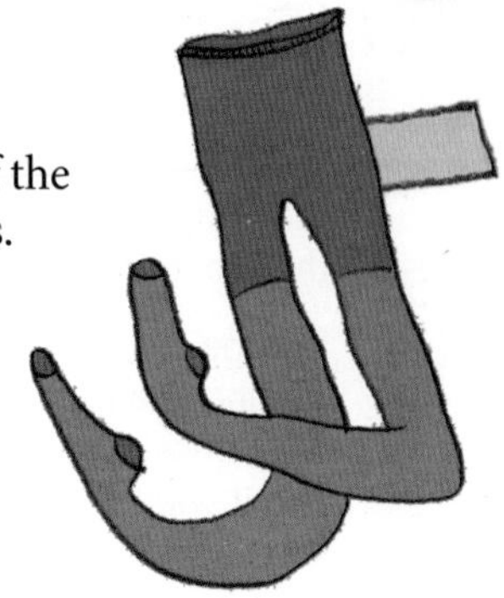

At the doctor's

1 Match the pictures with a health issue from the box.

| a sore throat   diarrhea /ˌdaɪəˈriːə/   the flu   an allergy   a twisted ankle   food poisoning   a cold |

2 Read the symptoms and complete the diagnosis with a health issue.

Patient's symptoms	**Doctor's diagnosis**
1 I can't stop coughing and blowing my nose.	You have _____ .
2 I have a fever and my whole body aches.	You have _____ .
3 It hurts when I walk on it.	You have _____ .
4 I keep going to the bathroom.	You have _____ .
5 My glands are swollen, and it hurts when I swallow.	You have _____ .
6 I keep throwing up, and I have terrible diarrhea.	You have _____ .
7 I start sneezing and itching when I'm near a cat.	You have _____ .

CD2 51 Listen and check. Practice saying the lines with a partner.

3 **CD2 52** Listen to a conversation between a doctor (**D**) and Edsom (**E**), a student from Brazil. Answer the questions.

1 What are Edsom's symptoms?
2 What questions does the doctor ask?
3 What does the doctor think is the matter with Edsom?
4 What does she prescribe?
5 What advice does she give him?
6 Does he have to pay for anything?

4 Read and complete Edsom's conversation with the doctor.

CD2 52 Listen again and check.

5 Act out the scene with your partner. Make similar conversations with other symptoms.

Seeing the doctor

D What seems to be the _____ ?
E Well, I haven't felt _____ for a few days. I've had a bad _____ and now I have a _____ .
D Any sickness or diarrhea?
E Well, I haven't been _____ .
D Do you feel hot?
E Yes, especially at night. I feel hot and start _____ when I lie down.
D OK, I'll just _____ your temperature. Ah, yes. You do have a _____ . Now, let me see your throat. Open your _____ wide, please.
E Can you see anything?
D Yes, your throat looks very red. Does this _____ ?
E Ouch!
D And your glands are _____ . You just have an infection. You need antibiotics. Are you allergic to penicillin?
E No, I'm not.
D Good. Now, you _____ take it easy for a couple of days and you _____ drink plenty of liquids. I'll write you a prescription.
E Thank you. Do I have to pay you?
D There's no charge for a sick visit. But you'll have to pay for the _____ .
E OK. Thank you very much.

9 Time for a story

Past Perfect and narrative tenses • Joining sentences
Feelings • Exclamations

1 Work in small groups. Who are these characters from literature?

2 What do you know about the stories they are from?

AESOP'S FABLES
Past Perfect and narrative tenses

1 Aesop was a storyteller who lived in Greece around 600 B.C. Look at the picture of one of his fables, *The Bear and the Travelers*. What can you see?

2 Read the story. What is the moral?

TRUE FRIENDS ARE HARD TO FIND.   CHOOSE YOUR FRIENDS CAREFULLY.

DON'T RUN AWAY FROM DANGER.

The Bear and the Travelers

Two travelers were walking slowly along a country road. They were going to the city because they were looking for work. They were tired (...) and they were hungry (...)

Suddenly, in the woods in front of them, they saw a huge bear. The men were terrified. One of them ran away, climbed a tree, and hid.

The other man fell to the ground and pretended to be dead. (...) The bear came toward him. It bent down, sniffed him, and whispered something in his ear. Then it wandered away.

(...) The other man came down from his tree and went to see how his friend was. (...)

"The bear gave me some advice," said his companion. "He said, 'Next time you go on a journey, travel with someone who won't leave you at the first sign of danger.'"

THE MORAL OF THIS STORY IS ...

_____

The bear whispered in his ear.

3 Complete the questions and the answers.

1 "Where _____ the travelers _____?"
  "Along a country road."

2 "Why _____ to the city?"
  "Because they were looking for work."

3 "What _____ in the woods?"
  "They saw a huge bear."

4 "What _____ the men do?"
  "One _____ in a tree, and the other _____
  to be dead."

5 "What _____ the bear _____?"
  "It bent down, sniffed, and then wandered away."

CD3 2 Listen and check.

4 Put these lines in one of the places (…) in the story.

1 … because they had walked 20 miles.

2 He wanted to know what the bear had said to him.

3 … because they hadn't eaten all day.

4 After the bear had gone, …

5 He had heard that bears don't like eating dead meat.

CD3 3 Listen to the complete story and check your
answers. Do you agree with the moral?

GRAMMAR SPOT

1 What tense are the verbs in **bold**?
   They **were looking** for work.
   They **saw** a bear.
   They **had walked** twenty miles.

2 *They didn't eat all day. They were hungry.* How is this
   expressed in the story?

3 The Past Perfect expresses an action before another
   time in the past. How do we form this tense?

   had + the _____ _____

▶▶ **Grammar Reference 9.1 p. 140**

---

5 Ask and answer the questions with a partner.
Use the Past Perfect.

1 Why were the travelers tired?
2 Why were they hungry?
3 Why did one of them pretend
   to be dead?
4 When did the other man come
   down from the tree?
5 What did he want to know?

CD3 4 Listen and check. Practice them again.

PRACTICE

Pronunciation

1 **CD3 5** The contraction **'d** can be difficult to
hear. Listen to the sentences. Select the ones
you hear **'d = had**.

1 _____ 2 _____ 3 _____
4 _____ 5 _____

Discussing grammar

2 What is the difference in meaning between
these sentences?

1 When I arrived,
     … she made dinner.
     … she was making dinner.
     … she'd made dinner.

2 She spoke good French because
     … she lived in France.
     … she had lived in France.

3 I listened to music
     … while I did my homework.
     … when I'd done my homework.

4 When I got home,
     … the children went to bed.
     … the children had gone to bed.

5 She gave me a book,
     … so I read it.
     … but I'd read it.

3 Match a phrase in **A** with a line in **B**.

A	
1	I was nervous on the plane because
2	When I'd had breakfast,
3	I met a girl at a party. Her face was familiar.
4	I felt tired all day yesterday because
5	My wife was angry with me because
6	The little girl was crying because

B	
___	I was sure I'd seen her somewhere before.
___	I'd never flown before.
___	I'd forgotten our anniversary.
___	she'd fallen and hurt herself.
___	I went to work.
___	I hadn't slept the night before.

CD3 6 Listen and check.

THE SHEPHERD BOY
Joining sentences

1 Here is another one of Aesop's fables. Work with a partner. Tell the story from the pictures.

2 Read the story. Choose the correct word or phrase to join the sentences.

What do you think the moral of the story is?
CD3 7 Listen and check.

3 Answer the questions.

When did the boy have his idea? *While …*
When did the villagers race to the hills? *As soon as …*
When did the shepherd boy smile? *After …*
When did the wolf appear? *As …*

> ### GRAMMAR SPOT
>
> **1** Conjunctions are used to join sentences.
>
> He wanted to have some fun **because** he was bored.
> **Although** they were all busy, they stopped work.
> No one believed the boy, **so** he climbed back up the hill.
>
> **2** *When, while, before, after, as, until,* and *as soon as* are conjunctions of time.
>
> **As soon as** the villagers heard the boy, they went to help.
> **While** the boy was in the village, the wolf killed all the sheep.
>
> ▶▶ **Grammar Reference 9.2 p. 140**

4 Complete the sentences with *although, so,* or *because*.

1 They didn't find the wolf, _____ they went back to work.

2 They helped the boy _____ they were worried about their sheep.

3 _____ they heard his cries, they didn't do anything to help.

5 Look at the pictures, not the text. Tell the story again. Use these prompts.

Once … there was … shepherd boy who …
One day … bored … idea.
… ran … village … shouted …
As soon as the men … but … nothing.
… smiled …
A few days later … again.
The men … angry … laughed.
Next day … wolf …
… raced … shouted …
This time … didn't believe …
… climbed back … wolf … killed …
… ashamed … cried.

The boy who cried wolf

O NCE upon a time there was a shepherd boy who took care of the sheep in the hills near his village. He thought his job was very boring. One day, (1)*while / because* he was sitting under a tree, he had an idea. He decided to have some fun, (2)*so / but* he went down to the village and shouted "Wolf! Wolf!" loudly. (3)*As soon as / Until* the villagers heard the boy, they stopped work and raced to the hills to help him. But (4)*when / while* they got there, they saw nothing. They returned to their work. (5)*Before / After* they'd gone, the shepherd boy smiled to himself.

A few days later, the boy did the same thing again. He ran into the village and shouted "Wolf! Wolf!" The villagers didn't know whether to believe him or not, but they were worried about their sheep (6)*because / so* they went to the hills to help him. Again, there was no wolf. They were angry (7)*because / so* the shepherd boy had lied again, but he just laughed.

T HEN, the next day, just (8)*as / before* the sun was setting, a wolf really did appear, and it began attacking the sheep. In terror, the boy raced down the hill to the village, shouting "Wolf! Wolf!" (9)*But / Although* the villagers heard his cries, they did nothing to help. This time they really didn't believe him.

T HE shepherd boy climbed back up the hill to look for the sheep, but the wolf had killed them all. He was so ashamed that he sat down in the moonlight and cried.

PRACTICE

Discussing grammar

1 Join the sentences using the conjunction. Put one verb in the Past Perfect.

1 I went to bed. I did my homework.	WHEN
2 I stopped for coffee. I drove two hundred miles.	AFTER
3 She passed her driver's test. She bought a car.	AS SOON AS
4 I didn't go to Italy. I learned Italian.	UNTIL
5 I read the book. I didn't understand the movie.	ALTHOUGH
6 His mother sent him to bed. He was bad.	BECAUSE
7 She burned the food. We went out to eat.	SO
8 She made a delicious dinner. Unfortunately I ate a large lunch.	BUT

CD3 8 Listen and compare your answers.

2 Choose the correct words to join the sentences.

1 *When / While* I got home, I checked my emails.
2 I cut myself *before / while* I was shaving.
3 He worked for the same company *until / as* he retired.
4 I got out of bed *before / as soon as* I woke up.
5 She was thinking about her father *as / until* she was going to work.
6 *After / Before* I went to bed, I locked all the doors.
7 *After / Before* I graduated from school, I traveled for a year.

Your ideas

3 Complete the sentences with your own ideas.

1 We enjoyed the vacation although …
2 As I sat on the plane, I felt nervous because …
3 I lived in Thailand for a year, but I …
4 I met my wife while I …
5 I wanted to get in shape, so I …
6 My phone rang just as I …
7 Although I didn't feel well, I …
8 We watched TV until …

Compare your sentences with a partner.

LISTENING AND SPEAKING
My favorite writer

1 What do you know about the writer Harper Lee?

1 She was *American / Canadian / English*.
2 She wrote in the *18th / 19th / 20th* century.
3 She wrote about *politicians / adventurers / ordinary people*.

2 **CD3 9** Listen to the first part of a radio program. Check your answers to Exercise 1 and read the information about Lee in the chart. Some of it is wrong. Correct it.

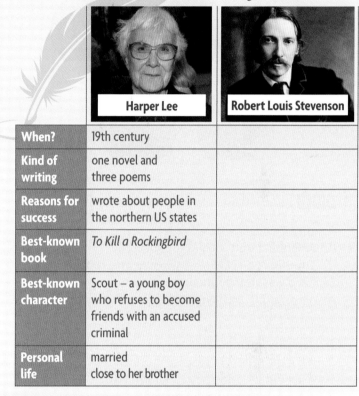

	Harper Lee	Robert Louis Stevenson
When?	19th century	
Kind of writing	one novel and three poems	
Reasons for success	wrote about people in the northern US states	
Best-known book	*To Kill a Rockingbird*	
Best-known character	Scout – a young boy who refuses to become friends with an accused criminal	
Personal life	married close to her brother	

3 Work with a partner. Compare your answers.

4 **CD3 10** Listen to the second part. Fill in some information about Robert Louis Stevenson. Compare your answers.

Speaking

What was the last book you read? What was it about?

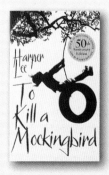
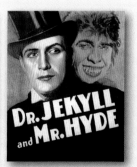

Good and evil

1 Look at the pictures in the story of *The Strange Case of Dr. Jekyll and Mr. Hyde.*

  1 When and where is it set?
  2 Is it a romance, a horror story, or a crime story?
  3 Is it fact or fiction?

2 Read the story quickly. Label these characters.

3 **CD3 11** Read and listen to the story. Answer the questions.

Frames 1–3
1 Describe the attack and the attacker.
2 How did Mr. Hyde react when he was caught?
3 What was strange about the check?
4 Why was Dr. Jekyll angry? Why was Utterson confused?

Frames 4–7
1 Describe the murder.
2 What did Utterson suspect?
3 What did Dr. Jekyll say about Mr. Hyde?
4 Why were the servants worried?
5 What did they see when they broke down the door?

Frames 8–12
1 What was Jekyll's theory about personality?
2 What happened when he took the first potion?
3 Why did Dr. Jekyll like being Mr. Hyde?
4 How was Mr. Hyde cruel?
5 In what way did Dr. Jekyll lose control?
6 Why did Dr. Jekyll have to die?

4 With a partner look at the pictures and retell the story.

What do you think?

• *The Strange Case of Dr. Jekyll and Mr. Hyde* was published in 1886. It was an immediate best-seller. Why do you think?
• We sometimes describe a person as being "a Jekyll and Hyde character." What do you think this means? Is it a compliment?
• What stories can you remember from your childhood? Who are the good characters? Who are the bad ones? Who usually wins?

The Strange Case

1 Late one night, a lawyer, Gabriel Utterson, was walking home through dark, silent streets when he saw a man attacking a woman. Utterson ran after him and caught him. The man's name was Mr. Hyde, and he looked ugly and evil.

4 A year passed. One night an old man was murdered as he was walking home. A maid witnessed the crime and recognized the killer. Mr. Hyde had struck again! The police went looking for Hyde, but he had disappeared.

7 Utterson and the servants broke down the door. Mr. Hyde was lying dead on the floor. He had taken poison. But why was he wearing Dr. Jekyll's clothes? And where was the doctor? Were Dr. Jekyll and Mr. Hyde one and the same person?

10 But after a time Jekyll found that he liked changing into Mr. Hyde. He enjoyed being bad. He became more and more violent and cruel. He took pleasure in hurting innocent people.

# of Dr. Jekyll and Mr. Hyde

by Robert Louis Stevenson

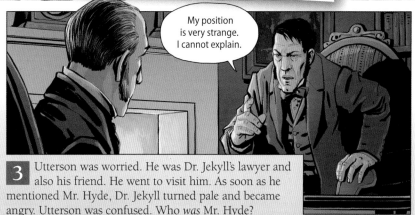

2 Mr. Hyde showed no regret for what he had done. To buy the woman's silence, he wrote her a check. Utterson noticed that the check was signed in the name of Dr. Jekyll, a well-known and well-respected man.

3 Utterson was worried. He was Dr. Jekyll's lawyer and also his friend. He went to visit him. As soon as he mentioned Mr. Hyde, Dr. Jekyll turned pale and became angry. Utterson was confused. Who *was* Mr. Hyde?

5 Again, Utterson went to visit his friend Dr. Jekyll. He suspected that Dr. Jekyll had helped Mr. Hyde to escape. When questioned, the doctor replied in a strange, wild voice that Mr. Hyde had gone forever.

6 Over the next few weeks Dr. Jekyll's behavior became more and more unusual. He locked himself in his laboratory and refused to open the door. His servants were worried. When they heard his voice, it sounded different. They asked Utterson for help.

8 On the desk was a letter addressed to Mr. Utterson. In it, Dr. Jekyll tried to explain himself. He said he believed that inside every human being there was a good side and an evil side.

9 Jekyll had created a potion. When he drank it, his whole body changed. The good, kind doctor became cruel, ugly, and evil. He called this other man Mr. Hyde. To change back, he had to drink another potion.

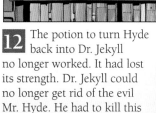

11 Finally Dr. Jekyll couldn't control Mr. Hyde anymore. He began to change into this monster even without taking the potion. Jekyll hoped and prayed that Hyde would disappear. But Hyde always returned.

12 The potion to turn Hyde back into Dr. Jekyll no longer worked. It had lost its strength. Dr. Jekyll could no longer get rid of the evil Mr. Hyde. He had to kill this monster. But to kill Mr. Hyde, Dr. Jekyll also had to die.

VOCABULARY AND SPEAKING

Feelings

1 Look at the adjectives in the box that describe feelings. Which are positive? Which are negative?

angry	nervous	delighted	stressed	upset	homesick	jealous	proud	scared	amazed	lonely	disappointed

2 How would you feel in these situations?

1 It's the day before a big test.

2 You got your test score. You failed.

3 Your son or daughter wins a race.

4 You have no friends.

5 You're a long way from home and you miss everyone.

6 You get a parking ticket.

7 It's night, and you're alone in the house. Suddenly there's a noise.

8 People are saying horrible things about you.

3 Complete the sentences with your own ideas. Tell a partner.

1 I was delighted because _I'd won $500 in a dance competition_.

2 I was stressed because _____.

3 I was proud because _____.

4 I was amazed because _____.

5 I was upset because _____.

CD3 12 Listen and compare.

9 Your boyfriend is getting very close to another girl.

4 Match a phrase in **A** with a line in **B**.

A	B
1 Sometimes I feel really lonely.	___ Yes, but people can be really nice, too.
2 I have so much to do! And the baby's crying! Help!	___ Cheer up! You have me. I'm your best friend!
3 Guess what? I just won $10,000!	___ Calm down! Don't stress yourself out.
4 When I watch the news on TV, I get scared.	___ I know what you mean. The world's a scary place.
5 I get upset when people are so horrible.	___ I'm happy for you! Can I have some?

CD3 13 Listen and check. Work with a partner. Practice the conversations and continue them.

EVERYDAY ENGLISH

Exclamations with *so* and *such*

1 **CD3 14** Read and listen to the sentences.

What an amazing movie!

I was scared!

I was really scared!

I was SO scared!

Do you think this use of *so* is more spoken or written?

2 Look at the sentences. When do we use *so*, *such*, *so many* …?

I was **so** surprised! It was **such a** shock!

It was **such an** awful day! You have **such** crazy ideas!

We had **such** terrible weather!

There were **so many** problems! I have **so much** work!

▶▶ **Grammar Reference 9.3 p. 140**

CD3 15 Listen and practice the sentences. Copy the stress and intonation.

3 Complete the sentences with words from the box.

so such such a(n) so many so much

1 That was _____ good book! You have to read it!

2 The movie was _____ scary that I couldn't watch it!

3 Jane and Pete are _____ nice people!

4 But their children are _____ badly-behaved!

5 There were _____ people at the party!

6 They made _____ mess!

7 I've spent _____ money this week!

8 I've had _____ awful day!

4 Match these sentences with lines in Exercise 3.

__ I'm glad I didn't have to clean up.

__ I'll lend it to you. You'll really like it.

__ They're always so welcoming and happy to see you.

__ I hate the sight of blood and people killing each other.

__ The parents have no control at all!

__ I don't have a single penny left!

__ I didn't get to talk to everyone.

__ I need some chocolate to cheer me up!

CD3 16 Listen and check. Cover Exercise 3. Try to remember the lines. Then cover Exercise 4 and do the same.

5 Work with a partner. Write a conversation on one or two of these topics. Include some exclamations.

- a great party
- a tiring trip
- a lot of problems
- a scary experience
- a disgusting meal
- an amazing apartment
- an annoying girlfriend/boyfriend

▶▶ **WRITING** Writing about a book or a movie *p. 110*

10 Our interactive world

Passives • Compound nouns • Words that go together • On the phone

 STARTER

1 Look at the signs. Where might you find them?

> **English is spoken here**

> **Cell phones must be turned off**

> **Calling cards are sold here**

2 <u>Underline</u> the past participles on the signs. Which is regular? Which are irregular?

THE CELL PHONE
Passives

1 What is the cell phone called in your country? What is it called in British English? Do you always have yours with you? When do you turn it off?

2 Read the introduction to *A phone call that changed the world*. Answer the questions.

   1 Who made the first cell phone call?
   2 When and where did he make it?
   3 How was the phone different from cell phones today?

3 **CD3 17** Read and listen to the *Fact File*. Correct the false information in these sentences.

   1 124 million phones are sold worldwide every year.
   2 The first text message was sent in the 1980s.
   3 Smartphones have been sold since 2002.
   4 Apple's iPhone now has over one million cameras.
   5 The most expensive phone costs $9,400.
   6 We throw away close to a million cell phones a year.

A phone call that

 The cell phone was once an oversized luxury item. Now it's a pocket-sized minicomputer.

The first cell phone call **was made** on April 3, 1973, by Martin Cooper, an American engineer, while he was walking along a street in New York City. People stopped and stared in amazement. Martin's phone was like a brick. It was almost 8 inches long and weighed 2.8 pounds. The battery lasted only 36 minutes.

1 Many of the verb forms in the text are in the passive.

> Cell phones **are owned** by almost six billion people.
> The first cell phone call **was made** in 1973.

How do we form the passive?

2 Read the text again. Write the passive verb forms in the chart.

Simple Present	Simple Past	Present Perfect	*will* future
are sold		have been sold	

▶▶ **Grammar Reference 10.1 p. 140**

Active to passive

4 Read the text again. How are these verbs expressed in the passive?

1 Martin Cooper **made** the first cell phone call in 1973.
2 Almost six billion people worldwide **own** cell phones.
3 Stores in the US **sell** 124 million phones every year.
4 They **have sold** camera phones since 2002.
5 Engineers **have added** a lot of amazing features.
6 They **decorate** the Goldstriker iPhone with over 550 diamonds.
7 We **throw away** 133 million cell phones every year.
8 Some people believe that cell phones **will** eventually **replace** all landline phones.

CD3 18 Listen and check.

5 What can you do on *your* cell phone? What do you think they will be used for in the future?

> I can play Scrabble on mine!
> Maybe they'll be used as credit cards.
> They might be used as passports.

changed the world

📁 FACT FILE

- Today, cell phones **are owned** by almost six billion people worldwide. In the US, 124 million **are sold** every year.

- The first text message **was sent** in 1992. Last year 8 trillion texts **were sent** worldwide.

- Camera phones **have been sold** in the US since 2002.

- "Smartphones" **were introduced** in 2007. The cell phone had become a multimedia gadget.

- Over the years a lot of amazing features **have been added**, including Internet browsing, email, MP3 players, video, and camera.

- In 2008, Apple's iPhone had 10,000 applications (apps). Now there are over 1,000,000 apps.

- The most expensive cell phone is the Goldstriker iPhone 4S Elite Gold. It **is made** of 24-karat gold and **decorated** with over 550 diamonds. It costs $9.4 million.

- 133 million cell phones **are thrown** away every year.

- Some people believe that before long, all landline telephones **will be replaced** by cell phones.

Goldstriker iPhone 4S Elite Gold

PRACTICE

Inventions that changed the world

1 Work with a partner. Look at the list of inventions. Which is the oldest? Which is the newest? Match them with the dates.

> I think the telephone was invented in 1901. What do you think?

> I'm not sure. I think it was invented in...

the telephone	105 AD
the printing press	1440
paper	1876
the ballpoint pen	1896
the personal computer (PC)	1924
television	1938
the radio	1976

CD3 19 Listen and check. What nationality were the inventors? What were their jobs?

Speaking

2 Which inventions do you think are most important? Why? Order them 1–7 (1 = most important). Discuss your ideas as a class.

Passive forms

3 Read *All things online!* Complete the sentences with the correct passive form. Which numbers and dates do you think are correct?

CD3 20 Listen and check.

4 Make questions about the information in Exercise 3. Ask and answer them with a partner.

1 How many emails/every day?

> How many emails are sent every day?

> Over 150 ...

2 How many queries/by Google/every day?
3 When/eBay? Who/by?
4 How many items/on eBay/it began?
5 How many video clips/YouTube every week?
6 When/the first Twitter message? Who/by?
7 How many languages/Facebook?
8 When/Amazon.com? Who/by?

CD3 21 Listen and check.

All things online!

1 Over *150 billion / 150 billion* emails **are sent** (send) every day.

2 Nearly *3.5 million / 3.5 billion* queries _____ (search) by Google every day.

3 eBay _____ (invent) in *1985 / 1995* by Pierre Omidyar, a French scientist.

4 Nearly *5 / 10* billion items _____ (sell) on eBay since it began.

5 *30,000 / 60,000* new video clips _____ (post) on YouTube every week.

6 The first Twitter message _____ (send) by American businessman, Jack Dorsey, in *2006 / 2009*.

7 Facebook _____ (translate) into *29 / 79* languages since it began.

8 The online store, Amazon.com, _____ (found) by Jeff Besoz, in his garage in *1989 / 1994*.

VOCABULARY AND SPEAKING
Words that go together

Noun + noun

> Two nouns can go together to make a compound noun.
> text + message = **text message**
> business + man = **businessman**
> news + paper = **newspaper**
> cell + phone = **cell phone**

1 **CD3 22** Listen to the compound nouns. Which word is stressed? Practice them.

2 Work with a partner. How many compound nouns can you make from these lists? Use your dictionary to help.

business		call	number
computer		card	site
lap	**+**	deal top	games
phone		waves	man
radio		virus	news
web		program	

CD3 23 Listen and check. Read the words aloud.

Verb + noun

3 In each box below, *one* noun does not go with the verb. Which one?

| 1 send | a text message   an email |
| | a phone call   a present   a postcard |

| 2 start | a business   a car   a family |
| | work   an idea |

| 3 make | a complaint   a discovery   a phone call |
| | the housework   a lot of money |

| 4 do | research   the shopping   a photo |
| | homework   the housework |

| 5 take | notes   a photo   sleep |
| | a long time   a walk |

| 6 play | games   the piano   yoga |
| | a part   baseball |

4 Choose a noun from each group and write a sentence using the verb. Read your sentences to the class.

I sent you a text message.
Are you taking notes in this class?

Adverb + adjective

> The adverbs *well* and *badly* can combine with past participles to form adjectives.
> **well known   badly behaved**

5 Complete the sentences with an adjective formed with *well* or *badly* and a past participle from the box.

done	paid	written	equipped
behaved	dressed	known	

1 She has a wonderful job. She's very _____ .
2 I didn't enjoy that novel. It was really _____ .
3 You don't need to spend a lot of money on clothes to look _____ .
4 Our office is really _____ . We have all the latest machines.
5 I hope their children don't come. They're so _____ .

6 Can I have my steak very _____ , please? I don't like it rare.
7 You haven't heard of Elizabeth Taylor? She was really _____ .

CD3 24 Listen and check. Practice the sentences.

Talking about you

6 Ask and answer these questions with your partner.

1 Do you ever play computer games? Which ones?
2 Which websites do you visit most often?
3 Do you send a lot of text messages? How many per day?
4 Who does the most housework in your home?
5 Does it take you a long time to get to school?
6 How do you like your steak?
7 Is your school well equipped?

CD3 25 Listen and compare.

There's a first time for everything

1 Work in groups. What do you use the Internet for? Make a list. Read the introduction and compare your ideas.

2 Match the headings in *Five Internet firsts* with these lines.

A | He built a single, easily searchable database for students to access information.

B | But soon his main topic became his personal life. He wrote openly about his relationships, passions, plans, and fears.

C | They are simply computer programs that replicate themselves again and again.

D | It quickly became the place for fashionable people to be seen.

E | People loved exchanging life stories with old schoolmates, and school romances were reignited.

3 You're going to read some of the articles. Divide them among your group. Read and take notes about …
- names and nationalities of the people
- what and where was the first
- important dates and events in its history

4 Use your notes to report back to your group. Do any of the *Five Internet Firsts* play a part in your life? How?

5 Read *all* the articles. Answer the questions.
1. What is there less need for these days? Why?
2. What is PCBang?
3. What was "Archie"? How did it get its name?
4. How did "blogging" get its name? Who named it?
5. Which virus broke hearts? How?
6. Which has more users, LinkedIn or Facebook? How many do they have?

Listening

6 **CD3 26** Listen to five people. Which of the Internet firsts are they talking about? What do they say that helped you figure it out?

Henry | Sandy | Liz | Martin | Barry

7 All these words are connected with the Internet. What do you think they mean? Discuss in your groups.

| bookmark | download | inbox | mouse | log in | spam |

▶▶ **WRITING** Discussing pros and cons *p. 111*

http://www...

No technology has evolved so much in so little time as the Internet. We not only shop, bank, work, and meet people online, but we share what we are doing at any given moment with sites such as Facebook and Twitter. So how did all this begin?

The first Internet café ①

A café with full Internet access (sometimes called a Cybercafé) was designed in early 1994 by Ivan Pope. He was asked to develop an Internet event for an arts weekend in London. Pope created a café with Internet access from the tables.

Inspired by this, the first commercial Internet café, called Cyberia, was opened later that year in central London. It quickly became the fashionable place to be seen.

Internet cafés soon extended across the world under a variety of names, for example, the Binary Café in Canada, CompuCaféin Finland, PCBang in South Korea, and the @Café in New York.

Cafés have always been places to exchange information, talk with friends, read newspapers, and play games. Internet cafés were a natural evolution of this. Now, people can connect to the Internet in any cafés using their own laptops and smartphones. There is less need for Internet cafés.

Five Internet firsts

The first search engine 2

For many people, using search engines has become a routine part of their lives. But how did they begin?

In 1989, a young computer scientist from Barbados, Alan Emtage, was studying at Montreal's McGill University in Canada. He built a single, easily searchable database for students to access information. This created a lot of interest and Alan was joined by two colleagues, Mike Parker and Bill Heelan, who helped develop the system. They called it "Archie." Why was it named Archie? Simply the word "archive" without the "v."

Emtage found himself at the heart of an Internet revolution. It didn't take long for search engines to become big business. Many more followed such as Excite in 1993, created by six Stanford University students, Yahoo in 1994, and Lycos also in 1994. With 60 million documents this was the largest of its time until Google was launched in 1998. Google now has 620 million visitors every day.

The first blog 3

The first ever blogger may never be identified, but the most likely candidate is an American journalist, Justin Hall. He began blogging in 1994 (before the word "blog" existed) with a website called "Justin's Links from the Underground." At first, his website just gave rather boring information about the Internet. But soon his main topic became his personal life. He wrote openly about his relationships, his passions, his plans, and his fears. More and more readers were attracted to his site, fascinated by his daily blogs. They began to share their lives with his.

The word "blog" wasn't used until 1997. It is short for "WebLog" (web log), a name invented by Jorn Barger in December of that year.

Now the number of active bloggers is estimated to be about 100 million worldwide, and Justin Hall has been named "the founding father of personal blogging" by *The New York Times*.

The first virus 4

What exactly are computer viruses? They are simply computer programs that replicate themselves again and again. This ability was predicted as early as 1949 by a German mathematician, John von Neumann. It is generally believed that the very first was a virus called Creeper. It was detected on ARPANET (the ancestor of the Internet) in the early 1970s. It was written by an engineer named Bob Thomas from Cambridge, Massachusetts in 1971. However, the Creeper was not a bad virus; it did not damage computers. When a machine was infected, a message simply appeared on the screen saying "I'm the Creeper, catch me if you can!" More damaging viruses appeared in the 1980s with the spread of personal computers.

In 1986, Brain was the first virus to infect PCs; in 1991, Michelangelo was the first to make international news; in 2000, Love Letter broke hearts by sending emails saying "I love you" to tens of millions of computers; and in 2007, Storm Worm spread with a message saying "230 dead as storm batters Europe!"

The first social networking site 5

In the 1990s, more and more homes had Internet access. People could connect easily with each other. Would they also like to reconnect with old friends? In 1995 Classmates.com, the first social networking site, began life in the basement of Randy Conrads, a Boeing employee in the US. It was immediately popular. People loved exchanging life stories with old schoolmates and school romances were reignited. In one year, this led to 100 marriages.

The idea was copied in many countries, including Friends Reunited in the UK. In 2003, the business networking site LinkedIn began. It now has over 300 million members. In the same year and with three times that number was MySpace. However, one name leads all other global social networking sites, Facebook. Created in 2004 by students at Harvard University, it went worldwide in 2006 and has more than 800 million users. There has even been a movie, *The Social Network*, made about it.

It seems people love talking about themselves. On the micro-blogging site, Twitter, users inform their followers about tiny details of their lives: "I'm having honey with my toast this morning!"

Modern life drives me crazy!

1 What things annoy you in a typical day? Write down one or two and give them to your teacher.

Jack's stressful day

2 Look at the photos of Jack. What do you think is annoying him?

3 **CD3 27** Alan is meeting Jack at the train station. Jack has not had a good trip. Listen and check (✓) what he complains about.

- the train is late
- the girl behind him
- the train is overcrowded
- the little boy
- parking
- booking a ticket
- the food
- traffic
- coffee shops

4 **CD3 27** Work in small groups. Listen again. What exactly are his complaints?

5 Have you ever had similar complaints to Jack's? Tell the class.

What do you think?

6 What do different generations complain about? Think of typical complaints for these people. Share ideas as a class.

- very young children
- teenagers
- parents
- the middle-aged
- old people

7 Your teacher will read aloud some of the things that annoy you. Can you guess who wrote it?

Role play

It's the end of a difficult day and you have just gotten home to your roommate/husband/wife/parents. Work with a partner and write a conversation about all the problems you had that day. Begin like this:

A I had a really terrible day!
B Why? What happened?
A Well, I …

Act out your conversations for the class.

⚬⚬⚬ EVERYDAY ENGLISH

On the phone

1 **CD3 28** Listen and practice saying these telephone numbers.

(919) 677-1303
555-1212
(212) 726-6389
1-800-451-7556

How were these numbers expressed?

0   555   800

2 **CD3 29** Listen and write the numbers. Compare your answers with a partner.

3 In your country what are the telephone numbers for …?

• your house   • your cell phone   • emergency services   • directory assistance

How many telephone numbers do you know by heart? Give examples. Whose are they?

4 **CD3 30** Listen to four phone conversations. Answer these questions after each one.

1 Who is speaking to who?
2 Are they on a landline or a cell phone?
3 Where are they?
4 What they are talking about?
5 How well do they know each other?

5 **CD3 30** Listen again and complete the expressions from the telephone conversations.

1 A Sorry Brian, you're _____ up. I couldn't hear that.
   B I know, Adam. It's not a good _____ . But, listen, I'm calling because I can't _____ it on Thursday. Are you free on Friday?
   A Friday? I'm not sure. Can I get _____ to you?
   B Sure. That's fine. Text me. Talk to you _____ !

2 A Hello, Carol? It's Adam. I'm trying to get a _____ of Brian.
   C I'm afraid he's not here. Have you _____ his cell phone?
   A Yeah. I tried that first, but he's not _____ .
   C It's probably _____ off.
   A Oh, OK. Can you give him a _____ ?
   C Sure.

3 D I'm sorry. Brian's line's _____ . Would you like to _____ ?
   E Yes, please.
   D It's _____ for you now.
   E Thank you.
   F Hello. Brian Doyle's office. Flora _____ .
   E _____ is Emma Smith from Digby and Moss Associates.
   F Oh, good morning, Ms. Smith. I'll put you _____ immediately.

4 C Hi, Flora. Can I speak to Brian, please?
   F Oh, I'm _____ he has _____ with him right now. Is it _____ ?
   C Just tell him Carol _____ and I'll see him tonight.
   F Will _____ . I hope there isn't a problem.

CD3 30 Listen again and check.

6 Work with a partner. Learn one of the conversations by heart. Act it out for the class.

Role play

Work in pairs. You are going to have three telephone conversations.

Student A Look at p. 148.   **Student B** Look at p. 150.

> Hi, Maria. I'm calling because I can't make it on Tuesday.

> Sorry, you're breaking up …

11 Life's what you make it!

Present Perfect Continuous • Tense review
Birth, marriage, and death • Good news, bad news

STARTER

1 Ask and answer these questions with a partner.
- How long have you been learning English?
- When did you start?

2 Ask your teacher the same questions about *teaching* English.

ANYONE CAN SING!

Present Perfect Continuous and tense review

1 How many students in your class think they can sing? How many think they can't? Take a survey and *prove* your answers.

2 Choirmaster and TV host, Gareth Malone is passionate about teaching singing. Look quickly through the chart about his life. In what ways has music been part of his life?

3 Study the chart more closely and answer the questions.

1 Where and when was Gareth born?
2 When did he move to London?
3 What did he study in college?
4 How long did he work for the LSO?
5 How many awards has he won?
6 How long has he been married?
7 Does he have any children?
8 What is he doing now?

4 Match a question about Gareth with an answer.

1 When did he start playing the piano?	___ Three.
2 How long has he been playing the piano?	___ For about 30 years.
3 When did he start teaching singing?	___ When he was three.
4 How long has he been teaching singing?	___ Since he was three.
5 When did he make his first TV show?	___ When he was 23.
6 How long has he been making TV shows?	___ Since he was 23.
7 How many shows has he made?	___ In 2007.
8 How long has he been living in London?	___ Since 2007.

CD3 31 Listen and check. Ask and answer the questions with a partner.

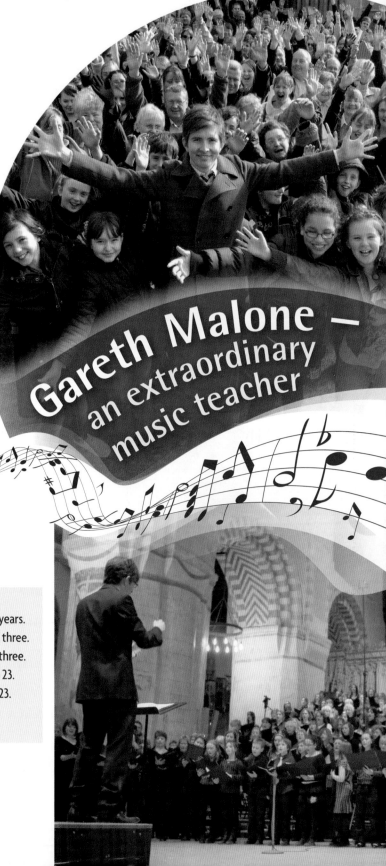

Gareth Malone –
an extraordinary
music teacher

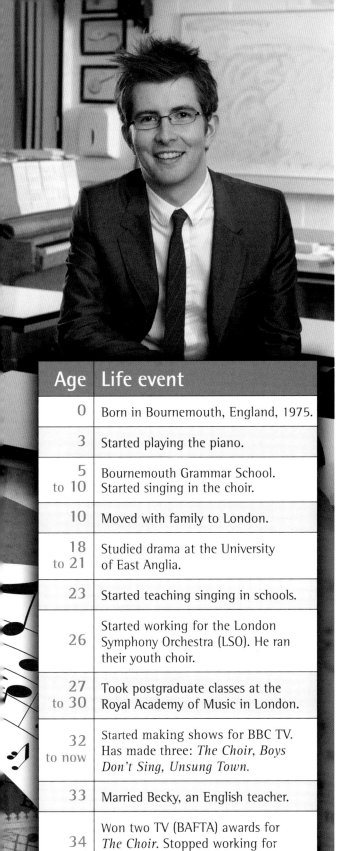

Age	Life event
0	Born in Bournemouth, England, 1975.
3	Started playing the piano.
5 to 10	Bournemouth Grammar School. Started singing in the choir.
10	Moved with family to London.
18 to 21	Studied drama at the University of East Anglia.
23	Started teaching singing in schools.
26	Started working for the London Symphony Orchestra (LSO). He ran their youth choir.
27 to 30	Took postgraduate classes at the Royal Academy of Music in London.
32 to now	Started making shows for BBC TV. Has made three: *The Choir, Boys Don't Sing, Unsung Town.*
33	Married Becky, an English teacher.
34	Won two TV (BAFTA) awards for *The Choir.* Stopped working for the LSO.
35	Daughter Esther born.
now	Still teaching music and making more radio and TV shows. Still living in London.

GRAMMAR SPOT

1 Read the sentences. What tenses are used?

He **made** his first TV show in 2007 and he still **makes** them.

He**'s been making** shows since 2007.

He**'s made** three so far.

The Present Perfect Continuous expresses an activity that began in the past and still continues.

2 Complete the questions. Answer them.

How long _____ he _____ TV shows?

How many shows _____ he _____ so far?

3 Remember! Stative verbs such as *be, have* (possession), *know*, and *love* are rarely used in continuous tenses.

I**'ve known** him for a long time.

▶▶ **Grammar Reference 11.1 p. 141**

PRACTICE

Discussing grammar

1 Choose the correct tense.

1 How long *have you been waiting / are you waiting* here?
2 I *bought / have bought* a computer a few weeks ago.
3 Alice *has been looking / has looked* for a new job for a long time.
4 How long *have you had / have you been having* your car?
5 Sue *has been talking / has talked* on her phone for a long time.
6 She*'s been speaking / has spoken* to at least six friends.

Asking questions

2 Work with a partner. Read the sentences aloud and reply using a question with *How long ...?* Think of an answer.

How long has she been working there?

Only a couple of months.

1 My sister's working in New York.
2 I'm training to run a marathon.
3 My boss is on vacation.
4 I'm learning how to drive.
5 I know Maria very well.
6 I have the new iPad.

CD3 32 Listen and compare.

Talking about you

3 Put the verbs in the Present Perfect, Present Perfect Continuous, or the Simple Past. Then ask and answer with a partner.

1 How long _____ you _____ (come) to this school?

2 How long _____ you _____ (use) this book?

3 Which book _____ you _____ (use) before this one?

4 How long _____ you _____ (know) your teacher?

What have they been doing?

4 Work with a partner. Ask questions with *Why?* about the people in the pictures. Reply with *because* and a reason.

> Why are the students bored?
>> Because the teacher's been talking for hours.

1 bored

2 sore throat

3 tired and dirty

4 backache

5 covered in paint

6 no money left

5 Complete these sentences in the Present Perfect about the people in Exercise 4.

1 They __haven't understood__ (not understand) a word.
2 He _____ (sing) every night for the last three weeks.
3 They're happy because they _____ (win) the game.
4 He _____ (plant) six rows of cabbage.
5 She _____ (paint) two walls already.
6 They _____ (spend) over $500.

CD3 33 Listen and check.

💬 SPEAKING

Tense review

1 Look at the pictures of Taylor Swift and read what she says. What kind of music do you think she sings? What do you learn about her mother?

Taylor Swift: From small-town girl to world-famous singer!

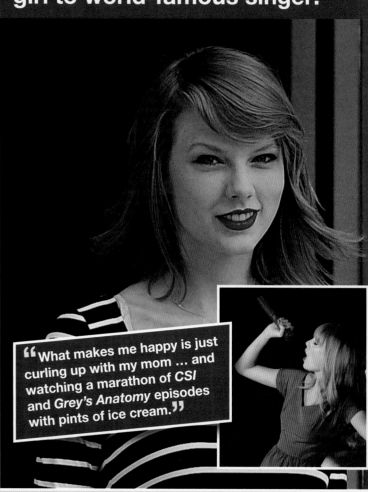

> " What makes me happy is just curling up with my mom ... and watching a marathon of *CSI* and *Grey's Anatomy* episodes with pints of ice cream. "

> " My mom and I have always been really close. She's always been the friend that was always there. There were times when, in middle school and junior high, I didn't have a lot of friends. But my mom was always my friend. Always. "

2 Work with a partner.

Student A Look at p. 148.
Student B Look at p. 150.

You have different information about Taylor Swift's life and career. Ask and answer questions.

> Where was Taylor Swift born?
>> In Wyomissing, Pennsylvania. When was she born?

I haven't seen you for a long time!

1 Write down the names of some friends you had when you were younger. Talk to a partner about them.

- Why were you friends?
- Do you still see them?
- What do you know about their lives now?

Friends

From: **SHansson6@chatchat.com**
Subject: **Hi**

MESSAGE

Are you **Mike Elliot** from Granville High School, 1996 – 2002? I hope so. I'm Sophie Roberts – yes – "Silly Sophie!" (Now **Sophie Hansson**). I've been trying to find information about you for a while. How's life? I'd love to hear your news. My email address is: SHansson6@chatchat.com

From: **Mikeyell@gargle.net**
Subject: **What a surprise!**

MESSAGE

Dear **Sophie**,
Great to hear from you! It's been a long time since we spoke – our last day at school, I think. What happened to all those promises about keeping in touch? How long have you been Mrs. Hansson? I'm not married, but I've been going out with a very nice girl for a while, so who knows? I'm working in Mexico City right now. What have you been doing with your life? We have to meet when I'm back in the US and catch up. **Mike**

2 Two old friends have just made contact again via a social networking site. Read their first messages.

- Who are they?
- When were they friends?
- What do you learn about their lives now?

3 **CD3 34** Sophie and Mike finally meet and catch up. Listen to the first part of their conversation. Are these statements about Mike true or false? Correct the false ones.

1 Mike thinks Sophie looks older.
2 He's been working in Mexico City for eight months.
3 The headquarters of his company is in Hong Kong.
4 His Mexican girlfriend speaks no English.
5 He's been learning Spanish for six months.
6 Now he's going to learn Swedish.

4 Read the second part of the conversation. Read what **Sophie** says. Answer the questions.

1 Who did she marry?
2 What and where was her first job?
3 Where does she work now?
4 What have they been trying to do?
5 Why do they need a place of their own?

5 **CD3 35** Complete **Mike's** questions. Listen and check. How does the conversation end?

Role play

6 Have a similar conversation with your partner. Pretend you have met again after a few years. Begin like this:

It's great to see you! It's been a long time. What have you been doing?

▶▶ **WRITING Filling out forms** *p. 112*

Sophie I got married a year ago to a Swedish guy. Ragnar, Ragnar Hansson.

Mike _____?

S We met while I was working in Stockholm.

M _____?

S Well, after school I studied fashion design and my first job was in Sweden, as a buyer for H&M Fashion.

M _____?

S I worked there for over three years. Ragnar was my boss.

M _____?

S Yes, we did. My parents came for the wedding.

M _____?

S No, we don't. We both work in the US.

M _____?

S About ten months. We've been trying to buy a small house since we got back.

M _____?

S With my parents. They're wonderful, but it's not great and we're expecting a baby next April, so we really need a place of our own.

M Oh, congratulations!

1 Who are the richest families in your country? How did they become rich? Describe their lifestyle.

2 Look at the pictures and read the introduction. What did you learn about the Getty family?

3 Work with a partner. Read about **Jean Paul Getty I**. Correct the information below about him.

  1 Jean Paul Getty I made his money from art and antiques.
  2 He was one of the world's first millionaires.
  3 He built the J. Paul Getty Museum in Guildford, England.
  4 He used his house in England to entertain British and American oil friends.
  5 He was famous for his generosity.
  6 He had five wives and four sons.

4 Read about **Jean Paul Getty II**. Answer the questions.

  1 Which adjectives best describe his relationship with his father. Give reasons.

close	distant	loving	cold	cruel	caring

  2 How many wives did he have? Who were they? How did each marriage end?
  3 What did he have in common with his father?
  4 Who was kidnapped? Where and why?
  5 Why did Paul I refuse to pay the ransom?
  6 Why did he change his mind?
  7 How much money did Paul II inherit? What did he do with it?
  8 Where was he living when he died? Where is he buried?

5 Read about **Jean Paul Getty III**. Make a list of the tragic events in his life. Who do you blame? Discuss as a class.

6 Read about **Balthazar Getty**. Complete the questions about him. Ask and answer them with a partner.

  1 Where/born?
  2 What/do?
  3 How long/working in movies?
  4 … made a lot of movies?
  5 Which TV series/appeared in?
  6 How many children/have?
  7 Why/marriage almost end?

What do you think?
1 Which Getty do you think is the most tragic? Which the least? Why?
2 What do you predict for Balthazar? Will he break the cycle of tragedy?

Project

Research the history of a famous family. Tell the class about it.

A Tragic Dynasty

The Getty family is one of the richest families in the world, yet it has been plagued by tragedy for generations. The family is proof that money cannot buy happiness.

Jean Paul Getty I (1892–1976)

Jean Paul Getty I was an American businessman. He founded the Getty Oil Company, and in 1957 was named the richest living American. He was one of the world's first billionaires.

An avid collector of art and antiques, he built the J. Paul Getty Museum in Los Angeles, California. He left over $661 million to the museum when he died.

> In 1957 he was named the richest living American

He moved to England in the 1950s and bought a 16th-century Tudor estate, Sutton Place, near Guildford. This house became the center of the Getty Oil Company and he used it to entertain his British and Arabian oil friends. Paul I was famous for his cheapness. He installed a pay phone in Sutton Place for his guests' use. He died there on June 6, 1976, at the age of 83.

Getty married and divorced five times in his life. He had five sons with four of his wives.

Jean Paul Getty II (1932–2003)

Jean Paul Getty II was the son of Paul I's fourth wife, Ann Rork. His parents divorced when he was three. The young Paul II rarely saw his father, but he wrote to him. His father never answered the letters. He just returned them with the spelling mistakes underlined.

In 1956, he married his childhood sweetheart, Gail Harris and had four children. They moved to Rome where Paul II ran Getty Oil Italiana. They were popular, but their party-loving ways took control of their lives. They divorced in 1964. Two years later Paul II married the Dutch model Talitha Pol (pictured). This also ended in disaster.

Paul II and Paul I had one thing in common – they were very bad fathers. In 1973 Paul II's eldest son, Jean Paul III, was kidnapped in Rome, and a ransom of $17 million was demanded. His grandfather refused to pay, saying "I have 14 other grandchildren." An envelope arrived from the kidnappers. Inside was Paul III's ear and a note:

This is Paul's ear. If we don't get some money within ten days, then the other ear will arrive.

Paul I finally paid $3 million and his grandson was released.

Paul II moved back to England and in 1997 became a British citizen. He had inherited $2.5 billion from his father. He donated over $2.25 million of this to the arts. In 1994, he married his third wife, Victoria Holdsworth. It was Victoria who helped him finally get his life together. He died in 2003 and is buried in Westminster Abbey.

Jean Paul Getty III (1956–2011)

Jean Paul Getty III spent his childhood in Italy. His parents divorced when he was nine and after that he saw very little of his father. By the age of 15 he had been expelled from seven schools and he was already taking drugs. Then in July 1973, when he was 16, the kidnapping happened. He was imprisoned in a cave in the mountains for five months until his ear was cut off and his grandfather finally paid a ransom. Paul III never recovered. He returned to his party lifestyle. In 1974, at the age of 18, he married Gisela Zacher, a German model, and moved to Los Angeles. He was just 19 when his son Balthazar was born.

Paul III was now an alcoholic and drug addict and in 1981, at just twenty-four years old, he had a stroke. He was in a coma for six weeks and afterward he was paralyzed, nearly blind, and unable to speak. His father, Paul II, like his grandfather before, refused to help. Paul III and Gisela divorced in 1993 and he was taken care of by his mother, Gail, until his death on February 5, 2011. He was 54.

Balthazar Getty (1975–)

Balthazar Getty, the great-grandson of Jean Paul Getty I, was born in California in 1975. He is an actor and a musician. When he was 11 he was sent to Gordonstoun School, an elite boarding school in Scotland that has educated three generations of the British royal family.

Balthazar has been working in movies since he was 12, when he was given the leading role of the schoolboy, Ralph, in the movie *Lord of the Flies*. He's made many movies since then, including *Young Guns II* and *Natural Born Killers*. He has also been in TV shows, like the hit ABC series, *Brothers and Sisters*.

Balthazar has also worked as a fashion model and in 2000, he married fashion designer Rosetta Millington. They have a son, Cassius Paul, and three daughters. The marriage almost ended in 2008 when Balthazar was photographed kissing the actress Sienna Miller. He has since returned to his wife.

So far Balthazar's life has been more successful than his father's and grandfather's. He says, "As a child, I really didn't know what it was to be a Getty. I had a pretty modest upbringing."

VOCABULARY AND LISTENING
Birth, marriage, and death

BIRTH

1 Work in small groups. When were you born? Do you know the exact time of your birth?

> I was born on March 21, 1991 at 2:40 in the morning.

2 Look at the pictures and complete the sentences with a word from the box.

birth   pregnant   expecting
weighed   born   due

Sophie's ¹ _pregnant_ . She's ² _____ a baby. The baby is ³ _____ in four weeks.

She gave ⁴ _____ to a baby boy. He was ⁵ _____ at 3:00 a.m. last night. He ⁶ _____ six pounds, four ounces.

MARRIAGE

3 When did you last go to a wedding? Whose was it? What was it like? Complete the sentences with a word from the box.

married   widowed   single   divorced   engaged

1 He's _____ .

2 They're _____ .

3 They're _____ .

4 They're _____ .

5 She's _____ .

4 These sentences describe the events in **Nina's** life. Put them in the correct order. Read them aloud as a class. What is a *honeymoon*?

Nina and Ted in 2002

___ They got married in 2002 at City Hall.

___ They went to Venice on their honeymoon.

___ The marriage started to go wrong.

___ In 2004, they had a son, **Sam**.

___ They separated and got divorced in 2008.

_9_ It's their anniversary today! They've been married since 2010.

___ **Nina** remarried. She married **Robert**, a colleague from work.

___ They got engaged two years later.

_1_ **Nina** and **Ted** started going out when they were both 17.

5 **CD3 36** Listen to **Alison** talking about her life. In what ways is her story different from Nina's? Who are Ben, Mark, Ellen, Tessa, and Tom?

DEATH

6 Complete the sentences with words on the right.

1 "Are your grandparents still _____ ?"

"My grandmother is. My grandfather _____ before I was born."

2 The _____ of his uncle came as a great shock. It was totally unexpected.

3 He _____ a heart attack. The _____ is next Thursday.

4 "Do you still have your dog?" "No. He's been _____ a long time. I _____ him so much."

died
funeral
dead
death
died of
miss
alive

Good news, bad news

1 Look at the pictures. What is the good news? What is the bad news?

2 **CD3 37** Work with a partner. Complete the conversations with words from the box. Listen and check.

1

> Congratulations
> had
> Give her my love
> doing
> weigh

A My wife ¹_____ a baby last night.
B ²_____! Was it a boy or girl?
A A boy! William James.
B How much did he ³_____?
A Nine pounds, six ounces.
B Oh! A big boy. How are mother and baby ⁴_____?
A They're fine.
B That's wonderful. ⁵_____ when you see her.

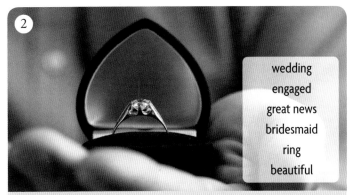

2

> wedding
> engaged
> great news
> bridesmaid
> ring
> beautiful

A Travis and I got ¹_____.
B That's ²_____! Congratulations!
A Do you like my ³_____?
B Wow! Diamonds! It's ⁴_____. When's the ⁵_____?
A We're thinking next spring.
B I hope I'm invited.
A Of course you are. I want you to be a ⁶_____.
B Really? I'd love that. I've never been one before.

3

> tough time
> break up
> getting along well
> What happened
> shame
> sorry to hear

A Did you hear about Brian and Josie?
B No! ¹_____?
A Well, they've been having a ²_____ recently.
B I know. They haven't been ³_____ at all.
A Mm. Well, they finally decided to ⁴_____.
B I'm so ⁵_____ that. What a ⁶_____!
A Yes, I always thought they were so good together.

4

> good man
> memories
> together
> coping
> so sorry
> fond of him

A We lost Grandpa last week.
B I know. Your dad told me. I'm ¹_____. He was a ²_____. Everyone was really ³_____.
A He and Grandma were ⁴_____ for almost 60 years.
B That's incredible! How old was he?
A 88.
B And how's your Grandma ⁵_____?
A She's OK. She has her family around her.
B Well, I'm sure you all have wonderful ⁶_____ of him.

3 Choose two of the conversations and practice them with your partner.
Act them out for the class.

12 Just wondering …

If + will/might/would conditionals • Prepositions • Thank you and goodbye!

 STARTER

What's the weather forecast where you are for …?
- today   • tomorrow   • the weekend

 86→

REAL POSSIBILITIES
First conditional + *will* and *might*

1 **CD3 38** Read and listen to the conversation.

> A What are you doing this weekend?
> B Mmm … if the weather's nice, we'll go for a picnic.
> A Sounds nice. Where to?
> B Not sure. We might go to the park, or we might go to the river.
> A Well, I'm sure you'll have fun!

What's the difference between …?
  We**'ll go** for a picnic.   We **might go** to the park.

Practice the conversation with a partner.

2 Have similar conversations with your partner.
   • sunny – go swimming – the pool / the lake
   • it rains – go shopping – Main Street / a shopping mall
   • have time – see some friends – a restaurant / a coffee shop

   CD3 39 Listen and compare.

3 What do you think you'll do this weekend?

   If it's a nice day on Saturday, I'll go to the beach.
   If it rains, I won't go to the beach.
   I might see some friends.

GRAMMAR SPOT

1 In first conditional sentences what tense comes after *if*? What is the other verb form?

> **If** it**'s** sunny, we**'ll go** for a picnic.
> We **won't** go out **if** it **rains**.

2 The first conditional refers to real time and real future situations.

> **If we have** time, **we'll see** some friends.

3 *Might* + base form expresses a future possibility. *Might = will perhaps.*

> I **might go out**, or I **might stay** at home. I'm not sure.

▶▶ **Grammar Reference 12.1 and 12.2 p. 142**

PRACTICE

Discussing grammar

1 Work with a partner. Choose the correct answer.

1 If I see Pete, *I might tell / I'll tell* him I saw you.
2 I'll come and see you if *I have / I'll have* time.
3 *I might see / I'll see* you later. I'm not sure.
4 *I might pick up / I'll pick up* the kids from school if you want.
5 If *you'll get / you get* there before me, wait by the door.
6 If you tell me, *I won't say / I'll say* a word to anyone else. I promise.

going to and *might*

2 Work with a partner. Make conversations about these future possibilities.

> **What are you going to do after school?**

> **I don't know. I might go home, or I might go to the store.**

1 What/do/after school?
   don't know – go home/go to the store

2 Where/go on your next vacation?
   not sure – Peru/Thailand

3 What/study in college?
   haven't decided – languages/business

4 What/buy Jane/birthday?
   not sure – a T-shirt/makeup

5 When/see your boyfriend again?
   don't know – Friday night/Saturday afternoon

CD3 40 Listen and check.

When I leave school ...

3 **CD3 41** Listen to Tara and Ben talking about when they graduate from high school. Who knows what they want to do? Who isn't sure?

Talk to a partner about Tara and Ben.

> **First, Tara's going to ...**

> **Ben might ...**

Tara   Ben

4 Ben has decided to go traveling with James but Tara sees a lot of problems. Use the prompts to continue his conversation with Tara.

Tara What will you do if you don't have any money?
Ben I'll get a job, of course!
Tara But what will you do if you ...?

- don't like the food   • get lonely
- are sick   • don't get along with James
- miss your family   • can't speak the language

Advice and warnings

5 Who is speaking? Complete their sentences.

1 If _____ these pills, _____ feel better.

2 If _____ junk food, _____ fat.

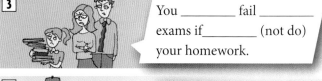

3 You _____ fail _____ exams if_____ (not do) your homework.

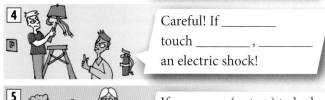

4 Careful! If _____ touch _____, _____ an electric shock!

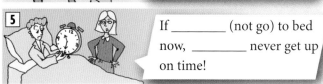

5 If _____ (not go) to bed now, _____ never get up on time!

CD3 42 Listen and check.

DREAMS AND WISHES
Second conditional *if + would*

1 Look at the picture of the genie? What can he do?

2 **CD3 43** Read and listen to Lily. How old do you think she is? What does she wish for?

Lily

I'd love a baby brother. If I had a baby brother, I would play with him all the time. We'd have a lot of fun. I'd be so happy! I wouldn't ask my mom and dad for anything else!

3 Answer the questions.

1 Does Lily have a brother?
   No, she …
2 How does she express her wish?
   If I had …, I would …
3 What would she do with her brother?
   They'd …
4 How would she feel?
   She'd …
5 Why would her mom and dad be happy?
   Because she …

CD3 43 Listen again and repeat what Lily says.

4 **CD3 44** Listen to Sam and Annie. What do they wish for? Complete their sentences.

Sam

I'd like to be taller. If I __were__ taller, I _____ on the travel team for soccer. And if I _____ really well, I _____ captain. And then if I _____ really hard, maybe one day I _____ professional soccer! My dad _____ so proud of me!

Annie

I have two kids. I love them, but I never have any time to myself. If I _____ a free weekend, I _____ in bed all day. I _____ magazines and watch TV. Then I _____ all night and my children _____ me up. Heaven!

5 What is the reality about Sam and Annie? What would they do if they could?

Sam isn't tall. If he were taller, he'd …

GRAMMAR SPOT

1 What verb forms do we use in second conditional sentences?
   If I **had** a brother, I **would play** with him.

2 The second conditional describes an improbable/impossible situation. Which sentence is more probable?
   If he trains hard, **he'll be** on the team.
   If he trained hard, **he'd be** on the team.

3 Notice that *was* can change to *were* in the *if* clause.
   If Sam **were** taller, he'd …
   If I **were** you, I'd stop smoking.

▶▶ **Grammar Reference 12.3 p. 142**

My wishes

6 Write down three wishes for you. Show a partner. Say what you would do.

I'd like to be rich. If I were rich, I'd …

PRACTICE

Discussing grammar

1 Put the verbs in the correct first or second conditional form.

1 If I _____ (win) the lottery, I _____ (give) all the money to you.

2 If you _____ (go) out, _____ you _____ (get) me a newspaper?

3 If I _____ (find) a wallet on the street, I _____ (not keep) it.

4 If I _____ (find) your book, I _____ (give) it back to you.

5 "I'm going to drive to the city today."
  "I _____ (not do) that if I _____ (be) you.
  You might get stuck in traffic. Take the train instead."

2 Work with a partner. How many sentences can you make from the chart? Read them aloud.

If I ...	were had knew didn't know	the answer, the president, you, a millionaire, the time,	I'd I wouldn't	tell you. travel the world. work for world peace. tell the truth. accept the job. help you. ask the teacher.

He's not much good at anything!

3 **CD3 45** Tony's dad is fed up with his son. Listen to him talking about Tony's life. Take notes.

Tony and his dad

Money
_____
Clothes
_____
Work
_____
Lazy
_____
Girlfriend
_____

4 Make sentences about Tony using these ideas.

- If / job / have money
- If / money / buy / new clothes
- If / nice clothes / look more well dressed
- If / a little more ambitious / apply for more jobs
- If / so lazy / get up before noon
- If / shave / shower / look better
- If / look better / get girlfriend

CD3 46 Listen and check.

At a crossroads

1 If you are at a crossroads in life, what does that mean? Give an example from your life.

2 **CD3 47** Jimmy and Fiona are at a crossroads in their lives. Listen to them talking to a friend and answer the questions after each one.

1 What is the problem?
2 Who are the people involved?
3 What are the possible options?
4 What are the pros and cons of each option?
5 What might happen as a result?
6 What does the friend advise?

What do you think?

3 What would you do if you were Jimmy or Fiona? What would you advise?

> If I were Jimmy, I'd ...

4 **CD3 48** Listen to the same two people talking a year later. Did they make the right decision?

Discussion

5 Work in small groups. Look at the situations on p. 153. They all describe dilemmas that people find themselves in and that require decisions.

Talk together. What would you do?

Life, the universe, and everything

1 Close your eyes. Do nothing for one minute. Did that seem like a long time? What *is* a long time?

2 What do you know about the universe? Take the quiz.

Time and the universe

1 The universe is **13.7 billion / 13.7 million** years old.

2 Our solar system was formed **5 billion / 1 billion** years ago.

3 The Earth was formed **4.5 billion / 500,000** years ago.

4 *Homo sapiens* appeared in East Africa **2 million / 200,000** years ago.

The answers are at the bottom of this page.

3 Read the introduction to *The Wonders of Our Universe*. Answer the questions.

 1 Why is it hard for us to understand the size of the universe?
 2 Why are the timescales involved difficult?

4 Read the rest of the article. Answer the questions after each part.

Part 1

 1 What is it about these features of the Earth that make it suitable for life?
 • distance from the sun   • rotation   • angle
 • water   • atmosphere   • size

 2 What would happen if these features were different?

Part 2

 3 What are the main objects in our solar system? What holds them all together?
 4 What are the planets made of?
 5 How would you give an alien directions to our solar system?
 6 How many stars are there in the Milky Way?
 7 How many galaxies are there in the universe?

Part 3

 8 Look at the diagram *The Life Cycle of the Sun*. Explain it. Where are we now? How will the universe end? When?
 9 What are the wonders of it all?

What do you think?

How does it make you feel to think
 … the universe is so old?   … it is infinite?   … one day it will end?

▶▶ WRITING **CD3 49** **CD3 50** Listening and note-taking *p. 113*

The Wonders

There are two things that are impossible for us to understand about the universe.

Part 1 > The Earth

The Earth is the only place in the universe where life is known to exist. It has all the conditions that are suitable for supporting life.

● It is a **perfect distance** from the sun. If it was closer, there would be too much radiation. The Earth would be too hot, and all the oceans would evaporate. If it was further from the sun, it would be too cold, and the planet would be covered in ice.

● The Earth **rotates** on its axis, so the whole surface is warmed and cooled once a day, every day. If it didn't rotate, one side would be permanently hot, and the other cold.

● It is at an **angle** (23.5°) to the sun, which gives us our seasons. At different times of the year, the northern hemisphere gets more or less sunlight than the southern hemisphere. Without seasons, our weather would be too extreme.

● 70% of the Earth is covered in **water**. If there was no water, there would be no life.

● Our **atmosphere** blocks harmful solar radiation, but it allows enough heat from the sun to warm us.

● The Earth is the right **size**. If it were bigger, gravity would be much stronger, and we wouldn't be able to move. If it were smaller and gravity were weaker, it wouldn't hold our oceans.

# of Our Universe

> One is its ... sIZE

It is probably **infinite**.
Which means it goes on forever ...
and **ever** ... and ever ... and ever ... and ever ...

> Another is its ... TIME MMMM E

If you think a year lasts a long time ...
If you think 20 is old ...
If you think 2,000 years ago is ancient history ...
think again. The universe is
13.7 billion years old.

The Earth

The Milky Way

Our Solar System

Part 2 > Our Solar System

The Earth is part of our solar system. At the center of this is the sun, which is the solar system's star.

Our solar system consists of the sun and objects connected to it by gravity – eight planets and their moons. The four smaller planets, Mercury, Venus, Earth, and Mars, are made of rock and metal. The two largest, Jupiter and Saturn, are called the gas giants. They consist mainly of hydrogen and helium gases. The two farthest from the sun, Uranus and Neptune, consist of ice.

> Our Galaxy

Our solar system is part of the galaxy known as the Milky Way. It is about half way out from the center.

Our sun is just one of the stars in the Milky Way. One of between 100 and 400 billion stars.

Our solar system goes around the center of the Milky Way once every 250 million earth years.

> The Universe

Our galaxy is just one of more than 170 billion galaxies in the observable universe. The universe is probably infinite. There is no end to it.

Part 3 > The End

Our sun is getting hotter. In one billion years, the Earth will become too hot for water to exist, and all life will end. Our sun will continue to burn until it uses all its supply of hydrogen. In five billion years, it will expand, and then explode and become a red giant. After that it will collapse and become smaller than the Earth.

Some scientists believe that the universe will continue to expand. All the stars, every single one, will burn out and it will go dark. The temperature will drop to zero. This will happen when the universe is 100 trillion years old. After that, there will be nothing. Forever.

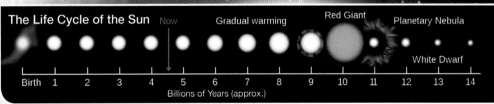

The Life Cycle of the Sun Now   Gradual warming   Red Giant   Planetary Nebula

White Dwarf

Birth   1   2   3   4   5   6   7   8   9   10   11   12   13   14
Billions of Years (approx.)

> The wonder of it all

There is a short period of time in the early years of the universe when life is possible. This period, in the history of time, lasts just a second, a flash, a snap of the fingers.

That miraculous time is **now**.
We are in the **most precious place** at the **most precious time**.

And it's now!

VOCABULARY
Prepositions

Prepositions are little words, but they're everywhere!

We are connected to the sun by gravity.
I'm going out on a date with Alice.

1 It's easy to make mistakes with prepositions. Correct these sentences. Sometimes no preposition is necessary.

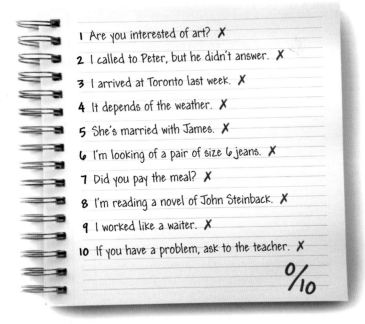

1 Are you interested of art? ✗
2 I called to Peter, but he didn't answer. ✗
3 I arrived at Toronto last week. ✗
4 It depends of the weather. ✗
5 She's married with James. ✗
6 I'm looking of a pair of size 6 jeans. ✗
7 Did you pay the meal? ✗
8 I'm reading a novel of John Steinback. ✗
9 I worked like a waiter. ✗
10 If you have a problem, ask to the teacher. ✗

%10

2 Complete each sentences with a preposition and a noun.

| in | by |
| for | on |

| strike | purpose | touch |
| dinner | myself | business |

1 It wasn't an accident. She broke it _____ _____ .
2 What's _____ _____ ? I'm starving!
3 He isn't in the office this week. He's away _____ _____ .
4 When you go, keep _____ _____ with me via email.
5 Transportation workers are _____ _____ for better pay.
6 I don't need other people. I like being _____ _____ .

CD3 51 Listen and check.

3 What prepositions go with these nouns?

some information _____ **Seoul**

a recipe _____ **paella**

be in love _____ **the girl next door**

a book _____ **butterflies**

a problem _____ **my central air-conditioning**

a lot of damage _____ **a building**

a meeting _____ **your boss**

a check _____ **$100**

a cure _____ **cancer**

the difference _____ **two cultures**

4 Complete the sentences with an adjective from the box and a preposition.

| good   used   afraid   angry   famous   worried   different |

1 I'm _____ _____ spiders. I can't even look at them.
2 Dave is very _____ _____ cooking. He makes amazing meals.
3 Why are you _____ _____ me? What did I do to annoy you?
4 I found the city noisy at first, but I'm _____ _____ it now.
5 New York City is _____ _____ its skyscrapers.
6 They're late. Where are they? I'm _____ _____ them.
7 I'm very _____ _____ my sister. She's very smart, and I'm not.

5 What prepositions go with these verbs? Sometimes there is more than one.

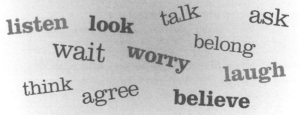

Write sentences with the verbs and a preposition.

I like listening to the radio.   What are you thinking about?

Thank you and goodbye!

1 Look at the pictures. Where are the people? Who are they? Complete the conversations with the words in the boxes.

pleasure	be going	glad	so much

A Well, it's late. I have to _____ now. Thank you _____ for a wonderful evening.

B My _____!

A And the food was delicious!

B I'm _____ you liked it. I hope you get home all right. Bye!

A Bye! And thanks again!

mention	nice	grateful	mind

A Thank you so much! It was so _____ of you.

B You're welcome.

A I'm so _____ for all your help.

B Don't _____ it!

A Uh ... Would you _____ helping me with just one more thing?

B No problem.

love	boarding	yourself	flight

A I hope you have a good _____! Who's meeting you?

B My sister, Sarah.

A Remember to give her my _____.

B I will. OK, it's _____. I have to go now. Bye!

A Take care of _____! Bye!

pleasure	kind	having	welcome

A Thanks for _____ me. I really enjoyed staying with you.

B You're _____. It was a _____. Come back and see us again sometime!

A That's very _____. Maybe next year!

C That would be great!

hello	I'll text	care	trip

A Have a safe _____!

B Thanks. _____ you when I get there.

A Say _____ to your parents for me.

B I will. Oh! The train's leaving!

A OK! Bye! Take _____!

B See you soon! Bye!

everything	luck	fun	will

A Goodbye! And thanks for _____! It was a lot of _____!

B I really enjoyed being your teacher.

C We learned so much with you!

B Thank you! Good _____ with your English. Keep practicing!

A We _____!

2 **CD3 52** Listen and check.

3 Work with a partner. Learn two of the conversations. Act them out for the class.

Oxford Online Skills Program
Log in for additional online learning

Writing and Reference Materials

Writing Contents

1 Look at the symbols often used to correct mistakes in writing. Correct the <u>underlined</u> mistakes in the sentences. Compare your answers with a partner.

Sp	Spelling	1	I'm <u>enjoing</u> the party. *Sp*
WW	Wrong word	2	They went <u>in</u> Brazil on vacation. *WW*
WO	Word order	3	I have <u>two brothers younger</u>. *WO*
Gr	Grammar	4	She has some new <u>reds</u> shoes. *Gr*
T	Tense	5	He <u>arrive</u> yesterday. *T*
P	Punctuation	6	They <u>arent</u> coming. *P*
⋏	Word missing	7	She's ⋏ doctor.

2 Work in two groups. In each of the sentences below there is one mistake.

Group A Find the mistakes in **A**. Use the symbols to mark them, but don't correct them.

Group B Find the mistakes in **B**. Use the symbols to mark them, but don't correct them.

A
1 I like Boston because is a beautiful city.
2 She studied for three years psychology.
3 There aren't any milk.
4 He's speaking French, German, and Spanish.
5 I watched TV, than I went to bed.
6 Did you by any bread at the supermarket?

B
1 I lost my all money.
2 What did you last night?
3 He always wear jeans.
4 My town is quite on weekends.
5 I want that I pass the exam.
6 She's married with Peter.

3 Find a partner from the other group. Correct each other's sentences.

4 Correct this piece of student writing.

My best friend

My best friend was my best man when I <u>get</u> married two <u>year</u> *T* *Gr*
ago. <u>He's</u> name is Antonio and we met <u>on</u> college in Miami. *Gr* *WW*
In fact we met on our very first day <u>their</u>. Antonio was ⋏ first *Sp* ⋏
person I spoke <u>with</u> and we discovered we were both studying *WW*
Spanish and that we were both soccer fans. When we gradu-
ated from college, we went <u>together traveling</u> for six <u>month</u>. *WO* *Gr*
We had a good time touring <u>central</u> and <u>south america</u>. When *P* *P*
we were in Mexico we met two sisters <u>of</u> California, Ally and *WW*
Chelsea. Now I'm married <u>with</u> Ally and next year Antonio and *WW*
Chelsea ⋏ going to get married. I like Antonio because he ⋏ very ⋏ *Gr* *Gr* ⋏
funny and we <u>has</u> really good times together. He <u>live</u> in a different state now, but we text or call <u>often each other</u>. I'm very *WO*
lucky that he's my friend.

5 Write about your own best friend.

6 Swap with a partner and see if you can find any mistakes. Read your work aloud to the class.

1 Read the postcard. Where are Gemma and Martin? Are they enjoying their vacation? Why? What is wrong with the style of the writing?

Dear Melanie,

Here we are in Boston having a nice time. The weather is very nice. We're staying in a really nice hotel in a nice part of town, Boston's Back Bay area. We have a nice view of Copley Square from our bedroom window. We think all the skyscrapers are nice. Yesterday we went on a really nice bus tour of the city and then in the evening we saw a nice concert at the Boston Pops Symphony Hall. Today we are going shopping in Macy's. It's a nice store for buying clothes. This evening we're going to eat at Legal Sea Food near the New England Aquarium. The restaurants here are nice and the food is really nice, but the servings are so huge that we often can't finish the meal.

See you soon,

Love,

Gemma and Martin

Melanie Baker
10 Wallasey Road
Brentwood,
Essex
CM15 7LE
ENGLAND

BOSTON

2 Gemma and Martin use *nice* eleven times. Complete the sentences below with other adjectives from the box. Sometimes more than one adjective is possible, but not always!

great	warm and sunny	interesting	excellent
delicious	luxurious	spectacular	amazing
exciting	brilliant	wonderful	

1 We're having a/an _____ time here in Boston.

2 The weather is _____ .

3 We're staying in a/an _____ hotel in a/an _____ part of town.

4 We have _____ views of Copley Square.

5 We think the skyscrapers are _____ .

6 We went on a/an _____ bus tour.

7 In the evening we saw a/an _____ concert.

8 Macy's is a/an _____ store for buying clothes.

9 The restaurants here are _____ .

10 The food here is really _____ .

3 Work with a partner. Read the postcard aloud using a variety of adjectives. Use *nice* once only. Discuss where you think is the best place to use it.

4 Think of a vacation you once took. Imagine you are still there. Write a postcard to a friend about it, but use the adjective *nice* only once! You can write about some of these things:

- the trip
- the weather
- the accommodations
- the food
- some things you did yesterday
- some things you are going to do today

Compare postcards with your partner, and then read them to the class.

1 Work with a partner. Look at the picture story. What is it about?

The burglar who fell asleep z ᶻ ᶻ ᶻ ᶻ ᶻ ᶻ Z

2 Read the sentences. They tell the story. Put the words in *italics* in a suitable position in the sentence. Change the punctuation if necessary.

1 A burglar broke into a house in Paris.
  Last Sunday evening   large, expensive   in the center of
  Last Sunday evening, a burglar broke into a large, expensive house in the center of Paris.

2 He went into the living room and he filled his bag with all the silverware and a Chinese vase.
  First   quickly and quietly   priceless

3 He went to the kitchen and found some cheese and two bottles of sparkling water.
  Next   delicious   the best

4 He was feeling hungry. He ate the cheese and drank the sparkling water.
  extremely   so   all

5 He felt very tired. He went to the bedroom and laid down on a big bed, and fell asleep.
  Suddenly   upstairs   comfortable   immediately   fast

6 He slept very well. When he woke up, three police officers were standing around his bed.
  Unfortunately   the next morning

CD1 44 Listen and check.

3 The pictures below illustrate a news story. What is it about? Match notes 1–6 with the pictures.

1 The phone was smelly and dirty. It still worked. Glen called some numbers.

2 Andrew Cheatle, a businessman was walking on the beach. He lost his cell phone. **(a)**

3 He was preparing the fish for sale. He noticed something metal inside a cod fish. It was a cell phone.

4 One week later, fisherman, Glen Kerley, was on his boat catching fish to sell in the market.

5 Glen returned the phone to Andrew. He still uses it.

6 Andrew was with his girlfriend, Rita. Her cell phone rang. She said, "It's for you! It's a call from your phone."

A fishy tale

4 Write the news story. Use suitable words to join the ideas and to make the story more interesting. Compare your stories in groups and with the sample answer on p. 153.

1 You receive an email from an old friend. It is many years since you heard from them. You want to reply and tell them about you and your life. Make some notes.

but, although, and *however*

2 Read these sentences. They all mean the same, but how are they different?

- I don't write many letters, **but** I send a lot of emails.
- **Although** I don't write many letters, I send a lot of emails.
- I don't write many letters. **However**, I send a lot of emails.

3 Join these pairs of sentences in different ways.

1 I love ice cream. I don't eat it often.
2 He's a good friend. We don't have a lot in common.
3 She isn't American. She speaks English very well.
4 It rained a lot. We enjoyed the vacation.

so and *because*

4 Read these sentences.

1 He lived in South Korea for many years, **so** he speaks Korean well.
2 He speaks Korean well **because** he lived in South Korea for many years.

Which pattern goes with which sentence?

a Result ⟶ Cause
b Cause ⟶ Result

5 Join the pairs of sentences in two different ways using *so* and *because*.

1 I don't eat broccoli. I don't like it.
2 She went home. She was tired.
3 We didn't enjoy our vacation. The weather was bad.
4 He worked hard. He passed all his exams.
5 I enjoy history class. I like the teacher.
6 It started to rain. We stopped playing tennis.

6 Read the email. Who is writing to whom? Why? What news does she give? Complete the email with these linking words.

but	although	however	so	because

Date: Wed, April 27 2016 11:07:36
From: "Lindy Cameron" <lindy.cam5@donwana.com>
Subject: RE: Do you remember me?
To: "Teresa Tate" <Teresa_Tate174@fsnet.com>

Dear Teresa,

How wonderful to hear from you. Of course I remember you (1) _____ it's been almost seven years since we were neighbors. How did you get my email address? You told me a little about yourself and your family, (2) _____ now I'd like to know more. You ask how we all are, (3) _____ here's some of our news.

First things first – George and I are now divorced. I know you never liked him much, (4) _____ you are probably not too surprised. (5) _____, we still see each other a lot (6) _____ of the twins. They're nine now and they're good girls, (7) _____, of course, sometimes a handful.

We moved from St. Louis (8) _____ I didn't want them to grow up in a big city. We now live in a beautiful, old farmhouse in Missouri. I love country life. We have lots of land, (9) _____ we grow all our own vegetables and keep a few chickens. (10) _____, it's all very expensive to take care of and (11) _____ I sell some of our produce to the local stores, we never have enough money for vacations and treats, (12) _____ we're happy and healthy.

I can't wait to hear more of your news. Write soon.

Please come to stay. I'd love to see you again.

Love,
Lindy XO

7 Write an email to your old friend. Use your notes from Exercise 1 and the phrases below. Compare your email with your partner's.

Dear X
How wonderful/amazing to hear from you.
I was so surprised./What a wonderful surprise.
How did you get my email address?
It was great to receive your email.
Let me tell you something about my life.
Let's keep in touch.
Love/Best wishes/All the best

1 Think about your future. How do you see your life …?

- next year
- in five years
- in ten years
- when you're 40 or 50

Write some notes about your hopes and ambitions for each of these times. Tell the class.

2 **CD2 6** Read and listen to Susannah talking about her future. What are her definite plans? What is she not sure about? What are her hopes, ambitions, and dreams?

3 Read Susannah's talk again carefully. Select any words or expressions that would be useful when you write a talk about your future. Compare with your partner. Did you choose the same ones?

4 Rewrite the first paragraph about you. Read it aloud.

5 Write a talk about your future plans and dreams. Mark pauses and words you want to stress. Practice reading it aloud. Give your talk to the class. Answer any questions.

My dreams for the future

Hello everyone. My name's Susannah – Susie for short. I'm 20 years old. Right now, I'm in my second year of art school, and I often dream about my future. I have big plans and I'd like to tell you a little bit about them.

My most immediate are vacation plans. I'm going to visit my brother who's working in Australia. My mom and I are going to spend two weeks with him in the summer sun. I'm very excited about that.

When I return, I need to decide what I'm going to study next year. I'm still not sure – I'm thinking either fashion design or landscape design. It's hard because I'm interested in both clothes and gardens. If I choose landscape I'd like to work with my friend, Jasper. He does amazing work with gardens and we've already worked on two together. It was a lot of fun and we get along really well.

In five or ten years I would like to have my own business and work for myself like my dad. He has his own building business. Maybe I'll study business after I graduate from art school.

Of course, one day I hope to marry and have children. Ideally before I'm 30, but I can't plan until I meet the right person, and I don't have a boyfriend right now.

In my dreams I see myself at 40 running a successful gardening company with about 20 employees. I'll design beautiful gardens for beautiful people. I'll have a beautiful house, two beautiful children, and of course a beautiful husband who's as successful as I am. Who knows? It could even be Jasper!

1 Complete this sentence in any way you can.

The town where I was born is / has …

Share the information with the class.

GRAMMAR SPOT

1 We use *who*, *that*, *which*, and *where* to join sentences. Look at these sentences.

> I met a man. He is from my town.
> I met a man **who** is from my town.

> I bought a house. It's on Market Street.
> I bought a house **that/which** is on Market Street.

> The hotel was very comfortable. We stayed in it.
> The hotel **where** we stayed was very comfortable.

2 *Who*, *that*, *which*, and *where* are relative pronouns. Complete the rules with a relative pronoun.

- _____ is for people.

- _____ or _____ is for things.

- _____ is for places.

---

2 Join the sentences with the correct relative pronoun.

1 There's the boy. He broke the window.
2 That's the farm. My uncle lives there.
3 There are the police officers. They caught the thief.
4 I bought a watch. It stopped after two days.
5 Here are the letters. They came this morning.
6 That's the hospital. I was born in it.

3 Look at the pictures of Denver. What do you learn about the city from them? Read the text and complete it with *who*, *that/which*, or *where*. Answer the questions.

> 1 Where is the city?
> 2 How many people live in Denver?
> 3 Who is the city named after?
> 4 What was it like 50 years ago?
> 5 What is it like now?
> 6 Which bands come from Denver?
> 7 What are the people like?

4 Write a similar description of your hometown in about 200 words. First, write some notes about it.

- Where is it?   • What's its history?   • What's it like now?

Next write some personal opinions.

- Do you like it?   • Why?/Why not?

5 Read your descriptions aloud and compare your towns.

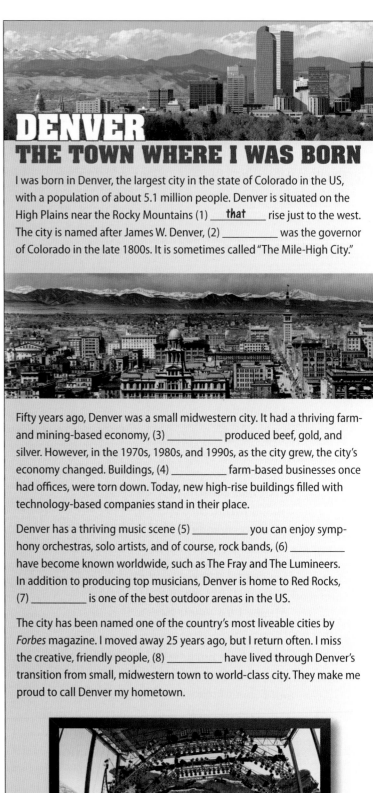

DENVER
THE TOWN WHERE I WAS BORN

I was born in Denver, the largest city in the state of Colorado in the US, with a population of about 5.1 million people. Denver is situated on the High Plains near the Rocky Mountains (1) __*that*__ rise just to the west. The city is named after James W. Denver, (2) _____ was the governor of Colorado in the late 1800s. It is sometimes called "The Mile-High City."

Fifty years ago, Denver was a small midwestern city. It had a thriving farm- and mining-based economy, (3) _____ produced beef, gold, and silver. However, in the 1970s, 1980s, and 1990s, as the city grew, the city's economy changed. Buildings, (4) _____ farm-based businesses once had offices, were torn down. Today, new high-rise buildings filled with technology-based companies stand in their place.

Denver has a thriving music scene (5) _____ you can enjoy symphony orchestras, solo artists, and of course, rock bands, (6) _____ have become known worldwide, such as The Fray and The Lumineers. In addition to producing top musicians, Denver is home to Red Rocks, (7) _____ is one of the best outdoor arenas in the US.

The city has been named one of the country's most liveable cities by *Forbes* magazine. I moved away 25 years ago, but I return often. I miss the creative, friendly people, (8) _____ have lived through Denver's transition from small, midwestern town to world-class city. They make me proud to call Denver my hometown.

1 Write down the names of any famous families you know. Share your ideas with the class. Why are they famous?

2 What do you know about John F. Kennedy? Discuss with a partner.

3 Read the seven paragraphs about John F. Kennedy. Work together to put the paragraphs in the correct order. Which words helped you decide the order?

THE LIFE OF A KENNEDY

1 John F. Kennedy 1917–1963

a ☐ This was a huge tragedy for Joseph, Sr. who had wanted his first son to become president. He now turned his attention to his second son, John. John wanted to please his father, and in 1952 he was elected to the US Senate.

b ☐ US President John Fitzgerald Kennedy (JFK) was born on May 29, 1917. He was the second of nine children in a wealthy and powerful American family. His father, Joseph, was the US ambassador to Britain, and his grandfather was the mayor of Boston. Despite all the money and fame, John's life was not easy.

c ☐ The following year, John joined the Navy and fought in World War II. He almost died when his boat sank in 1943. The following year his older brother, Joseph, Jr., was tragically killed in a military plane crash.

d ☐ As a child he was often sick and had to miss months of school. However, he was a smart and popular student. His high school classmates voted him "Most Likely To Become President"! He graduated from Harvard University in 1940.

e ☐ However, even as president, tragedy continued to follow JFK. In August, 1963, his son, Patrick, died two days after birth. And on November 22, 1963, John F. Kennedy was assassinated in Dallas, Texas. The nation was shocked, and even today millions of Americans remember what they were doing on that day.

f ☐ Around the time of John, Jr.'s birth, JFK became president. He was a popular, young leader during an important time in American history. Events during his presidency included the Cuban Missile Crisis, the building of the Berlin Wall, and the beginning of the space race.

g ☐ A year later, in 1953, he married Jacqueline Bouvier. In another tragedy, their first child died at birth in 1956. However, the couple had a daughter, Caroline, in 1957. In 1960, they had a son, John, Jr.

4 Read the notes about the life of John F. Kennedy's daughter, Caroline. Use the information to write her biography.

2 Caroline Kennedy Schlossberg 1957–

▼ Born November 27, 1957 … only surviving child of President John F. Kennedy.

▼ Brother John Fitzgerald Kennedy, Jr. born 1960.

▼ Just 5 in 1963 her father assassinated in …

▼ After father's death, moved from Washington, D.C., to New York City with mother. Grew up there.

▼ 1968, uncle, Robert F. Kennedy, also assassinated.

▼ Later in 1968, mother remarried – Greek billionaire Aristotle Onassis.

▼ Another uncle, Ted Kennedy, almost died in a car crash in 1969.

▼ 1980 graduated, Radcliffe College.

▼ 1980 started work in the Film and Television Department of the Metropolitan Museum of Art. Met her husband there.

▼ Married Edwin Schlossberg in 1986.

▼ Three children. Still lives in New York City.

▼ Her mother died in 1994, age 64.

▼ Has had many tragedies in her life. July 16, 1999, brother John, Jr. and his wife, Carolyn, died in an airplane crash.

▼ 2008 worked with Barack Obama in the US presidential election campaign.

5 Research information about a famous person (living or dead) that interests you. Make notes and write a biography.

1 Work with a partner. Discuss which beginnings can go with which endings. More than one is sometimes possible.

Which are formal? Which are informal?

1 Dear Peter,	a Lots and lots of love, Travis xo
2 Dear Mr. Smith,	b Love, Gianna
3 Hello Cathy,	c Warmly, George
4 Dear Sir or Madam,	d Bye for now, Sammy
5 Dear mom,	e Best regards, Daniel Miles
6 Hi Steve,	f Sincerely yours, Kay Macey
	g Best wishes, Dave

2 Look at the online advertisement for a school. Where is the school? What can you study there? Who do you contact?

The School | About PA | Classes | Fees | Accomodations

PHOENIX ACADEMY
OF ENGLISH

Welcome to our school

We are one of the US's most successful language schools. We welcome students from over 100 countries around the world to one of Arizona's most exciting cities. We offer quality English classes including general English, English for business, and test preparation.

Contact us:

Regina Camera (Director)	Phone: (623) 555-4566
Phoenix Academy of English	Fax: (623) 555-4567
6623 West Valley Road	
Phoenix, AZ 85383	info@phoenixacademyaz.net
USA	

We look forward to hearing from you.

A formal letter

3 Read the formal letter. Complete it with words or phrases from the box.

frequently	advertisement	However
interested in	Sincerely	to hearing
some information	application form	to improve

Via Morgagni 90,
1-00161 Rome, Italy
Tel: +39 06 44 11 97 08

March 29th

Regina Camera, Director
Phoenix Academy of English
6623 West Valley Road
Phoenix, AZ 85383

Dear Ms. Camera:

I saw your ¹_____ for English classes on your website and I am ²_____ coming to your school this summer.

I studied English for six years at school and I have to use English ³_____ in my job. ⁴_____, I now feel that it is necessary to study further. I would especially like ⁵_____ my pronunciation. Could you please send me more information about your classes, and an ⁶_____? I would also like ⁷_____ about accomodations.

I look forward ⁸_____ from you as soon as possible.

⁹_____ yours,

Gianna Lombardo

Gianna Lombardo

4 Look at the different parts of the letter. Compare with formal letters in your country.

Are the names, addresses, and the date in the same place? Do you have many different greetings and endings for formal and informal letters and emails?

An informal email

5 Match these phrases from an informal email and a formal letter.

A	B
It was great to hear from you.	Enclosed please find a photocopy of …
Thanks for …	I apologize for …
I want to ask about …	Thank you for your letter of November 1st.
I'm sorry about …	If you require additional assistance, …
I'm sorry to have to tell you that …	I regret to inform you that …
I'm sending you a copy of …	I would like to inquire about …
If you need more help, …	Thank you for …

6 Read Gianna's email to her American friend, Steve. Compare it with her letter to the school.

1 How does she express the highlighted lines from the email more formally in the letter?
2 What other informal words and phrases are in the email?

Your address

The date

Name and address of who you are writing to

Greeting

Introduction

Main parts

Conclusion

Ending

Signature

View Contact Details

Date: May 21, 2015 1:20 PM
From: "Gianna Lombardo" <gianna.lomb@aol.com>
To: stevojon@worldxnetz.net
Subject: Coming to the US

Hi Steve,

Just to let you know that I'm thinking of coming to the US this summer.

You know I have to use English a lot in my new job, so I want (need!) some

extra classes, especially for my pronunciation – as you are always telling me

I should try to improve this! Anyway, I saw an interesting ad on the Internet for

a school in Phoenix. Isn't that near you? I'd love to visit you while I'm there.

Can't wait to hear from you. See you soon I hope.

Love,

Gianna

---

7 Write a similar formal letter about yourself to the school in Phoenix. Then write an informal email to an American friend and tell them about it.

1 What movies are popular right now? Which have you seen? Complete these sentences. Then talk to a partner about it.

- The last movie I saw was …
- It starred …
- It was about …
- I enjoyed/didn't enjoy it because …

2 Read the paragraph below. What do the words in **bold** refer to?

> I saw a really good movie last week. **It** was a horror movie. I went with two friends. **They** didn't enjoy **it** at all. They said the acting was terrible. **That** surprised me because I thought **it** was excellent. My parents hardly ever go to the movies. **This** is because **they** wait until the movie comes out on DVD and then they watch **it** at home.

3 Have you heard of *Frankenstein*? Discuss these questions as a class.

1 Is *Frankenstein* a book or a movie? Or both?

2 What kind of story is it?
- a detective story
- science-fiction story
- a horror story
- a romance

3 Who or what is Frankenstein?
- a doctor
- a monster
- a scientist
- a student

4 What happens in the story?

5 Does it have a happy ending?

4 Read the review of the novel, *Frankenstein*. Check your answers to Exercise 3.

5 Read the review again. What do the words in **bold** refer to?

6 Look at these headings. Find the information in the review of *Frankenstein*.

- title and author
- type of book/movie
- characters
- the plot

Make some notes under the same headings about a book or movie that you have read or seen recently. Then write a short review. Read it aloud to the class and answer questions.

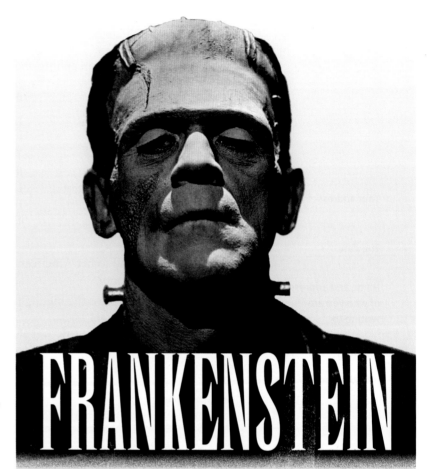

FRANKENSTEIN

The story of Frankenstein is famous all over the world. Written in 1818 by Mary Shelley, the wife of the English poet P.B. Shelley, **it** was immediately very popular. It's a horror story, and many people say it is the original science-fiction novel. However, **they** often think that Frankenstein is the name of the monster in the story, but in fact it is the name of the scientist who created **it**.

From the letters of an English explorer, Captain Robert Walton, we learn about Victor Frankenstein, a scientist from Geneva who has discovered the secret of life and decided to make a human being. So, at night he visits graveyards and collects bones and bodies. With **them** he creates a person who is more monster than man.

The monster is huge and ugly, but also intelligent. Of course when people see it they are terrified and as a result the poor monster has no friends and feels lonely and depressed. Finally, it asks Frankenstein to make **it** a wife. He refuses to do **this**. So the monster attacks and kills not only Frankenstein's bride, Elizabeth, but also his brother, and a friend. The scientist is heartbroken and now wants to kill the monster. He chases it across the world. However, he dies when they meet in the Arctic and the monster then kills **itself**.

There are over 40 movies that tell the story of Frankenstein, **the first** as long ago as 1910. It is a fascinating tale because of the complex character of the monster, **which** is both sad and frightening at the same time.

1 Do you use any **social networking sites** such as **Facebook**? Write down three things you like and three things you don't like about them. Compare your ideas with the class.

2 Read these notes. How many of your ideas are here? What do you think are the most important pros and cons?

Advantages of Facebook	Disadvantages of Facebook
You can: • keep in touch with friends • keep family up to date • find old friends • communicate with friends at any time you want • share photos • share favorite music and videos • join groups that interest you • advertise yourself and your work	• flooded with requests from unknown or unwanted "friends" • friends and family find out too much about your private life • hearing about boring events in friends' lives • tagged in pictures that you don't want others to see • wasting time on Facebook – can become addicted

3 Now read the text. What is the purpose of each paragraph?

4 Put the linking words on the right into the correct place on each line. Sometimes you will need to change the punctuation.

5 What ideas can you add to the text?

6 Make notes about the advantages and disadvantages of one of these topics. Then write a text similar to the one below.

• cell phones • Google • television

The Pros and Cons of Social Networking Sites

Social networking sites, such as **Facebook**, have many advantages. They are an excellent way of keeping in touch with people in your life, friends and family. They are a great way of finding old friends. You can communicate with these people at any time you want and in many ways, you can share your photos and your favorite music and videos with them. You can join groups with similar interests to yours, sports, hobbies, and your work.

Social networking sites have many disadvantages. You are often flooded with requests from unknown or unwanted "friends." Friends and family may find out too much about your private life and you may hear about boring events in their lives. You can be tagged in pictures that you don't want others to see. The biggest problem is that you can waste too much time on Facebook. Some people can become addicted to it.

Social networking sites are definitely here to stay. They are now one of the main means of communication worldwide. We can't imagine our lives without them.

clearly, First of all
both,
and, Also
for example
Another advantage is that
such as,

However, also, First,
Second,
what is more,
also,
Finally, perhaps
even

Despite the disadvantages,
The fact is that

1 When do you fill out forms? Give some examples.

2 Match the expressions and questions.

1	First name	a	Are you married or single?
2	Last name	b	What do you do in your free time?
3	Date of birth	c	What are your home and cell phone numbers?
4	Place of birth	d	What's your first name?
5	Permanent address	e	What do you do?
6	Marital status	f	Where were you born?
7	Occupation	g	When were you born?
8	Education	h	What's your last name?
9	Hobbies/Interests	i	What degrees, diplomas, certificates, etc., do you have?
10	Tel. nos.	j	Where do you live?

3 Follow these instructions. Write about you.

1 Write your name in capital letters.
2 Sex. Circle **F** or **M**.
3 Circle where applicable. **(Mr./Mrs./Ms.)**
4 Date of birth. **(mm/dd/yyyy)**
5 Phone no. including country code.
6 Write your zip code.
7 Signature.

4 Complete the form.

The Global School of English

PLEASE WRITE IN CAPITAL LETTERS

Mr./Mrs./Ms.   Last name   First name

Sex   Date of birth   Nationality

First language   Level of English

Address in your country   Occupation

Email address

Emergency contact & relationship to student

Type of accommodations required: homestay/hostel/dormitory/other (If other please specify)

Dietary requirements (if any)

Any medical conditions we should be aware of?

Where did you hear about the school?

Date of arrival   Date of departure

Reason for learning English: business/pleasure/exams/other (If other please specify.)

How many hours do you want to study?

Signature

1 **CD3|49** Listen to the first part of Professor Igor Petrov's talk about his vision of life in the future. Write down three things you remember. Tell the class.

2 Read the notes taken by two students during his talk. Work with a partner. Use the notes to help you remember more of the talk. Which kind of note-taking do you prefer?

3 **CD3|50** Listen to the second part of his talk. Complete Student 1's notes OR Student 2's notes.

4 **CD3|50** Compare your notes with a partner. Listen again and check.

Professor Igor Petrov

Student 1

LIFE IN THE FUTURE

OPTIMISTIC

- life expectancy = 50 → 80 USA – improved healthcare and technology

- last 20 years = DNA, microchips, Internet – in the future computers + Internet for all

- the environment – learning to control weather + natural disasters, no illness – new body parts: livers, etc.

- world population – if people educated and richer = decrease

- world government to manage global resources

- already world language = English + worldwide communication system = the Internet

PESSIMISTIC

_____
_____
_____
_____
_____
_____
_____
_____

Student 2

5 Use the notes to write a summary of Professor Petrov's talk.

Audio Scripts

UNIT 1

CD1 2 Getting to know you
A Where were you born?
B In Argentina.
A What do you do?
B I'm a teacher.
A Are you married?
B No, I'm not.
A Why are you studying English?
B Because I need it for my job.
A When did you start studying English?
B Two years ago.
A How often do you have English classes?
B Twice a week.

CD1 3 Where do you come from?
Hi! I'm Anton. I come from Canada, but right now I'm living here in New York. I'm working as a bike messenger. I really like New York. It's the center of the universe and it's very cosmopolitan. I have friends from all over the world. I earn about $150 a day in this job. That's good money. I'm saving money for my education.
I was born in Toronto, but my parents are from Bulgaria. They moved to Canada thirty years ago. When they first arrived, they didn't speak any English. They always worry about me. Last month, I had a bad accident on my bike, but I'm fine now.
Next September, I'm going back home to Toronto and I'm going to study for a master's degree, and then I hope to get a good job.

CD1 4
Hi, I'm Rowenna. I'm Australian, I come from Melbourne, but now I live in San Francisco, California, with my husband David. He's American. David and I run an art gallery. It's a gallery for Australian Aboriginal art. I just love Aboriginal art. I love all the colors and shapes. I'm preparing a new exhibition right now.
I came to the US in 2006 as a student. My parents wanted me to study law, but I didn't like it, uh, I hated it in fact. I left school after three months and got a job in an art gallery. That's where I met David. Then, we had the idea of opening our own gallery just for Aboriginal art, because most American people don't know anything about it. That was in 2006, and we borrowed $25,000 from the bank to do it. We're lucky because the gallery's really successful and we paid the money back after just five years. I go back to Australia every year. I usually go when it's winter in the US because it's summer in Australia. But I'm not going next year because I'm going to have a baby in December. It's my first so I'm very excited.

CD1 5
1 A Where does she live?
  B In San Francisco, California.
  A With who?
  B With her husband, David.
2 A What does she do?
  B She runs an art gallery.
3 A What is she doing right now?
  B She's preparing a new exhibition.
4 A When and why did she come to the US?
  B She came to the US in 2006 to study law.
5 A How long did she study law?
  B For three months.
6 A How much money did she borrow from the bank?
  B $25,000.
7 A How many children does she have?
  B She doesn't have any right now.
8 A Why is she excited?
  B Because she's going to have a baby.

CD1 6 Asking questions
I Hi, Serkan. Nice to meet you. Can I ask you one or two questions?
S Yes, of course.
I First of all, where do you come from?
S I'm from Istanbul in Turkey.
I And why are you here in the US?
S Well, I'm here mainly because I want to improve my English.
I How much English did you know before you came?
S Not a lot. I studied English in school, but I didn't learn much. Now I'm studying in a language school here.
I Which school?
S The A Plus School of English.
I That's a good name! Your English is very good now. Who's your teacher?
S Thank you very much. My teacher's name is David. He's great.
I What did you do back in Turkey?
S Well, actually, I was a teacher, a history teacher. I taught children from the ages of 14 to 18.
I How many children were in your classes?
S Sometimes as many as 40.
I Wow! That's a lot. How often do you go back home?
S Usually I go every year, but this year my brother is coming here. I'm very excited. I'm going to show him around.
I Well, I hope your brother has a great visit.

CD1 7 Whose or Who's?
1 A Whose phone is ringing?
  B It's mine.
2 A Who's calling?
  B It's my brother.

CD1 8
1 A Whose phone is ringing?
  B It's mine.
2 A Who's calling?
  B It's my brother.
3 Who's on the phone?
4 I'm going to the dance club. Who's coming?
5 Whose coat is this? It's not mine.
6 Whose are all these dirty clothes on the floor?
7 Who's going to Tina's wedding?
8 Do you know whose glasses they are?

CD1 9 Questions about you
1 What do you like doing in your free time?
2 Do you like listening to music?
3 What kind of music do you like?
4 What did you do last weekend?
5 What are you doing tonight?
6 What are you going to do after this class?
7 How many languages does your teacher speak?
8 What's your teacher wearing today?

CD1 10
1 A What do you like doing in your free time?
  B I like being with my friends. We go to each other's houses and talk.
2 A Do you like listening to music?
  B Of course. It helps me to relax.
3 A What kind of music do you like?
  B I like all kinds, rock, jazz, pop, but the thing I like best is listening to my dad's old Beatles albums.
4 A What did you do last weekend?
  B It was my mom's birthday so we all made a special meal for her.
5 A What are you doing tonight?
  B Nothing much. I want to do some things around the house before the weekend.
6 A What are you going to do after this class?
  B I have some shopping to do. Then I'm going home.
7 A How many languages does your teacher speak?
  B Only English! She says she's going to study Italian next year.
8 A What's your teacher wearing today?
  B A very pink sweater and red pants. Hmmm – not a great look!

CD1 11 My oldest friend
1 Judy and Kenny
J Kenny, I see you have more than 300 friends on Facebook!
K Amazing isn't it? I don't know how it happened. I think it's because my job takes me all over the world and I make friends wherever I go.
J I travel, too but I don't have so many friends.
K Come on Judy. I'm your friend. That's one at least!
J But what about close friends? How many of the 300 are close?
K I have no idea.
J No idea? More than ten? More than 20?
K Uh, probably no more than ten really close friends.
J So, who's your oldest friend?
K That's easy. Pete's my oldest friend – since we were both 16, and he went to my school. He lives in Canada now. But he was best man at my wedding and I was best man at his.
J How often do you see him?
K Not often. Maybe once or twice a year. I visited him last year when his son was born. Do you know, he named the baby Ken after me?
J Oh, that's nice! You and Pete are really good friends, aren't you?

K Yeah!

J Why do you think that is?

K It's because we both love baseball!

J Don't tell me, he loves the Yankees, too!

K Of course. Best team in the world. No, seriously, the best thing about Pete is that maybe we don't see each other for months, even years, but when we get together … right away we're talking …

J … about baseball

K No, about all kinds of things. Our families mainly. He's a great guy.

2 Damian and Toby

T Am I your best friend?

D No, silly, you're my brother!

T I'm not silly. Can't I be your best friend?

D No, you can't. No one's best friends with his brother!

T But I don't have many friends.

D That's your problem. Look, I'm going to hang out with Luke and the other guys now.

T Is Luke your best friend?

D No.

T Is he your oldest friend?

D No. Zac's my oldest friend. You know that – since we sat next to each other in the fourth grade. Zac and I are going to travel the world together when we graduate from school.

T Can I come?

D No, you can't! Just shut …

T Well, can Luke be my friend?

D Toby, be quiet about friends! You're so boring, I'm not surprised you have no friends.

T But can I …?

D No, no! I'm going now. See you!

T But …

3 Katie and Beth

B Katie, you're lucky, you have so many friends.

K Mmmm, I guess so. I do have a lot.

B Why do think that is?

K Well, I'm not sure, I think I kind of collect friends. I have friends from all different times in my life. You know high school, college, and now at work and I keep my friends.

B So, who's your oldest friend?

K You are, of course! You and me, Beth, we're the same age, 24, and you could say we met before we were born.

B I suppose you're right …

K Yeah, our moms met when they were …

B I know, at the hospital when they went for check-ups before we were born.

K Yeah, and we were born on the same day …

B I know, but I'm ten hours older than you!

K That's why you're wiser than me! You're my oldest and my best friend. You're like a sister to me.

CD1 12 A blind date

A survey of over 10,000 couples asked them how they first met. The top three were: first, with 22%, "at work"; second, with 20%, "through friends," and third, with 15%, "at school or college." Next, with 12%, was "meeting online." These days more and more couples are meeting this way. Just 8% met at a club and 5% through family, which was very surprising. Only 4% met on a blind date – maybe not so surprising. Last of all, just 1% met while shopping – so don't go looking for love in the supermarket. That leaves just 13% who didn't meet in any of these places.

CD1 13 What happened next?

Dominic

I sent Sally a text a couple of days after the date. She played it cool and didn't reply for two days. We met up a week later, went for a walk, and then to the movie. We're still seeing each other. She's helping me train for a marathon next month. She's going to come and watch me. Also, she came to the theater to watch my play and she said she liked it. I'm going to meet her parents next weekend. I'm a little bit worried but I enjoy being with her a lot.

Sally

When Dom texted, I knew I wanted to answer but I made him wait. I'm not sure why – silly, really – because I really do like him. I enjoyed seeing him act. I think he's a very good actor but I didn't really understand the play. He's coming to meet my family next weekend. I don't usually take boyfriends home so soon, but with Dom it's different. I have a good feeling about this relationship. Ask me again a year from now!

CD1 14 Words with two meanings

1 Turn **left** on Main Street and my house is the first on the right.
  She **left** in a hurry to catch her bus.
2 I love traveling by **train**.
  He's going to **train** to be a teacher.
3 I'm going to **run** a marathon next month.
  They **run** the art gallery together.
4 I'm working at home for the **rest** of the week.
  I need a **rest**! I'm so tired.
5 What **kind** of food do you like?
  How **kind** of you to bring me flowers!
6 Can you turn the **light** on, please?
  My bag is **light**, so it's easy to carry.
7 What do you **mean**? I don't understand you.
  He's so **mean**. He never has a nice thing to say about anyone.

CD1 15 Social expressions

1 **A** Hi, Anna. How are you?
  B I'm fine, thanks. How are you?
2 **A** Thank you very much.
  B You're welcome.
3 **A** Can I help you?
  B No, thank you. I'm just looking.
4 **A** Excuse me. Is this seat free?
  B No, sorry, I'm afraid it isn't.

CD1 16

1 **A** Good morning!
  B Good morning! Nice day today!
2 **A** See you tomorrow!
  B Yeah! About nine, in the coffee shop.
3 **A** How do you do?
  B Fine, thanks. Nice to meet you.
4 **A** Thank you very much.
  B You're welcome.
5 **A** I'm sorry. I can't come tonight.
  B That's OK. Maybe another time.
6 **A** Can you help me with this exercise?
  B Sure. What's the problem?
7 **A** Bye!
  B Bye! See you later!
8 **A** Bye! Have a good weekend!
  B Thanks! Same to you.
9 **A** Sorry I'm late.
  B Don't worry. You're here now.
10 **A** Cheers!
  B Cheers! Here's to your new job!

CD1 17

1 **A** Good morning!
  B Good morning! Nice day today!
  A Yes, it's really warm for this time of year.
2 **A** See you tomorrow!
  B Yeah! About nine, in the coffee shop.
  A OK. Nine is good for me, too.
3 **A** How do you do?
  B Fine, thanks. Nice to meet you.
  A Nice to meet you, too.
4 **A** Thank you very much.
  B You're welcome.
  A It was nice of you to pay.
5 **A** I'm sorry. I can't come tonight.
  B That's OK. Maybe another time.
  A I'm free tomorrow night. How about then?
6 **A** Can you help me with this exercise?
  B Sure. What's the problem?
  A I don't know what this word means.
7 **A** Bye!
  B Bye! See you later!
  A Yes. Let's meet after class.
8 **A** Bye! Have a good weekend!
  B Thanks! Same to you.
  A Thanks. Are you doing anything special?
9 **A** Sorry I'm late.
  B Don't worry. You're here now.
  A Yeah, I missed the bus.
10 **A** Cheers!
  B Cheers! Here's to your new job!
  A Thanks a lot. I'm excited, but a little bit nervous.

UNIT 2

CD1 18 Grandma Lee

Lee Strong is not an ordinary grandmother. She's in her 80s, and has an unusual job. She's a stand-up comic and works in comedy clubs in the US. She lives in Jacksonville, Florida. She has four children and ten grandchildren. They think what she's doing is very cool. She says, "I like telling jokes and making audiences laugh." She says the best part of performing stand-up comedy is when audience members thank her for being an inspiration. They like that she reaches for her dreams even though she is old.
She is currently touring around the US and making audiences laugh. Grandma Lee has a great life. She says, "I can't go anywhere without being recognized. It's awesome."

CD1 19 The Bow Tie Businessman

Moziah Bridges is an extraordinary young man. He has his own company, Mo's Bows, which he started when he was just nine. "I love dressing up," he says. "I look and feel so much better in nice clothes." He makes bow ties using sewing tips from his grandmother.
Mo's bow ties are online and in stores throughout the US. The business is growing fast with $30,000 from online sales alone in 2013. And he has a charity that sends kids to summer camp.
Mo is a busy boy – designing bow ties, going to school, and playing football – but he has his family to help him make his colorful bow ties.

CD1 20 Lee

1 A What does Lee do?
   B She's a stand-up comic.
2 A Where does she work?
   B She works in comedy clubs in the US.
3 A How many children does she have?
   B She has four children, and she also has ten grandchildren.
4 A What does she like doing?
   B She likes telling jokes and making audiences laugh.
5 A Why does she like her audience?
   B Because they thank her for being an inspiration.
6 A What is she doing right now?
   B She's touring around the US.

Moziah

1 A What does Moziah do?
   B He has his own company that makes bow ties.
2 A Why does he like nice clothes?
   B Because they make him look and feel better.
3 A Whose sewing tips does he use?
   B His great-grandmother's.
4 A Where can you buy his bow ties?
   B Online and in stores throughout the US.
5 A What is growing fast?
   B His business is growing fast.
6 A What does he like playing?
   B He likes playing football.

CD1 21

I = Interviewer, L = Lee
I Do you like being famous?
L Don't be silly. I'm not really famous. I'm just an old lady who's having fun.
I But it is unusual for someone your age, if you don't mind me saying, to be telling jokes in comedy clubs for young people.
L Well, I just like making people laugh. And I don't want to be an old woman in a retirement home watching television all day long.
I Why do you do it?
L I do stand-up comedy because the energy is amazing! Because I love to see people enjoying themselves. Because it makes me happy!
I Does your family agree with you?
L My family thinks it's great. Some of my friends say that it's not right for a woman my age to be telling jokes and staying out all night.
I And what do you say to them?
L I say to them, "It's none of your business. It doesn't matter how old you are. If you want to do something, you can."

CD1 22

I = Interviewer, M = Moziah
I Do you like being a businessman?
M Oh, yes, I love it! I like the planning, the marketing, and the selling. I like meeting people and talking about my business and everything about it!
I It seems to me you love what you're doing!
M It's true! I do!
I Do you have any free time?
M Um … yeah, but not a lot.
I What do you do in your free time?
M Well, I still go to school, so I do homework. And I love playing football.
I Do you have a girlfriend?
M Hmm, um … that's none of your business!
I Sorry. Uh … Who do you live with?
M I live with my mom and dad. And my aunts and uncles and grandparents live nearby.

CD1 23 Talking about you

A Do you have a car?
B Yes, I do.
C No, I don't
A Do you have a bike?
B Yes, I do.
C No, I don't.
D I don't have a camera.
E I don't have an iPhone.

CD1 24 Things I like doing

play games on my smartphone
go out with my friends
download music and movies
send emails and texts
shop for clothes online
take a nap
relax in front of the TV
meet friends for coffee
listen to music
go out for a meal
get take-out food
do nothing
read magazines
chat with friends online
go to the gym
watch basketball on TV

CD1 25

1 I like shopping at the mall, but mainly I shop online.
2 When I hear a band I like, I download their music from the Internet.
3 I listen to music on my phone when I go jogging.
4 I spend hours chatting with friends online, even though I'm with them all day at school!
5 Sometimes I like to chill out at home and do nothing.
6 I'm always so tired after work that I just want to relax in front of the TV.
7 On Saturdays, I take a nap, and I sleep all afternoon.
8 Do you want to cook tonight, or should we get take-out food?
9 It's Pete's birthday tonight, so we'll go out for a meal. Indian, I think.
10 I like staying in shape. I go to the gym three times a week.

CD1 26 Money

The best things in life are free
But you can give them to the birds and bees
I want money
That's what I want
That's what I want
Your love gives me such a thrill
But your love won't pay my bills
I want money

CD1 27 Two neighbors

Mrs. Boyle

I live in the apartment above that young man. I think his name is Nathan, because I see the mail carrier delivering his mail. He never says hello. He doesn't have a job, well he doesn't go to work in the morning – that's for sure! He doesn't get up until the afternoon, and he wears jeans and a T-shirt all the time. He always looks messy. He certainly never wears a suit. Who knows where he gets his money from! It's funny! I never hear him in the evening. I have no idea what he does in the evening.

There are people coming and going in and out of his apartment all day long. I have no idea how many people are staying. Four? Five? Don't any of them have jobs?

He has a girlfriend. She's very … pretty. Blond hair, dyed. She's living with him. I know a lot of young people live together these days, but I don't like it, living together and not married. It's not right. He always makes so much noise! Listen! There he is now! Music! He's listening to music! Why can't he turn it down? It's so loud!

Young people these days have no manners, they live in their own world, and they just don't care about other people. They don't even notice old people like me. He probably doesn't know who I am.

CD1 28 Two neighbors

Nathan

I have this new apartment. It's so nice! I really love it. I'm having such a good time. The only thing is that it's below an old lady, and that's a little bit difficult. Her name's Mrs. Boyle. I always say hello when I see her, "How are you, Mrs. Boyle?" "Nice day, Mrs. Boyle!" and all that, but she never answers back. She just looks at me. I think she's deaf.

She probably thinks I'm unemployed because I don't go out to work in the morning and I don't wear a suit. I think I wear really cool clothes. Well, I'm a musician. I play the saxophone, and right now I'm playing in a jazz club. I don't start until 8:00 at night, and I finish at 2:00 in the morning, so I sleep from 3:00 to 11:00.

There's only me living here, but my apartment's a little busy right now because some of the other guys in the band are using it to keep their instruments in, so they're always coming in and out.

I have an amazing girlfriend. She's the singer in the band, and she's so beautiful! She lives on the other side of town, but obviously I see her every day because we work together. She comes to my place sometimes.

I know I make noise, because I practice my saxophone sometimes. See what I mean? What can I do? I have to practice somewhere!

I know that old Mrs. Boyle is always watching me. It's sad because she has nothing to do. I feel sorry for her, and I'm always really kind to her like I am to my own grandmother, but she's so suspicious of young people. She thinks we're all no good and that we're lazy. It's just not true. I work really hard!

CD1 29 Making conversation

1 John and Maria
J Hello. My name's John. What's your name?
M Maria.
J Hi, Maria. Where are you from?
M Florida.
J Ah, OK. Where in Florida … are … you from?
M Tampa.
J Ah, Tampa. Right. And … what do you do there?
M I'm a student.
J I see … And … are you enjoying Los Angeles?
M Yes.
J Well, I have a class now, Maria. Bye! See you again!
M Bye.

2 Maggie and Jean-Jacques

M Hello. My name's Maggie. What's your name?
JJ My name is Jean-Jacques. Nice to meet you, Maggie.
M And you. Where are you from, Jean-Jacques?
JJ I'm French. I live in Paris – Paris, as you say in English – but I'm from the south, from Provence. Do you know the south of France?
M Yes, I do. It's beautiful.
JJ It is! And you, Maggie, where are you from?
M I'm from Canada.
JJ Oh, really! I've never been there, but I'd like to. It's a beautiful country, isn't it?
M Very. Lots of mountains and lakes. What … do you do in France, Jean-Jacques?
JJ I'm an architect. I design very expensive houses for rich people.
M Wow! That's an interesting job! Are you enjoying Los Angeles?
JJ Very much. I'm having a really good time. I think Los Angeles is an interesting city, and there's so much to do! And you, Maggie? What do you do?
M Well, I'm a teacher. I work here.
JJ Oh, really! What class are you teaching?
M 3B.
JJ Oh, that's my class! You're my teacher!
M Oh, how nice! Well, it's 9:00. Let's go!
JJ Good idea! I'll follow you …

CD1 30

1 A What a nice day it is today!
  B Yes, beautiful, isn't it! Much nicer than yesterday.
2 A Are you having a good time in Los Angeles?
  B Yes, I am. It's a very interesting city. There's so much to do. I love the stores.
3 A Have a good weekend!
  B Thanks. Same to you. Are you doing anything interesting?
4 A Did you have a nice weekend?
  B Yes, I did. It was really good. I saw some old friends. What did you do?
5 A What are you doing tonight?
  B Nothing special. Just staying at home. What about you?
6 A How's your mother these days?
  B She's OK, thanks. She's feeling a lot better. Thank you for asking.
7 A Did you watch the game last night?
  B No, I didn't. I missed it. Who won?
8 A I like your shoes.
  B Thank you! They're new. I got them last week on sale.
9 A If you have a problem, just ask me.
  B Thank you very much. That's very nice of you. I will.

CD1 31 Keeping a conversation going

A I went on vacation last month.
B Oh, really? Did you go away?
A Yes, I went to Italy.
B How nice! Italy's beautiful, isn't it?
A I think it's fabulous. I love all the history.
B Yes, and the buildings, and all the art!
A Where did you go?
B Well, I went to Florence and I spent a few days visiting the museums.
A Oh, fantastic! Did you see the statue of David?
B It's amazing! And then I went to see some friends near Sienna.
A Wow! Lucky you! Was the weather nice?
B Well, actually …

UNIT 3

CD1 32 Walking the Amazon

Amazing journey ends after 6,000 miles
Ed Stafford became the first man in history to walk the length of the Amazon River from the source to the ocean. He walked for 860 days. The journey began in April 2008 when Ed left the town of Camana on the Pacific coast of Peru. It ended in August 2010 when he arrived in Maruda, on the Atlantic coast of Brazil.
He went through three countries, Peru, Colombia, and Brazil. The journey took nearly two and a half years. "I did it for the adventure," says Ed.

CD1 33

1 A How far did Ed walk?
  B He walked 6,000 miles.
2 A When did the journey begin?
  B It began in April 2008.
3 A Where did the journey end?
  B It ended in Maruda on the Atlantic coast of Brazil.
4 A Which countries did he go through?
  B He went through Peru, Colombia, and Brazil.
5 A How long did the journey take?
  B It took nearly two and a half years.
6 A Why did he do it?
  B He did it for the adventure.

CD1 34 Cho's story

A What was Cho doing when he met Ed?
B He was working in the forest.
A Where were they walking when they saw the tribe?
B They were walking in a very dangerous part of the forest.
A Why did the tribe think Ed was crazy?
B Because he was walking along the Amazon for an adventure.

CD1 35 Ed's Blog

July 12
The day I nearly died
Today I was walking next to the river when I nearly stood on a snake. I stopped immediately. The snake's fangs were going in and out. I was terrified. I didn't move. One bite and you're dead in three hours.

September 10
Knives and guns!
Early this morning we were crossing the river by boat when we saw five canoes. The tribesmen were carrying knives and guns. They were angry because we didn't have permission to be on their land. We left as fast as we could.

November 24
The jungle at night
I was lying in my hammock last night trying to sleep, but it was impossible because the noise of the jungle was so loud. Monkeys were screaming in the trees, and millions of mosquitoes were buzzing around my head. I took a sleeping pill and finally fell asleep at 3:00 a.m.

CD1 36 Pronunciation

/d/ stayed, played, called, answered
/t/ stopped, worked, laughed, looked
/ɪd/ decided, ended, wanted, visited

CD1 37

We stayed in a hotel.
They played on the beach.
She called a friend.
I answered all the questions.
They stopped at lunchtime.
I worked in a bank.
We laughed and laughed.
I looked at the photo.
We decided immediately.
It ended in August.
She wanted a cup of tea.
I visited my grandma.

CD1 38

I was having dinner.
What was she wearing?
They were playing baseball.
Where were you going?
He wasn't listening.
They weren't enjoying the party.

CD1 39 The news

Here are the news headlines.
A gas leak in New York kills eight people.
Thieves steal paintings worth $80 million from a museum.
A national strike in France brings the country to a stop.
The 71-year-old actor James Robertson dies at his home in California.
And in ice hockey, the Pittsburgh Penguins beat the New York Rangers.

CD1 40

A gas leak was the cause of an explosion in Manhattan yesterday morning, killing eight people who were living in a nearby apartment building and injuring many more. Most of those injured were people who were walking to work or going to school in the early morning hours. Officials say the gas company is investigating the explosion.
Last night thieves in New York broke into the Museum of Modern Art, and escaped with three paintings by Picasso valued at $80 million. Cameras were recording the rooms at the time, but the guard who was watching the screens saw nothing. Museum officials didn't discover the theft until the next morning.
A national strike in France yesterday brought the country to a complete stop. Offices, banks, schools, and stores all closed, and there were no trains or buses throughout the whole country. Workers were protesting for higher pay, longer vacations, and a shorter working week.
The actor James Robertson died last night at his home in Hollywood, California. He was suffering from cancer. With him were his five children, his ex-wife, and his second wife, Cherie. The 71-year-old actor is best known for his role as the cowboy Dexter in *Mad Men of the West*.
And finally sports. The Pittsburgh Penguins last night beat the New York Rangers 2–1. At half time the Rangers were winning one to nothing, but then two goals by Sidney Crosby gave the Penguins a win.

CD1 41 Dictation

Last night thieves in New York broke into the Museum of Modern Art and escaped with three paintings by Picasso valued at $80 million. Cameras were recording the rooms at the time, but the guard who was watching the screens saw nothing. Museum officials didn't discover the theft until the next morning.

CD1 42 Adverbs

1 Please drive carefully through our town.
2 Romeo loved Juliet passionately.
3 My mother speaks three languages fluently.
4 It rained heavily every day last week.
5 He waited patiently for his girlfriend, but she didn't return.
6 The soldiers fought bravely, but many of them lost their lives.

CD1 43 Word order

1 My grandma is nearly 75, and she still goes swimming regularly.
2 "Do you really love me?"
   "Of course I do. I'll always love you."
3 I was just relaxing with a really good book when someone knocked loudly on the door.
4 My sister is only three, but she can already read, and she can write, too.
5 First, break the eggs into a bowl with some milk and butter. Then heat it gently. When it's ready, serve the scrambled eggs immediately with toast.
6 Almost all my friends have a smartphone. They're on Facebook as well. Even my dad's on Facebook.

CD1 44 The burglar who fell asleep

Last Sunday evening, a burglar broke into a large, expensive, house in the center of Paris. First, he went into the living room, and he quickly and quietly filled his bag with all the silverware and a priceless Chinese vase. Next, he went to the kitchen and found some delicious cheese and two bottles of the best sparkling water. He was feeling extremely hungry so he ate all the cheese and drank all the sparkling water. Suddenly, he felt very tired. He went upstairs to the bedroom and laid down on a big, comfortable bed and immediately fell fast asleep. He slept very well. Unfortunately, when he woke up the next morning, three police officers were standing around his bed.

CD1 45 Saying when

1 A What's the date today?
   B March eighteenth. Tomorrow's the nineteenth. The day after tomorrow's the twentieth.
2 A When's your birthday?
   B November eighth.
   A Oh! That's next week.
3 A What's your date of birth?
   B 9-12-87
   A What?
   B September twelfth, nineteen eighty-seven.
4 A What year were you born?
   B 1982.
   A Oh. You're the same age as me.

CD1 46

the third of February, February third
the sixth of April, April sixth
the twelfth of July, July twelfth
the twenty-first of June, June twenty-first
the first of May, May first
the sixteenth of August, August sixteenth
the thirteenth of January, January thirteenth
the thirty-first of October, October thirty-first

CD1 47

February the third
April the sixth
July the twelfth
June the twenty-first
May the first
August the sixteenth
January the thirteenth
October the thirty-first

CD1 48

1 A When did man first land on the moon?
   B On July twentieth, 1969.
2 A When's your wedding anniversary?
   B November eighth.
3 A When did the Berlin Wall come down?
   B The ninth of November, 1989.
4 A When was your son born?
   B July twenty-first, 2010.
5 A What's the expiration date on your credit card?
   B 6/18

UNIT 4

CD1 49 How to live to be 120!

1 Q Today we're talking to a couple on a calorie-restricted diet.
     So … do you eat any meat?
   A No, we don't eat any meat at all, but we eat some fish.
2 Q How much fish do you eat?
   A We eat a little fish like cod or salmon, but we love shellfish so we eat a lot of clams.
3 Q Do you eat much fruit?
   A Oh, yes, we eat a lot of fresh fruit – apples and grapes – everything.
4 Q And do you eat many vegetables?
   A Yes, of course, we eat lots of raw vegetables.
5 Q You don't cook any vegetables at all?
   A We cook some. Sometimes we steam a few carrots and a little broccoli.
6 Q And what do you drink?
   A Well, we don't drink any tea or coffee, and of course, there's no soda in our diet, but we do drink a lot of orange juice.
7 Q How many calories do you have every day?
   A About 1,500.
     That's about 1,000 fewer than most people.

CD1 50

Q Tell us some more about the diet.
A Well, I think we have a good diet. We enjoy the food we can eat. For breakfast we have cereal, homemade cereal, we make it ourselves. We have it with fruit. We eat all fruit.
A But we don't eat any dairy products – no milk, cheese, and we don't eat bread, so we don't need butter …
A We use olive oil instead. We often have it on salad for lunch with tomatoes and lots of nuts and sometimes green peppers stuffed with rice.
Q So you eat rice. What about pasta and potatoes?
A No, not at all. We don't eat anything made from potatoes.
Q No potato chips and French fries, right? And I'm guessing you eat nothing made with sugar.
A You're right. We make fresh juice to drink but with no sugar.
Q And no soda, of course. What about water?
A Well, we don't drink any tap water.

Q Really? Why not?
A It's not good for you. We drink a little bottled water sometimes.
Q You're amazing. I hope you live to be 120, but I'm sure I won't be around to see it.

CD1 51 something/someone/somewhere …

1 A Did you meet anyone nice at the party?
   B Yes. I met somebody who knows you!
   A Oh, who?
   B Your ex-boyfriend.
2 A Ouch! There's something in my eye!
   B Let me look. No, I can't see anything.
   A But I can feel it. Somewhere in the corner of my eye.
3 A Let's go somewhere hot for our vacation.
   B But we can't go anywhere that's too expensive.
   A I know, but we can afford this vacation package to Turkey.
4 A Where are my glasses? I can't find them anywhere.
   B What's on the top of your head?
   A There they are! Thank you.
5 A It was a great party. Everybody loved it.
   B They did. Nobody wanted to go home.
   A I know. A few people were still dancing at 3:00 a.m.
6 A Did you get anything nice at the sale?
   B No, nothing. I couldn't find anything I liked.
   A Why not try shopping online? You can buy everything online these days.

CD1 52

Do you know … famous?
The refrigerator is empty. There's … to eat!
The lights are off. There's … at home.
Pete's an awesome guy. … likes him.
We always go … nice to eat.
I can't go to the party. I don't have … nice to wear!
Has … seen my keys?
I can't find my keys …

CD1 53 The secret to a long life

My grandfather lived until he was 92 years old. He was a farmer with a cattle farm in a small town near a river in the southeastern part of New York State. He had two sons. The family lived in an old farmhouse. The oldest son, my uncle, owns the farm now.
In those days, people often bought beef directly from local farmers. My great uncle raised some of the best beef in the area. People came to his farm by car and truck to buy it.
Everybody loved my grandfather because he was such an honest and friendly man. He never went out to have dinner at restaurants, but every now and then he invited his family and friends to the farm for a picnic. He served hamburgers made from his beef. He didn't retire until he was 80. He said the secret to a long life was a happy marriage and a glass of warm milk before going to bed.

CD1 54 Reading aloud

My grandfather was a farmer.
He lived in a small town.
He had a cattle farm in the southeastern part of New York State.
His family lived in an old farmhouse.
He raised some of the best beef in the area.
Some people came by car to buy his beef.
He was such an honest man.
He never went out to have dinner at restaurants.
He liked to have a little warm milk before bed.

1 Alexander

We were on our honeymoon and we saw some brochures about this restaurant. It was my wife's birthday so I thought why not – it's expensive but you don't find many restaurants like this. It was difficult to get a reservation because it only takes 12 people. When we arrived, we had drinks on the deck above and someone gave us a talk about how they built the restaurant and then we took off our shoes and descended – down, down the spiral stairs and into the restaurant. Actually, the restaurant itself isn't very exciting, the decor I mean, but it doesn't need to be because of the view – it takes your breath away. All around and above your head are hundreds, maybe thousands, of fish, all colors in a blue ocean. I was sitting across from my wife when a turtle appeared just behind her head. In fact we were so busy looking at it all we almost forgot that we were there to eat. The food was delicious, fish of course, but to be honest we felt a little bad eating cod fish, surrounded by cod fish. There was just one problem, a guest at the next table. He spoke really loudly and complained about everything. We couldn't find anything to complain about. It was the perfect honeymoon restaurant.

2 Tomo

I booked online of course. It's the only way you can get a table. And I went with my sons – they're 5 and 6 years old and I thought they would like it a lot. They were very excited. They thought the servers were robots, so when we arrived and there was nobody there at all, they were a little disappointed. But the whole place was amazing. It was like walking inside a computer, so the boys soon became excited again. We picked up a card and sat down at one of the big round, red tables. The boys loved the touch-screen TVs. They got the idea immediately and started choosing food from the pictures. While we were waiting, they were texting their mother to tell her how amazing it all was. In just a few minutes pots with our meals inside came flying down. The boys couldn't believe it. They were shouting with excitement. We all had steak and salad and then the boys had baked bananas with ice cream and chocolate. It was delicious. There was an older lady sitting next to us. She was a little confused, so we helped her. She said, "I think this is more for young people than people my age." Maybe she's right.

3 Lucy

I was hungry when I arrived at the restaurant, but when I saw the crane, I forgot about being hungry. I was a little nervous. The host, David, said, "Don't worry, it's 100% safe." Huh! I'm sure a few of the other guests felt like me – they looked very pale. Anyway, we sat down at this huge table, fastened our seat belts, and up, up, up we went. I couldn't look down. Everyone was saying, "What a wonderful view," but I just couldn't look. When I finally felt safe enough, I opened my eyes and the view was amazing. People were waving to us from the ground. They probably thought we were crazy. The weather was perfect, thank goodness, just a little breeze. I began to enjoy it. The other guests were all a lot of fun. I didn't know anyone at the start, but I soon made some friends and the food was good, too, especially the clams. The chef cooked them in front of us on a tiny stove. But the best part of all was at the end. When everybody learned my name and they started singing, "Lucy in the sky with diamonds." No diamonds, but I was certainly in the sky. I was sorry when we came back down.

a piece of paper
a loaf of bread
a bottle of juice
a can of soda
a pound of apples
a gallon of gas
a pack of gum
a pair of jeans
a slice of cake
a bunch of bananas

1 A Just this copy of *The Times*, please.
  B That's $2.
  A Sorry, I only have a $20 bill.
  B No problem. I have change.
  A Thanks. Oh, and can I have a pack of gum, too?
  B OK. That's $3.50, please.

2 A Excuse me, how much is this pair of socks?
  B They're $3.99 a pair.
  A OK. Can I have two pairs, please? Do you have any in blue?
  B I'm afraid they only come in gray and black.
  A Never mind. A black and a gray pair, please.
  B That's $7.98 altogether. How would you like to pay?

3 A Good morning. Can we have two double espressos, and a latte, please?
  B What size latte?
  A Just medium, please. Oh, and three slices of chocolate cake. It looks delicious.
  B I'm afraid there are only two slices left, but the carrot cake's good, too.
  A OK. And one slice of carrot cake, then.
  B Certainly. That's $17.79.

4 A Can you help me? I need something for a very bad cold.
  B Yes, of course. Are you allergic to aspirin?
  A No, I'm not.
  B OK. Take these three times a day.
  A Thank you.
  B Do you want a bottle or a pack?
  A It doesn't matter. A bottle's fine. And can I have two packs of tissues, too, please?
  B Sure. Anything else?
  A No, that's all. How much is that?
  B That's $11.69 for everything.

5 A A pack of cards, please.
  B Sure. Anything else?
  A Do you have any cold soda?
  B I'm sorry, but the refrigerator is broken.
  A Oh. So you don't have anything cold to drink?
  B No. Unfortunately, we don't. We only have hot coffee and tea.
  A Oh, no thanks. Just the pack of cards, please.

6 A Good morning. What can I get for you?
  B Uh – three, no, four slices of turkey, please. Organic turkey.
  A OK. That's, uh, four slices. Anything else?
  B Yes, can I have that large piece of cheese?
  A The cheddar?
  B That's right. How much is that?
  A $10.49. But you don't pay here. You pay at the checkout with your other items.
  B Oh, OK. And can you tell me where the fruit and vegetables are?
  A They're in the first aisle, over there.
  B Oh, thanks very much. I'm lost in this place. It's my first time and it's so big.

1 A Would you like some more rice?
  B No, thanks. But could I have another piece of bread?
  A Of course. Do you want white or brown?

2 A Could you pass the salt, please?
  B Yes, of course. Do you want the pepper, too?
  A No, thanks. Just the salt.

3 A Can I have some water, please?
  B Do you want tap or bottled?
  A Just a glass of tap water is fine. Thank you.

4 A Please, just help yourselves to the dessert.
  B We will. It looks fantastic. Did you make it yourself?
  A I did. It's my grandmother's recipe.

5 A Would anybody like some more ice cream?
  B No, but I'd love some more fruit. Is there any left?
  A There's a little. It's all yours.

6 A How do you take your coffee?
  B Black, no sugar. Do you have any decaf?
  A I'm afraid not, but we have decaf tea. Would that be OK?

7 A This is delicious! Would you mind giving me the recipe?
  B No, not at all. I got it online. I'll give you the website.
  A Thanks. I get lots of my recipes online, too.

8 A Do you want some help with the dishes?
  B No, of course not. You're our guests!
  A Well, I hope you have a dishwasher 'cause there's a lot.

1 A Can I have some apple juice, please?
  B Sorry, we don't have any apple juice. Is orange juice OK?

2 A Could you tell me where Market Street is, please?
  B Sorry, I'm afraid I'm a stranger here myself.

3 A Could I see the menu, please?
  B Here you are. Today's specials are on the board over there.

4 A Could I use your iPad for a few minutes, please?
  B Eva's using it right now. But you can have it after her.

5 A Could you lend me $20, please?
  B Mmmm … I only have a ten.

6 A Can you take me to school, please?
  B Oh, is it time? We're going to be late!

7 A Can you help me with my homework, please?
  B OK, but I'm not very good at math.

8 A Could you give me a ride to the train station, please?
  B Of course. What time's your train?

5 A Would you mind lending me $20? I'll pay you back tomorrow.
  B Not at all. Is twenty enough?

6 A Would you mind taking me to school today, please? I missed the bus.
  B Not again! That's the third time this week!

7 A Would you mind helping me with my homework? I have no idea how to do it.
  B I don't mind helping you, but I'm not doing it for you!

8 A Would you mind giving me a ride to the train station? I have a lot of heavy bags.
  B Not at all. Are you ready to go now?

UNIT 5

CD2 2 **Verb patterns**

Tom
I'm 16 and I'm fed up with school and exams. I'd like to quit now and get a job, any job. I hope to earn some money, but my parents say that I can't quit school. They think I'll regret it later, but I don't think I will.

Abby
I'm a student in my last year of college. I have almost $50,000 of student loan debt. I'm going to study hard for my final exams because I want to get a well-paid job. I hate owing so much money. I'm going for an interview next Friday. Wish me luck!

Martin
I work in I.T. There's nothing I don't know about computers, but I need a change. I'm thinking of applying for another job with a company in New York. I saw it advertised online and it looks like the job for me. I'd love to work there for a couple of years.

Kelly
I'm a paramedic. I love my job, but it's very stressful. I'm looking forward to taking a break. We're going to the Caribbean this summer. I'm planning to do nothing but read on the beach for two whole weeks!

Alison
I have three kids under seven and my husband travels for work a lot of the time. I enjoy taking care of the kids, but I'd love to travel, too. Sometimes I get fed up with staying home all day. I'm looking forward to going back to work in a year or two.

Bill
I'm a retired newspaper delivery man, and I didn't have a day off for 40 years. Now I like sleeping late and planning vacations online for me and my wife. I'm pretty good at using a computer. We're going on vacation to Tuscany next year, so I'm going to learn some Italian before leaving.

CD2 3 **Discussing grammar**
1 I want to work in Paris.
  I'd like to work in Paris.
2 We like going to Florida for our vacation.
  We're thinking of going to Florida for our vacation.
3 She can't leave work early tonight.
4 I hope to see you again soon.
  I'd like to see you again soon.
5 He's good at playing sports games on the computer.
  He enjoys playing sports games on the computer.
6 Are you good at learning languages?
7 We're looking forward to taking a few days off soon.
8 I'm fed up with doing housework.
  I hate doing housework.

CD2 4
1 I enjoy working in Paris.
2 We're hoping to go to Florida for our vacation.
3 She wants to leave work early tonight.
  She'd like to leave work early tonight.
4 I'm looking forward to seeing you again soon.
5 He wants to play sports games on the computer.
6 Do you want to learn foreign languages?
  Do you like learning foreign languages?

7 We're going to take a few days off soon.
  We'd love to take a few days off soon.
8 I don't want to do housework.

CD2 5 **Making questions**
1 A I hope to go to college.
  B What do you want to study?
  A I'm going to study philosophy and politics. I'd like to be president.
  B I think that's the worst job in the world!
2 A One of my favorite hobbies is baking.
  B What do you like to bake?
  A Well, cakes, all kinds of cakes.
  B OK, Can I have a big chocolate cake for my birthday?
3 A I'm bored.
  B What would you like to do?
  A Nothing. I'm happy being bored.
  B Well, OK then!
4 A I'm looking forward to the party.
  B Who are you hoping to see there?
  A No one special. I just like parties.
  B Me too!
5 A We're planning our summer vacation.
  B Where are you thinking of going?
  A We want to go camping this year.
  B Ugh! I hate sleeping in tents.

CD2 6 **My dreams for the future**
Hello everyone. My name's Susannah – Susie for short. I'm 20 years old. Right now, I'm in my second year of art school, and I often dream about my future. I have big plans and I'd like to tell you a little bit about them.
My most immediate are vacation plans. I'm going to visit my brother who's working in Australia. My mom and I are going to spend two weeks with him in the summer sun. I'm very excited about that.
When I return, I need to decide about what I'm going to study next year. I'm still not sure – I'm thinking either fashion design or landscape design. It's hard because I'm interested in both clothes and gardens. If I choose landscape, I'd like to work with my friend, Jasper. He does amazing work with gardens, and we've already worked on two together. It was a lot of fun, and we get along really well.
In five or ten years I would like to have my own business and work for myself like my dad. He has his own building business. Maybe I'll study business after I graduate from art school.
Of course, one day I hope to marry and have children. Ideally before I'm 30, but I can't plan until I meet the right person, and I don't have a boyfriend right now.
In my dreams I see myself at 40 running a successful gardening company with about 20 employees. I'll design beautiful gardens for beautiful people. I'll have a beautiful house, two beautiful children, and of course, a beautiful husband who's as successful as I am. Who knows? It could even be Jasper!

CD2 7 **Do you have any plans?**
1 Pete and Ben
B Hi, Pete! What are you doing this evening??
P I'm meeting my brother for dinner. Would you like to come, Ben?
B Sorry, I can't. I'm working late tonight. But – are you doing anything interesting this weekend?
P Yes, I'm going to stay with an old friend from school. It's his birthday and he's having a party.
B Are you going to have a party for your birthday?

P Of course! I'm going to invite all my friends.
B Great! I'll look forward to that! Hey, where are you going on vacation this year?
P I'm going surfing in Costa Rica. I'm really excited.
B Wow, that sounds amazing. I'm not going anywhere this year. I can't afford it.
P Yeah, but that's 'cause you're saving to buy a car.
B I know. You can't have everything. Give my regards to your brother. I'll see you later.

2 Debbie and Ella
E Hey, Debbie! It's the weekend. Are you doing anything interesting?
D No, I'm not. I'll call you and maybe we can do something together.
E Sorry, I can't this weekend. I'm going on vacation on Saturday.
D Oh, nice! Where?
E Mexico, for a week. Where are you going on vacation this year?
D I can't decide. Maybe I'll go bike riding in Colorado. Hey, will you be back from vacation for my birthday on the 25th?
E Yes, I am. Are you going to have a party?
D I haven't thought about it. Maybe I'll just celebrate at home with a few friends.
E Nice idea! So what about tonight? I'd like to see you before I go away. What are you doing tonight?
D Nothing much. I think I'll just watch a movie and order a pizza. Come and join me!
E OK, I'll do that, but I won't stay late. My flight leaves at eight in the morning.

CD2 8 **Discussing grammar**
1 A Have you decided which college to apply to?
  B Yes. I'm going to apply to Reed College.
  A Good luck! It's difficult to get into.
2 A I don't have your number.
  B Really? I'll text it to you right now.
  A Thanks.
3 A We don't have any fruit in the house.
  B I'm going shopping this afternoon. I'll get some apples.
  A Great. I'll give you money.
4 A My bag is really heavy.
  B Give it to me. I'll carry it for you.
  A Thanks.
  B Wow! What do you have in here?
5 A Tony's back from vacation.
  B Is he? I'll give him a call.
  A I'm seeing him tonight. Do you want to come?
6 A What are we having for dinner?
  B I'm going to make spaghetti and meatballs.
  A Not again. We had that twice last week.

CD2 9 **What can you say?**
1 Why are you looking forward to the weekend?
2 I don't have your brother's new address.
3 Mary says she hasn't seen you for months.
4 Why are you dressed in old clothes?
5 Congratulations! I hear you have a new job.
6 Are you doing anything interesting after class?

CD2 10
1 A Why are you looking forward to the weekend?
  B Because I'm going to the theater with friends.
2 A I don't have your brother's new address.
  B You don't? I'll give it to you now.
3 A Mary says she hasn't seen you for months.
  B I know. I'll call her tonight.

4 A Why are you dressed in old clothes?
  B Because I'm going to help my dad in the yard.
5 A Congratulations! I hear you have a new job.
  B Thanks! It's at a software company in Boston.
6 A Are you doing anything interesting after class?
  B No I'm just going home.

CD2 11 Will you, won't you?

1 I think you'll pass your driver's test. You won't fail again. It's your fourth time!
2 I think my team will win. They won't lose this time. There's a new coach.
3 I think it'll be warm today. You won't need your sweater. Just take a T-shirt.
4 I think I'll join a gym. I won't go on a diet. I like my food too much.
5 I think they'll get divorced. They won't stay together. They're always arguing.
6 I think I'll go by train. I won't fly. I hate flying.

CD2 12 How does it feel to be 20-something?

Leo, 28
I had a real shock the other day. My little nephew, he's six, said to me "Uncle Leo, when you were a little boy, did you have telephones?" I couldn't believe it. I said, "Of course we did. How old do you think I am?" Then he said, "But did you have cell phones?" And I thought, "Did we?" I can't remember life without cell phones, but in fact, uh, I think I was about eight when my dad got our first one. "Yeah," I said, "When I was eight." "Aha!" said my nephew "I knew it. You are old." I didn't like hearing that! Even though I'm 28, I don't feel grown up at all. I have a great life – a good job, lots of friends. I go out with them most nights. I go to the gym every morning. I'm going to buy a condo next year. Maybe when I'm in my 30s, I'll get married and start a family.

Elsa, 26
I started studying to be a paralegal after I graduated from college. I was making good money, and in many ways I had a good life, but, uh, the more I studied law, the more I hated it. I was bored and miserable – so I decided to give it all up and travel. I was away for a year. I went to Australia, New Zealand, Central and South America – it was amazing, but then I went back home. I was 24 and with no money, no job, and nowhere to live. I moved back with my mom and dad. They're wonderful, and they don't make me pay rent, but – oh my gosh – it's like being a little girl again. Right now, I'm working as a waitress just to make a little bit of money and my dad keeps asking, "When are you going to find a real job?" My mom says, "When I was your age, I was married with two children." Married with kids! I don't feel old enough for that. I have a boyfriend, but we're not thinking about getting married! Maybe I'll study to be a teacher. Now that's a real job.

Dan, 24
When I left home at 18, I thought that was it – "goodbye mom and dad." Now six years later I'm back! My college years were great. I worked hard and played hard, but I left with huge debts – over $20,000 in student loans. I thought, "No problem, I'll just get a job and pay it back." I moved into an apartment with some friends and I was lucky – I got a job pretty quickly, but ... I want to be a journalist and the only way is to begin at the bottom. I'm a very junior reporter for a small local newspaper. I like working there, but it only

pays $25,000 a year. I couldn't afford the rent for the apartment, so here I am, back with the parents. They call us the "Boomerang Kids" – you know, kids who grow up, leave home, and then move back again, like a boomerang. A lot of my friends are doing the same thing. My girlfriend is back with her mom, too. One day we're hoping to get married and get a place of our own, but that probably won't be for a few years. You can't grow up when you're still at home with your parents. I'm fed up.

CD2 13 An Interview with Palina Yanachkina

I = Interviewer, P = Palina

I Today I'm talking to Palina Yanachkina. Nice to meet you, Palina. Can I ask you some questions?
P Sure.
I I hear that you call yourself the girl with two families. Why is that?
P Well, I have my family back home in Belarus and my family in Ireland.
I Where exactly do you come from?
P I come from the village of Polessye not far from Chernobyl. I was born in 1988 just two years after the nuclear accident there. It was a terrible time for us.
I I can understand that. What happened to your family?
P My parents are farmers, and after the accident they couldn't sell any of their produce. No one wanted to buy our meat or vegetables. We were poor and sick – like many people in the village.
I How awful.
P But I was lucky. I had the chance to go to Ireland and that was when I met my second family. I loved staying with them. They were so kind to me. They looked after me so well.
I Your English is excellent now. Did you speak English then?
P Not a word. But I learned quickly, especially from the children. I got along really well with them.
I So you picked up English little by little?
P I took some classes, too and I went back to Ireland many times.
I What are you doing now?
P I'm studying in Ireland. My Irish family is paying for my studies. I'm hoping to become a doctor one day and return to my village to help the people there. That's my big hope for the future.
I Well, I'm sure you'll do that one day. Thank you, Palina. It was a pleasure talking to you.

CD2 14 Talking about you

1 Where did you grow up? Do you still live in the same house?
2 How do you get along with your parents?
3 Did you ever break up with a boyfriend or girlfriend?
4 Would you like to be a doctor or nurse and take care of people?
5 Are you good at picking up foreign languages?
6 Do you look up a lot of words in your dictionary?

CD2 15 Expressing doubt and certainty

1 A Do you think Tom will pass his final exams?
  B I doubt it. He's fed up with school.
  C I know. He has no chance at all. He wants to leave and get a job.

2 A Does Martin earn a lot of money?
  B Yes, absolutely. He earns a fortune.
  C Mmm … I'm not sure. He wants to change his job.
3 A Is the US going to win?
  B They might. Anything's possible, but I think it's very unlikely.
  A Definitely not. I don't think they have a chance.

CD2 16

1 A Kelly's job is stressful, isn't it?
  B Absolutely. She's a paramedic.
  A Is she going on vacation soon?
  B I think so. She says she might go to the Caribbean.
2 A It's Rob's birthday next week, isn't it?
  B Yes, definitely. It's on the 22nd.
  A So he's a Capricorn.
  B No, I don't think so. I think he's an Aquarius.
3 A Do you think Anita and Paul are in love?
  B Definitely. They're getting married in Hawaii.
  A How nice! Are you going to the wedding?
  B Not a chance. I can't afford it.

CD2 17

1 A Did Leo Tolstoy write *War and Peace*?
  B Definitely. He wrote it in 1869.
2 A Is Nicole Kidman American?
  B I don't think so. I think she's Australian.
3 A Was Sherlock Holmes a real person?
  B Definitely not. He's from a book by the writer Sir Arthur Conan Doyle.
4 A Is the population of China more than two billion?
  B It might be. I don't know. It's definitely more than one billion.
5 A Do some vegetarians eat fish?
  B I think so. I have a friend who's vegetarian and she eats fish.
6 A Is the weather going to be nice next weekend?
  B I doubt it. It's cold and rainy today.
7 A Are you going to be rich and famous one day?
  B Not a chance. I'd like to be richer than I am now, but I wouldn't like to be famous.
8 A Is your school the best in town?
  B Absolutely. It's definitely the best.

UNIT 6

CD2 18 Tell me about her

1 A Do you like Mia?
  B Yes, I do. I like her a lot.
2 A How's Mia?
  B She's doing very well.
3 A What's Mia like?
  B She's really nice. Very friendly.
4 A What does Mia look like?
  B She's tall with brown eyes and black hair.

CD2 19

1 A What's your teacher like?
  B She's great! She helps us a lot.
2 A What sports do you like?
  B Bike riding and skiing.
3 A What does your brother look like?
  B He has blond hair and blue eyes.
4 A Do you like pizza?
  B Mmm, I love it!

5 A What's the weather like today?
  B Beautiful! Warm and sunny.
6 A How are your parents?
  B They're OK. Busy as usual.

CD2 20 What's it like?

T = Tom, M = Mia

T What's Shanghai like?
M It's very big and noisy, but it's very exciting.
T What's the food like?
M It's the best in the world! I just love Chinese food!
T What are the people like?
M They're very friendly, and they really want to do business.
T What was the weather like?
M When I was there, it was hot and humid.
T What are the buildings like?
M There are new buildings everywhere, but if you look hard, you can still find some older ones, too.

CD2 21 Singapore, Shanghai, and Dubai

T What did you think of Singapore? What's it like?
M Well, Singapore is very old. It's older than Shanghai, but it's a lot smaller. Shanghai has a population of 20 million, and it's enormous! Shanghai is much bigger than Singapore, and it's much noisier, too.
T Oh, OK. What about business? What's it like to do business in these places?
M Well, they're both top financial centers, but Singapore is more important. It's better for investment.
T Ah, right. And the buildings? Are they all new?
M Yeah, there are a lot of new buildings in Shanghai, so it's more modern than Singapore, but it isn't as cosmopolitan as Singapore. Half the population of Singapore is foreigners.
T Wow! Really? What about Dubai? What's that like?
M Dubai is the newest and youngest city, and it's the most modern. I like it because it has a "can-do" feel to it.
T What about the climate in these places? What was the weather like?
M It's interesting. Singapore is near the equator, so it's a lot hotter than Shanghai. But it isn't as hot as Dubai. Dubai is the hottest place. When I was there the temperature was over 100 degrees Fahrenheit.
T Wow! That's incredible!
M Singapore is very humid, so it's wetter than Shanghai. But Dubai is the driest. It only rains for a few days a year.
T Where did you like most of all? Where was best for you?
M For me Shanghai is the best because it's the busiest and the most exciting. There are so many things to do – the best restaurants, theaters, stores. It has everything!

CD2 22 Pronunciation

I'm older than Jane.
But I'm not as old as John.
He's the oldest.

CD2 23

A Who's smarter, you or Ben?
B Me, of course! He's smart, but he isn't nearly as smart as me.

CD2 24

A Who's kinder, you or Ben?
B Me, of course! He's kind, but he isn't nearly as kind as me!
A Who's funnier, you or Ben?
B Me, of course! He's funny, but he isn't nearly as funny as me!
A Who's better looking, you or Ben?
B Me, of course! He's good-looking, but he isn't nearly as good-looking as me!
A Who's more ambitious, you or Ben?
B Me, of course! He's ambitious, but he isn't nearly as ambitious as me!

CD2 25 My family

Sally
Well, I'm very much like my mom. We're interested in the same kind of things, and we can talk forever. We like the same movies and the same books. I look like my mom, too. We have the same hair and eyes. And she's the same size as me, so I can wear her clothes! My sister's a little older than me. Her name's Lena. We're pretty different. She's very neat, and I'm messy. She's much neater than me. And she's very ambitious. She wants to be a doctor. I'm a lot lazier. I don't know what I want to do.

Jamie
I'm not really like my mom or my dad, but I'm a twin. I have a twin brother, Rob, and we look a lot like each other. He has darker hair than me. Mine's blonder. His is dark brown. But people are always mixing us up. People come up to me and say hello and start a conversation, and I have no idea who they are. It's pretty funny. I just say "OK! Really?" We have similar interests. We both love art, theater, and books, but he's a little moody and quiet. I'm a lot noisier. I guess he's pretty shy. And I'm definitely smarter than him!

Rachel
People say I'm like my father. Hmm. I'm not sure about that. We do look the same. We're both tall, and I guess our faces are similar. But my father's a selfish man, and I hope I'm different from him. I hope I'm a little bit kinder than him. He doesn't talk much. He isn't very happy. I'm a happier person. He doesn't sound very nice, does he? He's OK, but there are things about him that I really don't like. I have a sister, Jenny, and we do everything together. I love her to pieces. But she's prettier and thinner than me, so I don't like that part about her!

CD2 26 Synonyms

1 A Maria comes from a very rich family.
  B Really? I knew her uncle was very wealthy. They have a house in the Caribbean, don't they?
2 A Was Sophie angry when you were late?
  B Yeah. She was pretty annoyed, that's for sure. She was yelling a little, but then she calmed down.
3 A Jack's such an intelligent boy!
  B Mm. He's very smart for a ten-year-old. He has some interesting things to say, too.
4 A I've had enough of this long, cold winter.
  B I know. I'm fed up with the dark nights. I need some sunshine.
5 A Dave and Sarah's apartment is small, isn't it?
  B It's tiny. I don't know how they live there. It's only big enough for one person.
6 A Are you happy with your new car?
  B Yes, I'm very satisfied with it. It runs well. And it's much more reliable than my old one.

CD2 27 Antonyms

1 A That man was so rude to me!
  B Yes, he wasn't very polite, was he?
2 A Some people are so generous!
  B Well, not everyone's as stingy as you!
3 A Dave's apartment is always so dirty!
  B Mm, it isn't very clean, is it?
4 A His wife always looks so miserable!
  B Yeah, she never looks very happy, does she?
5 A Their children are so loud!
  B Yes, they aren't very quiet, are they?
6 A This class is boring!
  B True. It isn't very interesting. Let's go home.

CD2 28 What's happening?

1 A What do you want to do today?
  B I'm not sure. How about going to the movie theater?
  A Mmm … I don't really feel like seeing a movie.
2 B OK. Would you like to go to an exhibition?
  A That sounds interesting! What is it?
  B Well, there's a Jackson Pollock exhibition.
  A Is it any good?
  B I think it looks good!
3 A Where is it?
  B It's on at The Getty Center.
  A How much is it?
  B It's free.
  A What time is it open?
  B From ten till five-thirty.
  A Great! Let's go!

 UNIT 7

CD2 29 A house with history
Hi! I'm Max. I live in New York City in an apartment on East 51st Street. I've lived here for three years. I'm a press photographer. I've worked for *The Daily News* since 2012. My wife's name is Meg. We've been married for two years. We met in college. Meg's a receptionist at Lennox Hill Hospital. I get around the city on a bicycle. I've done this since I moved here. Meg goes by bus. We don't have any children yet.

CD2 30

1 How long has he lived in the apartment?
  Max has lived in the apartment for three years.
2 How long did he live in the apartment?
  John Steinbeck lived in the apartment for one year.
3 Where does he work?
  Max works for *The Daily News.*
4 How long has he worked there?
  Max has worked there since 2012.
5 What was his job in New York City?
  Steinbeck was a war correspondent for a newspaper.
6 Which newspaper did he write for?
  Steinbeck wrote for the *New York Herald Tribune.*
7 How long has he been married?
  Max has been married for two years.
8 How long was he married to his second wife?
  Steinbeck was married to his second wife for five years.

CD2 31 *for* or *since*?

1 I've known John for three years. We met in college.
2 I last went to the movies two weeks ago. The movie was really boring.

3 I've had this watch since I was a child. My grandpa gave it to me.

4 I lived in New York from 2005 to 2007. I had a great time there.

5 I've lived in this house since 2008. It has a big backyard.

6 We last took a vacation two years ago. We went to Brazil.

7 I haven't seen you for years. What have you been up to?

8 We haven't had a break for over an hour. I really need some coffee.

CD2 32 Asking questions

A Where do you live, Susan?
B In an apartment near the river.
A How long have you lived there?
B For three years.
A Why did you move there?
B Because we wanted to be in a nicer area.

CD2 33

1 A What do you do?
B I work for an international company.
A How long have you worked there?
B For two years.
A What did you do before that?
B I worked in an office.

2 A Do you know Dave Brown?
B Yes, I do.
A How long have you known him?
B For five or six years.
A Where did you meet him?
B We went to college together.

CD2 34 Frieda Hoffman

I = Interviewer, F = Frieda

I Frieda, you've traveled a lot in your lifetime. Which countries have you been to?
F Well, I've been to a lot of countries in Africa and Asia, but I've never been to South America.
I When did you first go abroad?
F When I was six, my family moved to England.
I Why did you move there?
F Because my father got a job as a professor of history at Cambridge University.
I Have you always been interested in archaeology?
F Yes, I have. When I was ten, there was an exhibition of Tutankhamun, the Egyptian king, in London. My father took me to see it, and I was fascinated! After that I knew that I wanted to go to Egypt and be an archaeologist.
I How many times have you been to Egypt?
F At least twenty times! I go as often as I can.
I Have you ever discovered anything?
F Yes, I've made some very important discoveries. I was the leader of a team that discovered ancient tombs near Cairo.
I You've written about Egypt, haven't you? How many books have you written?
F I've written three about the pharaohs. And I've written a book about a journey I made from Cairo to Cape Town.
I How did you travel? By train? By car?
F In a Land Rover, of course!
I In all of your travels, have you ever been in danger?
F Oh, my gosh, yes! Many times! But in situations like that you learn so much about yourself.

CD2 35 Present Perfect or Simple Past?

I = Interviewer, F = Frieda

1 I You moved to England when you were six. Do you go back to Germany much?
F No, I don't. I've been back a few times, but I've never lived there again. I feel more English than German.

2 I What did you study in college?
F I studied ancient history at Cambridge.
I Did you enjoy it?
F Yes, I did. The classes were amazing, and Cambridge was a great place to live.

3 I Have you ever had an ordinary job?
F Of course I have! I've done all kinds of things! After college I didn't have any money.
I So what did you do?
F I worked in a restaurant. I hated it!
I Why didn't you like it?
F Because the hours were so long, and the people I was working with were horrible.

4 I You said you've often been in danger. What's the most dangerous situation you've been in?
F Well, I had a very bad car accident in Cairo. I was seriously injured and broke several bones. I spent three months in the hospital. I was very lucky. I nearly died.

CD2 36 Word endings

photographer
politician
interpreter
receptionist
musician
librarian
scientist
accountant
electrician
farmer
decorator
lawyer
artist
actor

CD2 37 Word stress

Two-syllabled noun and adjectives
Nouns
danger
kindness
critic
artist
difference

Adjectives
dangerous
healthy
friendly
famous
different

Two-syllabled verbs
invite
explain
discuss
employ
decide
compete

Nouns ending in -tion and -sion
invitation
explanation
competition
ambition
decision

CD2 38 A Family History: Part One

I come from Newcastle in England, but now I live in Perth, Australia. I've been here nearly ten years. My wife, Jodie, is Australian and our children Russel and Alice were born here. Alice is named after my grandmother, her great-grandmother, Alice Bews. She's 89 now and still lives in Newcastle. Lately I've become really interested in my family history back in the UK. I've started speaking to my grandmother about it. I've found out that she was the youngest of nine children and the only one to have been born in England. Her eight brothers and sisters were all born in Scotland. They came from the very north of Scotland, from some islands called the Orkneys. They worked there as farmers over a hundred years ago. My grandmother told me that hundreds of years ago our family's ancestors were actually Norwegian – they came over to Scotland in the 9th century. She says that's why we all have blond hair in our family. Anyway, it became more and more difficult for my great-grandparents to make a living farming, so they traveled south. They finally arrived in the north of England, in Newcastle with their eight children. Alice was born soon after they arrived.

CD2 39 A Family History: Part Two

D = David, A = Alice Bews

D So Grandma, your parents were both born in the Orkney Islands, is that right?
A Yes, my mother was called Jane. She grew up there and she married when she was just 17.
D And you were her ninth child?
A Yes, I was the only one born in England. Times were really hard for my mother – you see my father died when I was three. I can't remember him at all.
D So what did your mother do?
A She worked as a cleaner and a dressmaker.
D She had two jobs and a big family, that's …
A Oh, yes, she was an amazing lady. But my two eldest brothers … they got work in the shipyards so that helped, too. All my brothers and sisters have died now – I'm the only one left.
D I know. Did you marry young, Grandma?
A Oh, no. I didn't marry until I was 22.
D That's still young.
A It wasn't unusual in those days. And I had only three children.
D But now you have lots of grandchildren and great-grandchildren.
A I do. They live all over the world – not just in Australia.
D I know. I have cousins in New Zealand and America. But cousin Peter still lives near you, doesn't he?
A Yes, he does. He helps me keep in touch with you all with this Skype thing.
D Yeah, this Skype is amazing, isn't it?
A Oh, yes. I love it. I talk to all my grandchildren and I've seen all my great-grandchildren. I email sometimes, too. Email, Skype, and texting – it's all really wonderful, isn't it?
D It is, Grandma. It's just great talking to you. I've got lots more questions for you next time.

CD2 40 Agree with me!

It's really wonderful, isn't it?
You come from a small town, don't you?
Life wasn't easy then, was it?
You've lived here for years, haven't you?

1 A It's a beautiful day, isn't it?
  B Yes, it is! Amazing!
  A We all love days like this, don't we?
  B We sure do!
2 A Mommy! Our cat isn't very big, is she?
  B No, she isn't. She's just a kitten.
  A And she loves fish, doesn't she?
  B She does! It's her favorite food!
3 A We had such a good vacation, didn't we?
  B We did. We had a great time.
  A And it wasn't too expensive, was it?
  B No, it wasn't. It wasn't expensive at all.
4 A The baby looks just like her mother, doesn't she?
  B Uh huh. Same brown eyes, same nose.
  A But she doesn't have her father's curly hair, does she?
  B No, she doesn't. Her hair is very straight.

CD2 42

1 A It was a great party last night, wasn't it?
  B Yes, it was. I really enjoyed it.
2 A Dave knows everything about computers, doesn't he?
  B Yes, he does. He can fix them and program them.
3 A You went to school with my brother, didn't you?
  B Yes, I did. We were really good friends.
4 A Learning a language isn't easy, is it?
  B No, it isn't. It takes a lot of practice and patience.
5 A Our English has improved a lot, hasn't it?
  B Yes, it has. We're all much better now.
6 A We haven't had a break for hours, have we?
  B No, we haven't. It's time for one right now.

CD2 43

1 A The weather is just horrible today, isn't it?
  B Awful!
  A The rain makes you miserable, doesn't it?
  B And wet!
  A Oh, well. We need the rain, don't we?
  B I guess so.
2 A It's so romantic here, isn't it?
  B Yes, it's beautiful!
  A And the ocean looks so inviting, doesn't it?
  B I think I'll take a swim before breakfast. I have time, don't I?
  A Of course you have time! We're on vacation, aren't we?
3 A You don't like Ann, do you?
  B Um … she's all right.
  A But you didn't talk to her all night, did you?
  B Well … she was talking to Jim, wasn't she?
  A Actually, she's very interesting.
  B But she never listens, does she? She just talks and talks and talks!
4 A I'd love to buy that car!
  B But we don't have any money, do we?
  A I thought we had a lot.
  B But we spent it all on a new kitchen, didn't we?
  A Oh, yes! That's right. I forgot.
  B We can save up, can't we?
  A Uh … OK.
5 S We had an amazing vacation, didn't we, Dave?
  D We did. It was very relaxing.
  S And the weather was fabulous, wasn't it, Dave?
  D Yup. We were lucky.
  S And we met some nice people, didn't we, Dave?
  D We did. Charming people.

6 A Amanda Seyfried's a fabulous actor, isn't she?
  B Very good.
  A And her voice is really good, isn't it?
  B Yes, it's amazing!
  A She can hit the highest notes, can't she?
  B Yeah, I don't know how she does it.
7 A We love each other very much, don't we?
  B We do.
  A And we want to get married one day, don't we?
  B One day, yeah.
  A And we'll have six children, won't we?
  B Uh … yeah. Six, that's right.
8 A That was a terrible game, wasn't it?
  B Awful! What a waste of money!
  A Lopez played really badly, didn't he?
  B He was horrible! He didn't do anything right all night, did he?
  A We deserved to lose, didn't we?
  B We did! I don't know why I root for them!

 # UNIT 8

CD2 44 An interview with Tilly Parkins

I = Interviewer, T = Tilly Parkins

I Tilly, I'm sure you have to be in great shape to go climbing. How often do you have to train?
T I don't have to train every day, just two or three times a week, that's enough. I go to the gym. On weekends I try to get out of the city to train, but sometimes I have to work at the hospital.
I What do you do at the hospital?
T I'm a cardiac technologist. I help doctors treat people with heart disease.
I Oh, wow! That's interesting. The photograph of Moon Hill Crag is amazing. Was it a difficult climb?
T Difficult but very beautiful.
I I can see that. It's like a painting. What time of day was it?
T It was just after dawn. I had to climb very early in the morning. You can't climb later in the day – it's too hot, over 95°F.
I Who took the picture?
T An amazing sports photographer named Adam Pretty.
I He's a brave man.
T Oh, he didn't have to climb with me. He took the picture from a nearby tourist spot.
I Smart man! Rock climbing is such a dangerous sport and you've climbed in some of the most difficult places in the world. Why do you do it?
T It's what I love doing. It's my life. It's who I am.

CD2 45

1 "How often does she have to train?"
   "Two or three times a week."
2 "Does she have to work on weekends?"
   "Yes, she does sometimes."
3 "Why did she have to climb Moon Hill Crag just after dawn?"
   "Because later it gets too hot and you can't climb in the heat."
4 "Did Adam have to climb the rock?"
   "No, he didn't. He took the picture from a tourist spot."

CD2 46 Pronunciation

1 I have a good job.
   I have to work hard.
2 He has a nice camera.
   She has to train a lot.
3 We had a good time.
   We had to get up early.

CD2 47 Advice from Annie

Dear Mark,
Good preparation is the answer. You must prepare well and practice a lot. The first thirty seconds are the most important. You should begin with a personal story. It will relax you and the audience. You should write your speech down, but I don't think you should read it aloud to the group. Just make notes to help you remember it. For more help, you should visit speechtips.com.

Dear Paula,
More and more people worldwide have become addicted to this. He must get professional help, but this is difficult because he won't accept that he has a problem. I think you should show him this letter, and tell him to visit the website olganon.org. Tell him firmly that he must change his ways or he'll lose his wife and family. Talk to all your friends and family about the problem – you shouldn't suffer alone.

Dear Billy,
These feelings are very common between brothers and sisters. I'm sure your parents love you and your brother just the same, so you shouldn't worry about this. When you're older, you'll get your own phone – and your own clothes! You must talk to your parents about how you feel. And you shouldn't feel jealous of your brother. He's older than you – that's all!

Dear Tracy,
The fact is, that to get to the top in sports, you do have to train very hard. You should talk to someone else about your doubts. I don't think you should listen to just your friends. You should explain how you feel to your coach and your mother. However, in the end, the decision is yours and yours alone. You must decide your own future.

CD2 48 Giving advice

1 A I can't sleep at night.
  B You must exercise more during the day. Why don't you walk to work? And you shouldn't drink so much coffee just before bedtime.
2 A I don't like my brother's new girlfriend.
  B I don't think you should tell your brother. I think you should try to find some good things about her.
3 A I have an important exam tomorrow, and I'm really nervous.
  B I don't think you should study any more today. You must get a good night's sleep tonight. Don't worry. I'm sure you'll pass and if you don't, it's not the end of the world.
4 A A boy in my class is bullying me.
  B You must tell your teacher or ask your parents to talk to the teacher.
5 A I'm horrible at all sports.
  B You shouldn't worry about that. A lot of people aren't very athletic. Think about all the things you are good at.

6 **A** I fell and I think I twisted my ankle.
 B Oh it looks bad! You must go to the doctor or even an emergency room and ask for an X-ray. I'll drive you. I don't think you should walk on it.

7 **A** My computer's being really weird.
 B Mine does that all the time. You should do what I do. Turn it off, wait a while, and then turn it on again. It's the only thing that ever works for me.

8 **A** My car's making a funny noise.
 B It sounds bad, you shouldn't drive it. You must bring it to a mechanic right away.

CD2 49 **Jessica Ennis – 2012 Olympic heptathlon champion**

I = Interviewer, J = Jessica Ennis

I Nice to meet you, Jessica. Congratulations on your gold medal at the 2012 Olympic Games in London.

J Thank you very much.

I You won in London, but I know that several years ago you injured your ankle badly. Were you worried that your track and field career was over?

J Yes, I was, very worried. I missed the 2008 Olympics, and I had to work hard with physical therapists and doctors for nine months – but I'm fine now.

I You are obviously a very determined woman.

J Yes, my mom always said that from a young age I was very determined. I knew what I wanted.

I Is your mom a big influence in your life?

J Yes, she is. She works for a non-profit organization. She helps people with drug problems. You have to have a lot of patience for that. My mom has that. My dad's a painter and decorator. He was born in Jamaica, and he moved here when he was 13.

I I can see your parents are important to you. I'm sure you have a good coach, too.

J Yes, Tony Minichiello. He's a really good coach, but we fight a lot, I…

I You fight!

J Well, we do spend a lot of time together. He's always saying "Come on, come on, you have to be more aggressive," and I'm not really like that. He says that I should only think about track and field. He didn't even want me to get a dog.

I Did you get a dog?

J Oh, yes. I have a beautiful chocolate Labrador. Her name is Myla.

I So, do you think that you should have other interests, not just track and field?

J Yes, but when I'm competing I go into my own little world. I don't see my boyfriend, I…

I You have a boyfriend?

J Yes, Andy. I only speak to him once or twice when I'm at competition. I have to concentrate on competing. I know I won an Olympic gold medal, but I can still improve. I have to work on my long jump and javelin, and I know I can run faster. It's the small things that make a difference in the end.

I I hope you have time to feel proud about winning the gold medal.

J Oh, yes. I keep my medal by my bed, and when I look at it I think, "Oh my goodness, I won. I'm an Olympic champion." Sometimes I can't believe it.

I It's an amazing achievement. Good job and good luck at your next competition.

J Thank you.

CD2 50 **Brothers and sisters**

1 David
I'm the middle of three brothers. There was just Mark, my elder brother, and me for years. I liked that, I liked being the baby, but then Rob was born when I was seven, and I was so jealous. I thought he was our mom's favorite. We fought a lot as kids, but now it's great. I'd like to have at least three kids – three boys like us would be great.

2 Peta
My mom and dad named me Peta when I was born because they wanted a boy! Then they had four boys after me. I don't like being the oldest of so many boys, and I don't like my name. I'm going to change it to Petra when I'm 18. I like my youngest brother, Henry – he's everybody's favorite – but I hate the others. They're annoying and very boring – all they do is play noisy computer games and talk about sports. I don't want any children when I grow up – well, maybe just one daughter.

3 Stewart
I'm an only child. My parents divorced when I was just three years old, so I grew up with just my mom. I love her, but I didn't like the situation. I was her whole world. This was hard for me. When I was thirteen, she married again and that was hard, too. It took me a long time to get along with my step-dad. He's really nice, but I was jealous of him for years. I just got married. My wife's an only child, too, and we both definitely want to have lots of kids.

CD2 51 **At the doctor's**

1 I can't stop coughing and blowing my nose.
 You have a cold.
2 I have a fever and my whole body aches.
 You have the flu.
3 It hurts when I walk on it.
 You have a twisted ankle.
4 I keep going to the bathroom.
 You have diarrhea.
5 My glands are swollen, and it hurts when I swallow.
 You have a sore throat.
6 I keep throwing up, and I have terrible diarrhea.
 You have food poisoning.
7 I start sneezing and itching when I'm near a cat.
 You have an allergy.

CD2 52

D = doctor, E = Edsom
D What seems to be the problem?
E Well, I haven't felt well for a few days. I've had a bad headache and now I have a sore throat.
D Any sickness or diarrhea?
E Well, I haven't been sick.
D Do you feel hot?
E Yes, especially at night. I feel hot and start coughing when I lie down.
D OK. I'll just take your temperature. Ah, yes. You do have a fever. Now, let me see your throat. Open your mouth wide, please.
E Can you see anything?
D Yes, your throat looks very red. Does this hurt?
E Ouch!
D And your glands are swollen. You just have an infection. You need antibiotics. Are you allergic to penicillin?

E No, I'm not.
D Good. Now, you should take it easy for a couple of days and you should drink plenty of liquids. I'll write you a prescription.
E Thank you. Do I have to pay you?
D There's no charge for a sick visit. But you'll have to pay for the prescription.
E OK. Thank you very much.

UNIT 9

CD3 2 **The Bear and the Travelers**
1 Where were the travelers walking?
 Along a country road.
2 Why were they going to the city?
 Because they were looking for work.
3 What did they see in the woods?
 They saw a huge bear.
4 What did the men do?
 One hid in a tree, and the other pretended to be dead.
5 What did the bear do?
 It bent down, sniffed, and then wandered away.

CD3 3
Two travelers were walking slowly along a country road. They were going to the city because they were looking for work. They were tired because they had walked twenty miles and they were hungry because they hadn't eaten all day. Suddenly, in the woods in front of them, they saw a huge bear. The men were terrified. One of them ran away, climbed a tree and hid.
The other man fell to the ground and pretended to be dead. He had heard that bears don't like eating dead meat. The bear came toward him. It bent down, sniffed him, and whispered something in his ear. Then it wandered away.
After the bear had gone, the other man came down from his tree and went to see how his friend was. He wanted to know what the bear had said to him.
"The bear gave me some advice," said his companion. "He said, 'Next time you go on a journey, travel with someone who won't leave you at the first sign of danger.'"
The moral of the story is … choose your friends carefully!

CD3 4
1 Why were the travelers tired?
 Because they had walked twenty miles.
2 Why were they hungry?
 Because they hadn't eaten all day.
3 Why did one of them pretend to be dead?
 Because he had heard that bears don't like eating dead meat.
4 When did the other man come down from the tree?
 After the bear had gone.
5 What did he want to know?
 He wanted to know what the bear had said to him.

CD3 5 **Pronunciation**
1 They'd walked twenty miles.
2 One man hid in a tree.
3 The other pretended to be dead.
4 When the bear had gone, the man came down.
5 He'd left his friend when danger came.

CD3 6

1 I was nervous on the plane because I'd never flown before.
2 When I'd had breakfast, I went to work.
3 I met a girl at a party. Her face was familiar. I was sure I'd seen her somewhere before.
4 I felt tired all day yesterday because I hadn't slept the night before.
5 My wife was angry with me because I'd forgotten our anniversary.
6 The little girl was crying because she'd fallen and hurt herself.

CD3 7 The boy who cried wolf

Once upon a time there was a shepherd boy who took care of the sheep in the hills near his village. His job was very boring. One day, while he was sitting under a tree, he had an idea. He decided to have some fun, so he went down to the village and shouted, "Wolf! Wolf!" loudly.
As soon as the villagers heard the boy, they stopped work and raced to the hills to help him. But when they got there, they saw nothing. They returned to their work. After they'd gone, the shepherd boy smiled to himself.
A few days later, the boy did the same thing again. He ran into the village and shouted, "Wolf! Wolf!" The villagers didn't know whether to believe him or not, but they were worried about their sheep so they went to the hills to help him. Again there was no wolf. They were angry because the shepherd boy had lied again, but he just laughed.
Then, the next day, just as the sun was setting, a wolf really did appear, and it began attacking the sheep. In terror, the boy raced down the hill to the village, shouting, "Wolf! Wolf!" Although the villagers heard his cries, they did nothing to help. This time they really didn't believe him.
The shepherd boy climbed back up the hill to look for the sheep, but the wolf had killed them all. He was so ashamed that he sat down in the moonlight and cried.
The moral of the story is … we should not lie. A liar will not be believed, even when telling the truth.

CD3 8 Discussing grammar

1 I went to bed when I'd done my homework.
2 After I had driven two hundred miles, I stopped for coffee.
3 As soon as she had passed her driver's test, she bought a car.
4 I didn't go to Italy until I had learned Italian.
5 Although I had read the book, I didn't understand the movie.
6 His mother sent him to bed because he had been bad.
7 She had burned the food, so we went out to eat.
8 She made a delicious dinner, but unfortunately I had eaten a large lunch.

CD3 9 My favorite writer

I = Interviewer, T = Tom
Part 1
I Tom, you chose American Harper Lee as your favorite writer. Can you tell us a little about her? When was she alive?
T She wrote in the middle of the twentieth century. She was born in the US in 1926, and she's still alive today.
I What did she write? What kind of books?

T Interestingly, she only wrote one novel, but it won a Pulitzer Prize in 1961.
I And tell us … Why is she famous?
T At the time she was writing, there was a lot of inequality between blacks and whites in the southern US states. Lee wanted to bring attention to this problem. She wrote about racism – specifically the racism she saw while growing up in a small town in Alabama. Lee created some of the most famous characters in American literature.
I What is the name of her book?
T It's called *To Kill a Mockingbird*. It's about a young white girl whose name is Scout and how she becomes friends with a black man, who is accused of a crime he did not commit. As the story unfolds, Scout realizes that people are the same inside no matter what color their skin is. In fact, it has a lot of autobiography in it.
I Fascinating! Did she write anything else?
T She wrote several magazine articles, but mostly she stopped writing after the great success of her only book.
I What was Lee's personal life like?
T Mmm. It's hard to say. After writing *To Kill a Mockingbird*, she disappeared from public life. She refuses almost every request for interview. She has said, "I have said what I wanted to say and I will not say it again."
I Did she ever marry?
T No, she never married. But she's very close to her older sister, who's 98 years old and still practices law in Alabama!
I Amazing!

CD3 10 My favorite writer

I = Interviewer, A = Alice
Part 2
I Now, Alice. You chose the British writer Robert Louis Stevenson. Tell us about him. When was he writing?
A Well, he was born in 1850, and he died in 1894, so he was writing well before Lee, in the second half of the nineteenth century.
I And … what did he write?
A He wrote novels, and poetry, and he was also a travel writer.
I Oh! Tell us … why is he famous?
A Well, he isn't as famous as other writers of his time. But he's very popular because he's a great storyteller. His stories are about adventure, danger, and horror. His heroes are pure, and his villains are dark.
I What are his best-known books?
A There's a children's book called *Treasure Island*, and there's a travel story about France, but the most famous is *The Strange Case of Dr. Jekyll and Mr. Hyde*.
I And they, I suppose, are his most well-known characters?
A Yes. The book was a great success. It's about a man who has two sides to his character, one good and one bad. The man, Dr. Jekyll, has a battle inside himself between his good side and his evil side.
I This is the psychological idea of someone with a split personality?
A Yes. In everyday speech we say about someone, "Oh, he's a real Jekyll and Hyde," meaning there are two sides to their personality.
I Fascinating! Tell us about his personal life.

A As a child he was sick a lot. He married an American woman who had children from an earlier marriage, but they didn't have any children together. He traveled a lot, to Europe and the US. He died very young, when he was just 44.
I Well, thank you, Alice, for telling us about Robert Louis Stevenson.

CD3 11 *The strange case of Dr. Jekyll and Mr. Hyde*

1 Late one night, a lawyer, Gabriel Utterson, was walking home through dark, silent streets when he saw a man attacking a woman. Utterson ran after him and caught him. The man's name was Mr. Hyde, and he looked ugly and evil.
2 Mr. Hyde showed no regret for what he had done. To buy the woman's silence, he wrote her a check. Uttersson noticed that the check was signed in the name of Dr, Jekyll, a well-known and well-respected man.
3 Utterson was worried. He was Dr. Jekyll's lawyer and also his friend. He went to visit him. As soon as he mentioned Mr. Hyde, Dr. Jekyll turned pale and became angry. Utterson was confused. Who was Mr. Hyde?
4 A year passed. One night an old man was murdered as he was walking home. A maid witnessed the crime and recognized the killer. Mr. Hyde had struck again! The police went looking for Hyde, but he had disappeared.
5 Again, Utterson went to visit his friend Dr. Jekyll. He suspected that Dr. Jekyll had helped Mr. Hyde to escape. When questioned, the doctor replied in a strange, wild voice that Mr. Hyde had gone forever.
6 Over the next few weeks Dr. Jekyll's behavior became more and more unusual. He locked himself in his laboratory and refused to open the door. His servants were worried. When they heard his voice, it sounded different. They asked Utterson for help.
7 Utterson and the servants broke down the door. Mr. Hyde was lying dead on the floor. He had taken poison. But why was he wearing Dr. Jekyll's clothes? And where was the doctor? Were Dr. Jekyll and Mr. Hyde one and the same person?
8 On the desk was a letter addressed to Mr. Utterson. In it, Dr. Jekyll tried to explain himself. He said he believed that inside every human being there was a good side and an evil side.
9 Jekyll had created a potion. When he drank it, his whole body changed. The good, kind doctor became cruel, ugly, and evil. He called this other man Mr. Hyde. To change back, he had to drink another potion.
10 But after a time Jekyll found that he liked changing into Mr. Hyde. He enjoyed being bad. He became more and more violent and cruel. He took pleasure in hurting innocent people.
11 Finally Dr. Jekyll couldn't control Mr. Hyde anymore. He began to change into this monster even without taking the potion. Jekyll hoped and prayed that Hyde would disappear. But Hyde always returned.
12 The potion to turn Hyde back into Dr. Jekyll no longer worked. It had lost its strength. Dr. Jekyll could no longer get rid of the evil Mr. Hyde. He had to kill this monster. But to kill Mr. Hyde, Dr. Jekyll also had to die.

CD3 12 Feelings

1 I was delighted because I'd won $500 in a dance competition.
2 I was stressed because I had so many bills and no money to pay them.
3 I was proud because I'd worked so hard and passed all my exams.
4 I was amazed because my teachers didn't expect me to pass.
5 I was upset because no one remembered my birthday.

CD3 13

1 A Sometimes I feel really lonely.
   B Cheer up! You have me. I'm your best friend!
2 A I have so much to do! And the baby's crying! Help!
   B Calm down! Don't stress yourself out.
3 A Guess what? I just won $10,000!
   B I'm happy for you! Can I have some?
4 A When I watch the news on TV, I get scared.
   B I know what you mean. The world's a scary place.
5 A I get upset when people are so horrible.
   B Yes, but people can be really nice, too.

CD3 14 Exclamations with *so* and *such*

What an amazing movie!
I was scared!
I was really scared!
I was SO scared!

CD3 15

I was so surprised!
It was such a shock!
It was such an awful day!
You have such crazy ideas!
We had such terrible weather!
There were so many problems!
I have so much work!

CD3 16

1 That was such a good book! You have to read it!
   I'll lend it to you. You'll really like it.
2 The movie was so scary that I couldn't watch it! I hate the sight of blood and people killing each other.
3 Jane and Pete are such nice people! They're always so welcoming and happy to see you.
4 But their children are so badly-behaved! The parents have no control at all!
5 There were so many people at the party! I didn't get to talk to everyone.
6 They made such a mess! I'm glad I didn't have to clean up.
7 I've spent so much money this week! I don't have a single penny left!
8 I've had such an awful day! I need some chocolate to cheer me up!

 UNIT 10

CD3 17 A phone call that changed the world

The cell phone was once an oversized luxury item. Now it's a pocket-sized minicomputer.
The first cell phone call was made on April 3, 1973, by Martin Cooper, an American engineer, while he was walking along a street in New York

City. People stopped and stared in amazement. Martin's phone was like a brick. It was almost 8 inches long and weighed 2.8 pounds. The battery lasted only 36 minutes.

Fact file

Today, cell phones are owned by almost six billion people worldwide. In the US, 124 million are sold every year.
The first text message was sent in 1992. Last year 8 trillion texts were sent worldwide.
Camera phones have been sold in the US since 2002.
"Smartphones" were introduced in 2007. The cell phone had become a multimedia gadget.
Over the years a lot of amazing features have been added, including Internet browsing, email, mp3 players, video, and camera.
In 2008, Apple's iPhone had 10,000 applications (apps). Now there are over one million apps.
The most expensive cell phone is the Goldstriker iPhone 4S Elite Gold. It is made of 24-karat gold and decorated with over 550 diamonds. It costs $9.4 million.
133 million cell phones are thrown away every year.
Some people believe that before long, all landline telephones will be replaced by cell phones.

CD3 18 Active to passive

1 The first cell phone call was made in 1973 by Martin Cooper.
2 Cell phones are owned by almost six billion people worldwide.
3 124 million phones are sold in the US every year.
4 Camera phones have been sold since 2002.
5 A lot of amazing features have been added.
6 The Goldstriker iPhone is decorated with over 550 diamonds.
7 133 million phones are thrown away every year.
8 Some people believe that eventually all landline phones will be replaced by cell phones.

CD3 19 Inventions that changed the world

1 Paper was invented in 105 A.D. by a Chinese government official, named Cai Lun.
2 The printing press was invented in 1440 by a German printer named Johannes Gutenberg.
3 The telephone was invented in 1876 by Alexander Graham Bell. Bell was born in Scotland, but he moved to the US.
4 The radio was invented in 1896 by Guglielmo Marconi, an Italian physicist.
5 Television was invented in 1924 by a Scottish engineer, John Logie Baird.
6 The ballpoint pen was invented in 1938 by the Hungarian journalist, Laszlo Biro.
7 The PC was invented in 1976 by two American computer engineers, Steve Jobs & Steve Wozniak. The name Apple was chosen for the company because it was Jobs's favorite fruit.

CD3 20 All things online

1 Over 150 billion emails are sent every day.
2 Nearly 3.5 billion queries are searched by Google every day.
3 eBay was invented in 1995 by Pierre Omidyar, a French scientist.
4 Nearly 5 billion items have been sold on eBay since it began.
5 60,000 new video clips are posted on YouTube every week.

6 The first Twitter message was sent by American businessman, Jack Dorsey, in 2006.
7 Facebook has been translated into 79 languages since it began.
8 The online store, Amazon.com, was founded by Jeff Besoz, in his garage in 1994.

CD3 21

1 A How many emails are sent every day?
   B Over 150 billion. Isn't that amazing?
2 A How many queries are searched by Google every day?
   B Nearly 3.5 billion. It's incredible.
3 A When was eBay invented?
   B In 1995.
   A Who was it invented by?
   B A French scientist named Pierre Omidyar.
4 A How many items have been sold on eBay since it began?
   B 5 billion. Actually 5 billion and one. I just bought something!
5 A How many video clips are posted on YouTube every week?
   B 60,000 new videos every week.
6 A When was the first Twitter message sent?
   B In 2006.
   A Who was it sent by?
   B An American businessman named Jack Dorsey.
7 A How many languages has Facebook been translated into?
   B 79. And there'll be more.
8 A When was Amazon.com founded?
   B In 1994.
   A Who was it founded by?
   B Jeff Besoz.

CD3 22 Words that go together

text message
businessman
newspaper
cell phone

CD3 23

business card
business deal
businessman
business news
computer games
computer program
computer virus
laptop
phone call
phone card
phone number
radio news
radio program
radio waves
website

CD3 24

1 She has a wonderful job. She's very well paid.
2 I didn't enjoy that novel. It was really badly written.
3 You don't need to spend a lot of money on clothes to look well dressed.
4 Our office is really well equipped. We have all the latest machines.
5 I hope their children don't come. They're so badly behaved.
6 Can I have my steak very well done, please? I don't like it rare.
7 You haven't heard of Elizabeth Taylor? She was really well known.

1 A Do you ever play computer games?
  B No, but my nephew does, all the time.
2 A Which websites do you visit most often?
  B Google, Wikipedia, and Grantland. I get all my sports scores online now.
3 A Do you send a lot of text messages?
  B I do. It's a great way to make plans. I text all the time.
  A How many per day?
  B I'd say about 100.
4 A Who does the most housework in your home?
  B Not me! My mom always says, "Oh, I'll do it, you're so slow."
5 A Does it take you a long time to get to school?
  B Not really … maybe half an hour at the most.
6 A How do you like your steak?
  B Medium-rare please. I don't like it too dry.
7 A Is your school well equipped?
  B Not really. But I think we're getting interactive whiteboards soon.

CD3 26 There's a first time for everything

1 Henry
It's made for me. I'm a frustrated writer. One day maybe I'll write a novel. I write about my thoughts, my work, all my travels, and I've even written a kind of work biography. I'm so happy that I have so many visitors and comments. I feel in touch with the world. I tweet, too.

2 Sandy
Yeah, I have an account and I go on it pretty often. I like sharing photos with friends. I love seeing their photos, too, and it's a nice way of keeping up to date with them and sometimes making contact with old friends. I don't use it for anything more. Some people communicate a lot about their lives on it – I couldn't do that.

3 Liz
Actually, it was a terrible shock. I went back to my machine and the screen was bright purple with large red letters across it saying "WARNING!" Everything was completely frozen. I called the helpline and they said they'd had over fifty calls from people with the same thing. It had even infected the Stock Exchange. Who are the sad individuals who do this, I want to know!

4 Martin
There aren't many left in my town. Just one, I think, on Main Street. It's because so many people have home computers and laptops these days, and there are more and more places where you can access the Internet. I used them a lot when I was traveling.

5 Barry
I do so much online – I think I conduct most of my life online. I book everything – movie tickets, travel, restaurant reservations; I shop online – clothes, food, presents; I check symptoms if I'm sick (actually, I stopped doing this because I got too scared by the answers); I download recipes. I could go on and on. I like the way "google" has become a verb. I'm always saying "I'll just google that and find out."

CD3 27 Jack's Stressful Day

A = Alan, J = Jack
A Hi, Jack! Over here! How was your trip?
J Huh! Not good! Not good at all.

A Why was that?
J Well, there was this girl in the seat behind me, and she was talking loudly on her cell phone the whole trip. I know everything about her life. I even know what she's going to wear when she goes out on Saturday night, and I know what she's not going to wear.
A That drives me crazy, too! You know, not long ago trains had quiet cars where you couldn't use your cell phone.
J Well, they don't anymore. I couldn't read my paper with her yak, yak, yakking behind me. She told the same thing to at least four friends. Then, I had this kid across from me with his mother. He …
A What was he doing to annoy you?
J He had one of these game things with a pen …
A A Nintendo 3DS?
J Yeah, one of those and he had his head down playing games all the time – zing, ping, bang – all these noises coming from it. He never looked up once. When his mother asked him to say hello, he just grunted, "Uh!" So impolite!
A I know. Kids these days, they're so badly behaved. Did you book your ticket online this time?
J I tried to.
J What happened?
A Well, I followed the instructions, one by one, and when I got to the end, it asked for my password. Password? I didn't know I had one for train travel. So I thought "OK, I'll call instead."
A Maybe not the best idea.
J Uh – no. So I called the train company and of course I got the usual recorded message – you know the usual kind of thing: "All our operators are busy right now." Then music and "Thank you for holding. Our operators are still busy." And more music, so I gave up. I bought a ticket at the train station.
A It drives you crazy, doesn't it? Life's too short to spend so long on the phone. Still, I usually do enjoy traveling by train.
J Me too, usually. It's better than driving. I hate driving into the city these days. There's too much traffic. It's just traffic jam after traffic jam. And it's impossible to find a parking space. Parking's a nightmare! And parking lots and parking meters are so expensive.
A I know. I remember when you could park all day for $10. Come on, let's get out of here. Let's get coffee.
J OK, but not Starbucks. I can't stand Starbucks.
A Why? I like the coffee.
J It's the size of the cups. They're all huge. Even the small one is too big for me, and the biggest is so big, it's enormous, and there are too many choices – latte, skinny latte, soy latte, cappuccino, Frappucino, single shot, double shot …
A OK! OK! Modern life! There's a small coffee shop around the corner. Let's go there.

CD3 28 On the phone
(919) 677-1303
555-1212
(212) 726-6389
1-800-451-7556

CD3 29
(847) 432-5655
(415) 440-2770
1-800-698-7395
555-6900

CD3 30

A = Adam, B = Brian, C = Carol, D = Donna,
E = Emma, F = Flora
1 Brian and Adam
A Sorry Brian, you're breaking up. I couldn't hear that.
B I know, Adam. It's not a good connection. But, listen, I'm calling because I can't make it on Thursday. Are you free on Friday?
A Friday? I'm not sure. Can I get back to you?
B Sure. That's fine. Text me. Talk to you later!
2 Adam and Carol
A Hello, Carol? It's Adam. I'm trying to get a hold of Brian.
C I'm afraid he's not here. Have you tried his cell phone?
A Yeah. I tried that first, but he's not answering.
C It's probably turned off.
A Oh, OK. Can you give him a message?
C Sure.
3 Emma, Donna, and Flora
D I'm sorry. Brian's line's busy. Would you like to hold?
E Yes, please.
D It's ringing for you now.
E Thank you.
F Hello. Brian Doyle's office. Flora speaking.
E This is Emma Smith from Digby and Moss Associates.
F Oh, good morning, Ms. Smith. I'll put you through immediately.
4 Flora and Carol
C Hi, Flora. Can I speak to Brian, please?
F Oh, I'm afraid he has someone with him right now. Is it urgent?
C Just tell him Carol called and I'll see him tonight.
F Will do. I hope there isn't a problem.

UNIT 11

CD3 31 Gareth Malone
1 A When did he start playing the piano?
  B When he was three.
2 A How long has he been playing the piano?
  B Since he was three.
3 A When did he start teaching singing?
  B When he was 23.
4 A How long has he been teaching singing?
  B Since he was 23.
5 A When did he make his first TV show?
  B In 2007.
6 A How long has he been making TV shows?
  B Since 2007.
7 A How many shows has he made?
  B Three.
8 A How long has he been living in London?
  B For about 30 years.

CD3 32 Asking questions
1 A My sister's working in New York.
  B How long has she been working there?
  A Only a couple of months.
2 A I'm training to run a marathon.
  B How long have you been training?
  A Since December. Wish me luck!
3 A My boss is on vacation.
  B How long has he been away?
  A Two weeks. It's great without him!

4 **A** I'm learning how to drive.
　B How long have you been learning?
　A Almost two years. I failed my driver's test three times.
5 **A** I know Maria very well.
　B How long have you known her?
　A Since we were in school together.
6 **A** I have the new iPad.
　B How long have you had it?
　A I just got it yesterday.

CD3 33 What have they been doing?

1 **A** Why are the students bored?
　B Because the teacher's been talking for hours and they haven't understood a word.
2 **A** Why does he have a sore throat?
　B Because he's been singing too much. He's sung every night for the last three weeks.
3 **A** Why are they so tired and dirty?
　B Because they've been playing soccer, but they're happy because they've won the game.
4 **A** Why does he have a backache?
　B Because he's been digging the garden. He's planted six rows of cabbage.
5 **A** Why is she covered in paint?
　B Because she's been decorating her apartment. She's painted two walls already.
6 **A** Why don't they have any money left?
　B Because they've been shopping. They've spent over $500.

CD3 34 I haven't seen you for a long time!

S = Sophie, M = Mike
S Mike! I'm over here!
M Sophie! You look great! You haven't changed a bit.
S Oh, I don't know. It's been over ten years. I'm definitely older if not wiser.
M Well, you look just the same to me. Come on! We have over ten years to catch up on and not a lot of time! My plane leaves in a few hours.
S Tell me about you first. How long have you been working in Mexico? What are you doing there?
M Well, I work for an international I.T. company and right now I'm based in Mexico City. I've been there about 18 months now.
S Wow, that sounds important. Are you enjoying it?
M Yeah, I really am. But there's a chance that I'll have to move to Hong Kong in three months. That's where the headquarters is.
S That sounds interesting, too.
M Yeah, but I have a Mexican girlfriend now.
S Ah, I see. What's her name?
M Rosa. You'd like her – she's a lot of fun. We've been going out for almost a year now.
S Whoah! That sounds serious. Does she speak English?
M Oh, yes. Her English is much better than my Spanish. I started taking Spanish classes six months ago, but I still find Spanish pronunciation really hard.
S I know.
M Oh, yes, you studied languages, didn't you?
S Yes, I studied French and German in college, but I've also been trying to learn Swedish for the last few years.
M Swedish! Come on, now it's your turn Sophie. Tell me about you.

CD3 35

S = Sophie, M = Mike
M Tell me about you.
S Well, I got married a year ago to a Swedish guy. Ragnar, Ragnar Hansson.
M Where did you meet him?
S We met while I was working in Stockholm.
M What were you doing there?
S Well, after school I studied fashion design and my first job was in Sweden, as a buyer for H&M Fashion.
M Really! How long did you do that?
S I worked there for over three years. Ragnar was my boss.
M Ah, did you get married in Sweden?
S Yes, we did. My parents came for the wedding.
M And do you still work in Sweden?
S No, we don't. We both work in the US.
M How long have you been back from Sweden?
S About ten months. We've been trying to buy a small house since we got back.
M So, where have you been living?
S With my parents. They're wonderful, but it's not great and we're expecting a baby next April, so we really need a place of our own.
M Oh, congratulations! I hope you find somewhere soon. Oh, look at the time, I'll have to rush to catch my plane.
S Bye, Mike. It's been great seeing you again. Let's keep in touch from now on.
M Yes, it's been great. Maybe next time you can meet Rosa and I can meet Ragnar.

CD3 36 Birth, marriage, and death

I didn't marry until later in my life. I met Ben when I was 30 and we didn't get married until I was 33, that was in 2006. We got married in a church close to where my mom lives. I had been engaged before that to another man, Mark. We'd been together over ten years, since high school in fact, and I think we just got bored with each other. Ben and I had a great honeymoon in Mexico. We were away for three weeks. And soon after that, I found I was pregnant. That was Ellen, our first baby. She was born the year after we got married, and two years after that, in 2009, we had the twins, Tessa and Tom. They've been keeping us busy ever since! I'm exhausted most of the time, but they're a lot of fun. I'm really glad I married Ben. He's a great dad. I want it to be forever. My mom and dad divorced when I was just thirteen and I don't want us to do that.

CD3 37 Good news, bad news

1 **A** My wife had a baby last night.
　B Congratulations! Was it a boy or girl?
　A A boy. William James.
　B How much did he weigh?
　A Nine pounds, six ounces.
　B Oh! A big boy! How are mother and baby doing?
　A They're fine.
　B That's wonderful. Give her my love when you see her.
2 **A** Travis and I got engaged.
　B That's great news! Congratulations!
　A Do you like my ring?
　B Wow! Diamonds! It's beautiful. When's the wedding?
　A We're thinking next spring.
　B I hope I'm invited.

A Of course you are. I want you to be a bridesmaid.
B Really? I'd love that. I've never been one before.
3 **A** Did you hear about Brian and Josie?
　B No! What happened?
　A Well, they've been having a tough time recently.
　B I know, they haven't been getting along well at all.
　A Mm. Well, they've finally decided to break up.
　B I'm so sorry to hear that. What a shame!
　A Yes, I always thought they were so good together.
4 **A** We lost Grandpa last week.
　B I know. Your dad told me. I'm so sorry. He was a good man. Everyone was really fond of him.
　A He and Grandma were together for almost 60 years.
　B That's incredible. How old was he?
　A 88.
　B And how's your Grandma coping?
　A She's OK. She has her family around her.
　B Well, I'm sure you all have wonderful memories of him.

UNIT 12

CD3 38 Real possibilities

A What are you doing this weekend?
B Mmm … if the weather's nice, we'll go for a picnic.
A Sounds nice. Where to?
B Not sure. We might go to the park, or we might go to the river.
A Well, I'm sure you'll have fun!

CD3 39

1 **A** What are you doing this weekend?
　B Mmm … if it's sunny, we'll go swimming.
　A Sounds great! Where?
　B Don't know. We might go to the pool, or we might go to the lake.
　A Well, I'm sure you'll have a good time!
2 **A** What are you doing this weekend?
　B Mmm, well … if it rains, we'll go shopping.
　A Sounds like a good idea! Where to?
　B Not sure. We might go to Main Street, or we might go to a shopping mall.
　A Well, I'm sure you'll enjoy it!
3 **A** What are you doing this weekend?
　B Mmm … if we have time, we'll see some friends.
　A Sounds good! Where will you go?
　B Don't know. We might go to a restaurant, or we might just go to a coffee shop.
　A Well, I'm sure you'll have fun!

CD3 40 going to and might

1 **A** What are you going to do after school?
　B I don't know. I might go home or I might go to the store.
2 **A** Where are you going on your next vacation?
　B I'm not sure. I might go to Peru or I might go to Thailand.
3 **A** What are you going to study in college?
　B I haven't decided. I might study languages or I might study business.

4 A What are you going to buy Jane for her birthday?
   B I'm not sure. I might buy her a T-shirt or I might buy her makeup.
5 A When are you going to see your boyfriend again?
   B I don't know. I might see him Friday night or I might see him Saturday afternoon.

CD3 41 When I leave school …

1 Tara
When I graduate from high school, first I'm going to take a few weeks of vacation. I'm going to see my brother in Florida. Then I'm going to college. I'm going to study economics. If I do well in college, I'll get a good job and if I get a good job, I'll earn lots of money! I hope so anyway!

2 Ben
I'm not very good at decisions. I don't really know what I want to do. I might work for my father. He has a store, but that's not very interesting. Or I might go traveling with my friend James. The problem is that I don't have much money. So I might get a job in a coffee shop and save some. I'm pretty good with computers, so I might take a class about computer programming. Who knows?

CD3 42 Advice and warnings

1 If you take these pills, you'll feel better.
2 If you eat junk food, you'll get fat.
3 You'll fail your exams if you don't do your homework.
4 Careful! If you touch that, you'll get an electric shock!
5 If you don't go to bed now, you'll never get up on time!

CD3 43 Dreams and wishes

Lily's Dream
I'd love a baby brother. If I had a baby brother, I would play with him all the time. We'd have a lot of fun. I'd be so happy! I wouldn't ask my mom and dad for anything else!

CD3 44

Sam's Dream
I'd like to be taller. If I were taller, I'd be on the travel team for soccer. And if I played really well, I'd be captain. And then if I practiced really hard, maybe one day I could play professional soccer! My dad would be so proud of me!

Annie's Dream
I have two kids. I love them, but I never have any time to myself. If I had a free weekend, I'd stay in bed all day. I'd read magazines and watch TV. Then I'd sleep all night and my children wouldn't wake me up. Heaven!

CD3 45 He's not much good at anything!
Well, he's not much good at anything. He hasn't had a job since he graduated from school … so he doesn't have any money … so he can't buy any new clothes. He never looks well dressed. And he doesn't know what kind of job he wants. He's not ambitious at all so he doesn't apply for jobs at all. I think the problem is that he's lazy. He doesn't get up until noon. And he doesn't shave. He doesn't even shower often. He doesn't look good. Maybe that's why he doesn't have a girlfriend. He's useless!

CD3 46
If Tony had a job, he'd have money.
If he had money, he could buy some new clothes.
If he had some nice clothes, he'd look more well dressed.
If he were a little more ambitious, he would apply for more jobs.
If he weren't so lazy, he'd get up before noon.
If he shaved and showered more, he'd look better.
If he looked better, he might get a girlfriend and that would help him a lot.

CD3 47 At a crossroads

1 Jimmy's problem
J = Jimmy, A = Amy
J Amy, can I talk to you for a minute?
A Sure. What about?
J Well, you know I'm in my first year of college. I enjoy the classes. And I love what I'm studying – physics – but …
A I was waiting for a but!
J Yes, you're right! But I'm also in a band. There are three of us, and we've been playing together for a couple of years, and we just got a recording contract, which is something we've been trying to get for a long time.
A And you can't do both. Is that it?
J Exactly! The other guys want me to drop out of college. If the record was a success, we'd go on tour. We might go to Europe for three months, or we might even go to South America! That would be amazing!
A But if you dropped out of college and the band wasn't a success, then what would you do?
J Well, that's the problem! But if I don't give the band a chance, I'll regret it for the rest of my life! This is our one big chance!
A But if the band doesn't work, you won't have a career.
J And my parents would go crazy! Help me, Amy! What do I do?
A Well, I think you should give the band a try. If it doesn't work, it's not the end of the world. You could always go back to college. And you might hit it big in the music business!

2 Fiona's problem
F = Fiona, J = Jenny
F Jenny! You have to help me!
J What is it? Are you all right?
F Yes, I'm fine, but I'm having boyfriend trouble.
J What, with Sam? I thought you two were fine.
F We are, sort of. I really like Sam. We've been going out for over a year, and we do things together, but …
J But, but …
F But … I met this guy at work, and he asked me out, and I don't know what to do!
J Wow! This is so sudden!
F Well, not really. The thing is, everyone thinks that Sam and I are a couple and we're going to get married. But for me, Sam is more like a brother! I can't marry him! If I married Sam, I'd be so unhappy! But if I broke up with him, he would be heart-broken! I don't know what he'd do.
J Well, it sounds like you have to say something. If you don't tell him now, it might be worse later. Who's this man at work?
F Well, he's really nice. His name's Frank. He's my age, and he's very good-looking. We work together, and he makes me laugh. He isn't pushing me to go out with him, but …

J But you'd really like to. I know.
F And if I don't say anything to him, he might think I don't like him. So what do I do?
J Well, if I were you, I wouldn't say anything to this guy at work yet. Be nice to him, but don't encourage him.
F But he might go out with another girl!
J If he started going out with another girl, then you'd know what kind of man he was. If he likes you, he'll wait. But you have to talk to Sam …

CD3 48 A year later

Jimmy
Well, we made a record, and we went on tour in Japan, and the band's doing OK! We're not rock stars yet, but we've had one or two hits, and we're well-known in some parts of the world. We haven't been to Australia yet, but we hope to soon. And my parents have been OK. Well, my mother has. My father keeps saying, "When are you going to get a real job?" but he doesn't approve of anything I do, so that's nothing new.

Fiona
Well, I told Sam, and as a matter of fact, he was fine about it! He also said that he thought we were more like brother and sister! I was kind of upset that he wasn't more upset! Anyway, he was all right about it. And of course, all our friends said that they had seen this all along …
So I broke up with Sam, and it didn't work out with Frank at all. It turned out that he was engaged and he was just being friendly with me. So I got the situation completely wrong! Never mind. I'm single, but that's fine. I'll just see what happens.

CD3 49 My vision for the 21st century

Part 1
Generally I am optimistic about the future. If you go back to the beginning of the 19th century, most Americans lived for only about 50 years. Nowadays life expectancy is nearly 80 years. This is because of great improvements in healthcare and technology. There's no reason why this won't continue far into the 21st century. The world has changed so much in the last 20 years – we have DNA, microchips, and the Internet. We must teach people to use this new technology. I believe that one day everybody will have computers and access to the Internet.
For over 2,000 years we have tried to understand our environment. Now we are beginning to control it as well. We are learning how to control the weather and one day will learn to control earthquakes and volcanoes. Eventually illness and disease will not exist because we will build new body parts – new livers, kidneys, hearts, lungs – like spare parts for a car.
People say world population is an increasing problem, but if people become more educated and richer, they won't need or want to have so many children and the population of many countries will decrease.
I believe that one day there will be a world government because the resources of the world will have to be managed at a global level. We need to make global decisions. We already have a world language called English, and there is now a worldwide communication system called the Internet.

CD3 50

Part 2

I do have some reasons to be pessimistic. I think people will remain fundamentally the same. There will always be stupid people as well as intelligent people. There will always be cruel people who want to fight and wage wars. There will be people who don't understand that we have to take care of our world, our forests, our oceans, our atmosphere. There will certainly always be people who think that money is everything. We have the technology, but we need the wisdom to go with it.

CD3 51 Prepositions

1 It wasn't an accident. She broke it on purpose.
2 What's for dinner? I'm starving.
3 He isn't in the office this week. He's away on business.
4 When you go, keep in touch with me via email.
5 Transportation workers are on strike for better pay.
6 I don't need other people. I like being by myself.

CD3 52 Thank you and goodbye!

1 A Well, it's late. I have to be going now. Thank you so much for a wonderful evening.
 B My pleasure!
 A And the food was delicious!
 B I'm glad you liked it. I hope you get home all right. Bye!
 A Bye! And thanks again!
2 A Thank you so much! It was so nice of you.
 B You're welcome.
 A I'm so grateful for all your help.
 B Don't mention it!
 A Uh ... Would you mind helping me with just one more thing?
 B No problem.
3 A I hope you have a good flight! Who's meeting you?
 B My sister, Sarah.
 A Remember to give her my love.
 B I will. OK, it's boarding. I have to go now. Bye!
 A Take care of yourself! Bye!
4 A Thanks for having me. I really enjoyed staying with you.
 B You're welcome. It was a pleasure. Come back and see us again sometime!
 A That's very kind. Maybe next year!
 C That would be great!
5 A Have a safe trip!
 B Thanks. I'll text you when I get there.
 A Say hello to your parents for me.
 B I will. Oh! The train's leaving!
 A OK! Bye! Take care!
 B See you soon! Bye!
6 A Goodbye! And thanks for everything! It was a lot of fun!
 B I really enjoyed being your teacher.
 C We learned so much with you!
 B Thank you! Good luck with your English. Keep practicing!
 A We will!

Grammar Reference

 1.1 Tenses

This unit has examples of the Simple Present and Present Continuous, the Simple Past, and two future forms: *going to* and the Present Continuous.

All these tenses are covered again in later units.

Present tenses   Unit 2
Past tenses   Units 3 and 9
Future forms   Unit 5

The unit reviews what you already know.

Present tenses
She **lives** in New York City.
I **earn** $100 a day.
I**'m saving** money for my education.
They**'re studying** in a language school.

Past tense
They **moved** to Canada 30 years ago.
I **had** a bad accident last month.

Future forms
I**'m going to** study for a master's degree.
What **are you doing** tonight?

 1.2 Auxiliary verbs

The Present Continuous uses the auxiliary verb *to be* in all forms.

Affirmative   **Question**
She **is** reading.   **Is** she reading?
They **are** watching a movie.   What **are** they watching?

Negative
He **isn't** learning French.
I**'m not** sleeping.

Verb forms with no auxiliary verb
In the Simple Present and the Simple Past there is no auxiliary verb in the affirmative. We use the auxiliary verb *do* in the questions and negatives.

Affirmative   **Question**
They live in Australia.   **Do** they live in London?
He arrived yesterday.   Where **did** Bill go?

Negative
I **don't** work in New York.
We **didn't** watch TV.

 1.3 Questions

1   *Yes/No questions have no question word.*
    Are you hot?   *Yes, I am./No, I'm not.*
    Does he speak English?   *Yes, he does./No, he doesn't.*

2   Other questions can begin with a question word.

what	where	which	how	who	when	why	whose

    Where's the train station?
    Why are you laughing?
    Whose is this?
    How does she go to work?

3   *What, which,* and *whose* can be followed by a noun.
    What size do you wear?
    Which coat is yours?
    Whose book is this?

4   *Which* is generally used when there is a limited choice.
    Which is your pen? The black one or the blue one?

    However, this rule is not always true.

    What | *newspaper do you read?*
    Which |

5   *How* can be followed by an adjective or an adverb.
    How big is his new car?
    How quickly can you finish this?

    How can also be followed by *much* or *many.*
    How much is this sandwich?
    How many brothers and sisters do you have?

 2.1 Simple Present

Form

Affirmative and negative

I You We They	live don't live	
He She It	lives doesn't live	near here.

Question

Where	do	I you we they	live?
	does	he she it	

                               Short answer
Do you like Peter?   **Yes**, I **do**.
Does he speak French?   **No**, he **doesn't**.

Use

The Simple Present is used to express:

1   a habit.
    I **get up** at 7:30 every morning.
    Jo **eats** too much junk food.

2   a fact that is always true.
    Vegetarians **don't eat** meat.
    We **come** from Spain.

3   a fact that is true for a long time.
    I **live** in Denver.
    She **works** in a bank.

▶ 2.2 Present Continuous

Form

am/is/are + *-ing* (present participle)

Affirmative and negative

I	'm (am) 'm not	
He She It	's (is) isn't	working.
You We They	're (are) aren't	

Question

	am	I	
What	is	he she it	wearing?
	are	you we they	

Short answer

Are you going? **Yes, I am./No, I'm not.**   NOT ~~Yes, I'm.~~
Is Anna working? **Yes, she is./No, she isn't.**   NOT ~~Yes, she's.~~

Use

The Present Continuous is used to express:

1 an activity happening now.
   *They**'re playing** soccer in the yard.*
   *She can't talk now because she**'s washing** her hair.*

2 an activity happening around now, but not right exactly at the moment of speaking.
   *He**'s studying** math in college.*
   *I**'m reading** a good book right now.*

3 a planned future arrangement.
   *I**'m seeing** the doctor at 10:00 tomorrow.*
   *What **are** you **doing** this evening?*

▶ 2.3 Simple Present and Present Continuous

1 Read the right and wrong sentences.
   *Ernesto **comes** from Peru.*
   NOT ~~Ernesto is coming from Peru.~~
   *I**'m reading** a good book right now.*
   NOT ~~I read a good book right now.~~

2 Some verbs express a state, not an activity, and are usually used in the Simple Present only.
   *She **likes** the band, Arctic Monkeys.*
   NOT ~~She's liking the Arctic Monkeys.~~
   *I **know** what you mean.*
   NOT ~~I'm knowing what you mean.~~
   Similar verbs are *think, agree, understand, love.*

▶ 2.4 *have*

Form

Affirmative

I/You/We/They	have	
He/She	has	two sisters.

Negative

I/You/We/They	don't have	
He/She	doesn't have	any money.

Question

Do	I/you/we/they		
Does	he/she	have	a new car?

Short answer

Do you have an iPhone?   **Yes, I do./No, I don't.**

Note

We can't use contractions with *have.*
*I **have** a sister.*   NOT ~~I've a sister.~~

Use

1 *Have* expresses possession.

I have	a new car.
She has	three children.
He has	blond hair.

2 In the past tense, we use *had* with *did* and *didn't* for questions and negative sentences.
   ***Did** you **have** a nice weekend?*
   *I **didn't have** any money when I was a student.*

UNIT 3

 3.1 Simple Past

Form

The form of the Simple Past is the same for all persons.

Affirmative

I He/She/It You We They	finished arrived went	yesterday.

Negative

The negative of the Simple Past is formed with *didn't*.

I He/She/It You We They	didn't (did not) arrive	yesterday.

Question

The question in the Simple Past is formed with *did*.

When	did	she/you/they/etc.	arrive?

	Short answer
Did you go to work yesterday?	**Yes, I did.**
Did it rain last night?	**No, it didn't.**

Spelling of regular verbs

1   The usual rule is to add *-ed* or *-d*.
    work/work**ed**   start/start**ed**   live/live**d**   love/love**d**

2   Some short verbs with only one syllable double the last consonant.
    stop/sto**pp**ed   plan/plan**n**ed

3   For verbs ending in a consonant + *-y* , change the *-y* to *-ied*.
    study/stud**ied**   carry/carr**ied**

    But …
    play/play**ed**   enjoy/enjoy**ed**
    There are many common irregular verbs. See the list on p. 154.

Use

The Simple Past expresses a completed past action. Notice some of the time expressions.

   *We **played** tennis last Sunday.*
   *I **worked** in Seoul in 2007.*
   *John **left** two minutes ago.*

 3.2 Past Continuous

Form

was/were + verb *-ing* (present participle)

Affirmative and negative

I/He/She/It	was wasn't (was not)	working.
You/We/They	were weren't (were not)	

Question

What	was	I he she it	doing?
	were	you we they	

	Short answer
Were you working yesterday?	**Yes, I was./No, I wasn't.**

Use

1   The Past Continuous expresses a past activity that has duration.
    *I had a good time while I **was living** in Paris.*
    *You **were making** a lot of noise last night. **Were** you **having** a party?*

2   The activity was in progress *before*, and probably *after*, a time in the past.
    *"What **were** you **doing** at 8:00 last night?" "I **was watching** TV."*
    *When I woke up this morning, the sun **was shining**.*

3.3 Simple Past and Past Continuous

1   The Simple Past expresses completed past actions. The Past Continuous expresses activities in progress. Compare these sentences.
    *I **washed** my hair last night.*
    *I **was washing** my hair when you **called**.*
    *"What **did** you **do** on the weekend?" "I **played** tennis."*
    *We **were playing** tennis when it **started** to rain.*

2   A Simple Past action can interrupt a Past Continuous activity in progress.
    *When I **called** Travis, he **was taking** a shower.*
    *I **was doing** my homework when Jane **arrived**.*

3   In stories, the Past Continuous can describe the scene. The Simple Past tells the action.
    *It **was** a beautiful day. The sun **was shining** and the birds **were singing**, so we **decided** to go for a picnic. We **put** everything in the car …*

3.4 Prepositions in time expressions

at	in	on
at six o' clock at midnight at dinner	in 2007 in the evening in the summer in two weeks	on Saturday on Monday morning on New Year's Day on January 18th on the weekend
no preposition		
two weeks ago yesterday morning this afternoon	next month tomorrow morning tonight	

4.1 Expressions of quantity

Count and noncount nouns

1 Notice the difference between count and noncount nouns.

Count nouns	Noncount nouns
a cup	water
a girl	sugar
an apple	milk
an egg	music
a dollar	money

We can say *three cups, two girls, ten dollars*. We can count them. We cannot say ~~*two waters, three musics, one money*~~. We cannot count them.

2 Count nouns can be singular or plural.
*This **cup** is full.*
*These **cups are** empty.*

Noncount nouns can only be singular.
*The **water is** cold.*
*The **weather was** terrible.*

much and many

1 We use *much* with noncount nouns in questions and negatives.
*How **much money** do you have?*
*There isn't **much milk** left.*

2 We use *many* with count nouns in questions and negatives.
*How **many people** were at the party?*
*I didn't take **many pictures** on vacation.*

some and any

1 *Some* is used in affirmative sentences.
*I'd like **some** sugar.*

2 *Any* is used in questions and negatives.
*Is there **any** sugar in this tea?*
*Do you have **any** brothers and sisters?*
*We don't have **any** soap.*
*I didn't buy **any** apples.*

3 We use *some* in questions that are requests or offers.
*Can I have **some** cake?*
*Would you like **some** tea?*

4 The rules are the same for *someone, anything, anybody, somewhere*, etc.
*I have **something** for you.*
*Hello? Is **anybody** here?*
*There isn't **anywhere** to go in my town.*

a few and a little

1 We use *a few* with count nouns.
*There are **a few cookies** left, but not many.*

2 We use *a little* with noncount nouns.
*I only have **a little time**.*

a lot/lots of

1 We use *a lot/lots of* with both count and noncount nouns.
*There's **a lot of butter**.*
*I have **lots of friends**.*

2 *A lot/lots of* can be used in questions and negatives.
*Are there **lots of tourists** in your country?*
*There isn't **a lot of butter**, but there's enough.*

 4.2 Articles – a, an, and the

1 The indefinite article *a* or *an* is used with singular, count nouns to refer to a thing or an idea for the first time.
*We have **a cat** and **a dog**.*
*There's **a supermarket** on Maple Street.*

2 The definite article *the* is used with singular and plural, count and noncount nouns when both the speaker and the listener know the thing or idea already.
*We have a cat and a dog. **The cat** is old, but **the dog** is just a puppy.*
*I'm going to **the supermarket**. Do you want anything? (We both know which supermarket.)*

Indefinite article

The indefinite article is used:

1 with professions.
*I'm **a teacher**.*
*She's **an architect**.*

2 with some expressions of quantity.
a pair of ***a little*** ***a couple of*** ***a few***

3 with some expressions of frequency.
once a week ***three times a day***

4 in exclamations with *what* + a count noun.
What a beautiful day!
What a pity!

Definite article

The definite article is used:

1 before oceans, rivers, hotels, theaters, museums, and newspapers.
the Atlantic ***the Guggenheim Museum***
The Times ***the Ritz***

2 if there is only one of something.
the sun ***the president*** ***the government***

3 with superlative adjectives.
*He's **the richest man** in the world.*
*Jane's **the oldest** in the class.*

No article

There is no article:

1 before plural and noncount nouns when talking about things in general.
I like potatoes.
Milk is good for you.

2 before countries, towns, streets, languages, magazines, meals, airports, train or bus stations, and mountains.
I had lunch with John.
I bought Cosmopolitan at Penn Station.

3 before some places and with some forms of transportation.

at home	in/to bed	at/to work
at/to school/college	by bus	by plane
by car	by train	on foot

*She goes to work **by bus**.*
*I was **at home** yesterday evening.*

4 in exclamations with *What* + a noncount noun.
***What** beautiful **weather**!* ***What** loud **music**!*

Note
In the phrase *go home*, there is no article and no preposition.
*I went **home** early.* NOT ~~*I went to home.*~~

5.1 Verb patterns

Here are four verb patterns. There is a list of verb patterns on p. 154.

1 Verb + infinitive
   *They **want to buy** a new car.*   *I'd **like to go** abroad.*

2 Verb + -*ing*
   *We **love going** to parties.*   *I **enjoy traveling** abroad.*

3 Verb + -*ing* or + infinitive with no change in meaning
   *It **started to rain/raining**.*
   *I **continued to work/working** in the library.*

4 Verb + preposition + -*ing*
   *We're **thinking of moving** to a new house.*
   *I'm **looking forward to having** more free time.*

like doing and *would like to do*

1 *Like doing* and *love doing* express a general enjoyment.
   *I **like working** as a teacher.* = I am a teacher and I enjoy it.
   *I **love dancing**.* = This is one of my hobbies.

2 *Would like to do* and *would love to do* express a preference now or at a specific time.
   *I'd **like to be** a teacher.* = When I grow up, I want to be a teacher.
   *Thanks. I'd **love to dance**.* = At a party. I'm glad you asked me.

Question	Short answer
Would you like to dance?	*Yes, I would./Yes, I'd love to.*
Would you like to go for a walk?	*Yes, I would./No, thank you.*

Note
No, I wouldn't is not common because it is impolite.

 ## 5.2 Future forms

will

Form

will + base form
Will is a modal auxiliary verb. There is an introduction to modal auxiliary verbs on p. 143. The forms of *will* are the same for all persons.

Affirmative and negative

I/He/She/It/You/We/They	'll (will) won't	come. help you. invite Tom.

Question
*What time **will** he **be back**?*

Short answer
Will you help me?   **Yes, I will.**

Note
No, I won't is impolite as an answer to a request. It means "I don't want to help you."
A polite way of saying "no" to a request is "*I'm afraid I can't.*"
"*Will you give me a ride?*" "*Sorry, **I'm afraid I can't.**"

Use

Will is used:

1 to express a future intention made *at* the moment of speaking.
   "*It's Jane's birthday.*" "*Is it? I'll buy her some flowers.*"
   *I'll **give** you my phone number.*
   "*Do you want the blue or the red pen?*" "*I'll **take** the red one.*"

2 to express an offer.
   *I'll **carry** your suitcase.*   *We'll **wash** the dishes.*"

3 to express a future fact. The speaker thinks it is sure to happen in the future.
   *I'll **be** 30 next week.*   *It will **be** a nice day tomorrow.*

The speaker is talking about the future without expressing an intention, plan, or personal opinion.

going to

Form

am/is/are + *going* + *to* + base form

Affirmative and negative

I	'm (am) 'm not	
He/She/It	's (is) isn't	going to leave.
You We They	're (are) aren't	

Question

When	am	I	
	is	he/she/it	going to arrive?
	are	you/we/they	

Short answer
Are they going to get married?   **Yes, they are./No, they aren't.**

Use

Going to is used:

1 to express a future decision, intention, or plan made *before* the moment of speaking.
   *How long **are** they **going to stay** in Tokyo?*
   *She **isn't going to have** a birthday party.*

2 when we can see or feel now that something is certain to happen in the future.
   *Look at these clouds! It's **going to rain**.*
   *Watch out! You're **going to drop** that vase.*

will or *going to*?

Look at the use of *will* and *going to* in these sentences.

*I'm **going to make** chicken for dinner.*
(I decided this morning and bought everything for it.)
*What can I cook for dinner? Uh ... I know! I'll **make** a chicken casserole!* (I decided at the moment of speaking.)

Present Continuous

The Present Continuous for the future is used:

1 to express a planned future arrangement.
   *I'm **meeting** my cousin for lunch.*
   "*What **are** you **doing** this weekend?*"
   "*We're **having** a party. Can you come?*"

2 with the verbs *go* and *come*.
   *She's **coming** on Friday.*
   *I'm **going** home early tonight.*

Sometimes there is little or no difference between *going to* and the Present Continuous to express a future arrangement.
*We're **seeing** a movie this evening.*
*We're **going to** see a movie this evening.*

UNIT 6

 6.1 What ... like?

Form

what + to be + subject + like?

A *What's your teacher* **like?**
A *What are his parents* **like?**
A *What was your vacation* **like?**
A *What were the beaches* **like?**

B *She's very patient.*
B *They're very kind.*
B *Wonderful. We swam a lot.*
B *OK, but a little small.*

Note

1 We don't use *like* in the answer.
   She's patient.   NOT   ~~*She's like patient.*~~

2 *Like* in this question is a preposition, not a verb:
   "What's Jim **like?***" "He's intelligent and kind, and very good-looking."*

3 In these sentences *like* is a verb:
   "What does Jim **like?***" "He* **likes** *motorcyles and playing tennis."*

Use

1 *What ... like?* means "Describe somebody or something. Tell me about it. I don't know anything about it."

2 *How's your mother?* asks about health. It doesn't ask for a description.
   "How's your mother?" "She's doing well, thank you."

 6.2 Comparative and superlative adjectives

Form

1 Look at the chart.

		Comparative	Superlative
Short adjectives	cheap small *big	cheaper smaller bigger	cheapest smallest biggest
Adjectives that end in -y	funny early heavy	funnier earlier heavier	funniest earliest heaviest
Adjectives with two syllables or more	careful boring expensive interesting	more careful more boring more expensive more interesting	most careful most boring most expensive most interesting
Irregular adjectives	far good bad	farther/further better worse	farthest/furthest best worst

*For short adjectives that end with consonant + vowel + consonant, double the last consonant: *hot/hotter/hottest*; *fat/fatter/fattest*.

2 *Than* is often used after a comparative adjective.
   I'm **younger than** *Barbara.*
   Barbara's **more intelligent than** *Sarah.*

   Much can come before the comparative to give emphasis.
   She's **much nicer than** *her sister.*
   Is Tokyo **much more modern than** *New York?*

3 *The* is used before superlative adjectives.
   He's **the funniest** *boy in the class.*
   Which is **the tallest** *building in the world?*

Use

1 Comparatives compare one thing, person, or action with another.
   She's **taller** *than me.*
   San Francisco's **more expensive** *than San Diego.*

2 We use superlatives to compare somebody or something with the whole group.
   She's the **tallest** *in the class.*
   It's the **most expensive** *hotel in the world.*

3 *As ... as* shows that something is the same or equal.
   Jim's **as tall as** *Peter.*
   I'm **as worried as** *you are.*

4 *Not as ... as* shows that something isn't the same or equal.
   She **isn't as tall as** *her mother.*
   He **isn't as smart as** *me!*

UNIT 7

7.1 Present Perfect

Form

have/has + past participle
The past participle of regular verbs ends in *-ed*. There are many common irregular verbs. See the list on p. 154.

Affirmative and negative

I You/We/They	've (have) haven't	won a competition.
He/She/It	's (has) hasn't	

Question

Have	I you/we/they	been to the United States?
Has	he/she/it	

Have you been to Las Vegas?
Has she ever written a novel?

Short answer
Yes, I have./No, I haven't.
Yes, she has./No, she hasn't.

Note

We cannot use contractions in short answers.
Yes, I have.   NOT   ~~*Yes, I've.*~~
Yes, we have.   NOT   ~~*Yes, we've.*~~

Use

1 The Present Perfect expresses an action or state that began in the past and continues to the present.
   I've known *John for six years.*
   How long **have** *you* **worked** *for the New York Daily News?*

   The time expressions *for* and *since* are common with this use.
   We use *for* with a period of time, and *since* with a point in time.
   We've lived here **for** *three years.* (a period of time)
   They've lived here **since** *2010.* (a point in time)

Note

In many languages, this use is expressed by a present tense. But in English, we say:

*Peter **has been** a teacher for ten years.*
NOT *Peter is a teacher for ten years.*

2 The Present Perfect connects the present and the past. It expresses experiences in life before now.

*I've **met** a lot of famous people.* (before now)
*She **has won** a lot of awards.* (in her life)
*I've **traveled** a lot in Africa.* (in my life)
*She's **written** three books.* (up to now)

The action can continue to the present, and probably into the future.

*He's **made** six TV shows.* (He'll probably make more.)

Ever and *never* are common with this use.

*Have you **ever** been to Africa?*
*I've **never** played Flappy Bird.*

3 The Present Perfect expresses a past action with results in the present. It is often a recent past action.

*I've **lost** my wallet.* (I don't have it now.)
*The taxi's **arrived**.* (It's outside the door now.)
***Has** the mail carrier delivered the mail?* (Is there mail for me?)

The adverbs *already* and *yet* are common with this use.

Yet is used in questions and negatives.

*I've **already** had breakfast.*
*Has the mail carrier delivered the mail **yet**?*
*It's 11:00 and she hasn't gotten up **yet**.*

 ## 7.2 Present Perfect and Simple Past

1 Read and compare the use of the Simple Past and the Present Perfect in these sentences.

*I **lived** in Paris for two years, from 2007–2009.* (The action is finished.)
*I've **lived** in London since 2009.* (I still do. The action is not finished.)
*I've **been** to South Korea.* (This is an experience in my life.)
*I **went** with my husband two years ago.* (At a definite past time.)
*"**Have** you **ever flown** in a helicopter?" "Yes, I **have**."*
*"Where **did** you **fly**?" "I **flew** over New York."*

2 These are common time expressions used with the Simple Past and the Present Perfect.

Simple Past	Present Perfect
last week	since Monday
yesterday	ever
the day before yesterday	never
in 1999	already
on July 21st	yet
three months ago	for two weeks (and continues)
for two weeks (but now ended)	

UNIT 8

8.1 *have to*

Form

has/have + *to* + base form

Affirmative and negative

I You/We/They	have don't have	to	work hard.
He/She/It	has doesn't have		

Question

Do Does	I/you/we/they	have to	work hard?
	he/she/it		

	Short answer
*Do you **have to** wear a uniform?*	*Yes, I **do**.*
*Does he **have to** pay with cash?*	*No, he **doesn't**.*

Past of *have to*

The past tense of *have to* is *had to*, with *did* and *didn't* in the question and negative.

*I **had to** get up early this morning.*
*Why **did** you **have to** work last weekend?*
*I **didn't have to** do any housework when I was a child.*

Use

1 *Have to* expresses strong obligation. The obligation comes from "outside" – a law, a rule at school or work, or someone in authority.

*You **have to** pass a driver's test if you want to drive a car.* (That's the law.)
*I **have to** start work at 8:00.* (My company says so.)
*The doctor says I **have to** exercise more.*

2 *Don't/doesn't have to* expresses absence of obligation (it isn't necessary).

*You **don't have to** wash the dishes. We have a dishwasher.*
*She **doesn't have to** work tomorrow. It's Saturday.*
*I **didn't have to** get up early this morning, but I did because I couldn't go back to sleep.*

8.2 Introduction to modal auxiliary verbs

Form

These are modal auxiliary verbs.

can	could	must	should	will	would

They have certain things in common:

1 They go with another verb and add meaning.
*He **can** play the guitar.*
*I **must** wash my hair.*

2 There is no *s* in the third person singular. The form is the same for all persons.
*She **can dance** very well.*
*He **should try** harder.*
*It **will rain** soon.*
*We **must hurry**.*

3 There is no *do/does* in the question.
Can** she **sing?
***Should** we **go** now?*

4 There is no *don't/doesn't* in the negative.
*I **wouldn't** like to be a teacher.*
*They **can't** speak French.*

Note
will not = won't
*It **won't** rain tomorrow.*

5 Most modal verbs refer to the present and future. Only the past tense form of *can, could,* refers to the past.
*I **could** swim when I was three.*

 8.3 *should*

Form

should + base form
The forms of *should* are the same for all persons.

Affirmative and negative

I You/We/They He/She	should shouldn't	exercise more. tell lies.

Question
***Should** I/she/they see a doctor?*
*Do you think I/he/we **should** see a doctor?*

	Short answer
Should I call home?	**Yes, you should.**
Should I buy a motorcycle?	**No, you shouldn't.**

Use

1 *Should* is used to express what the speaker thinks is the best thing to do. It expresses mild obligation, or advice.
*I **should** do more work.* (This is my opinion.)
*You **should** do more work.* (This is my advice.)
*Do you think we **should** stop?* (I'm asking for your opinion.)

2 *Shouldn't* also expresses advice.
*You **shouldn't** sit so close to the TV. It's bad for your eyes.*

3 *Should* expresses the opinion of the speaker, and it is often introduced by *I think* or *I don't think.*
***I think** politicians **should** listen more.*
***I don't think** people **should** get married until they're 21.*

 8.4 *must*

Form

must + base form
The forms of *must* are the same for all persons.

Afffirmative and negative

I You/We/They He/She	must must not	try harder. steal.

Note
Questions with *must* are possible, but *have to* is more common.
*What time **do we have to** leave?*

Use

1 *Must* expresses strong obligation. Generally, this obligation comes from "inside" the speaker.
*I **must** take a shower.* (I think this is necessary.)
*We **must** get going.*

2 *You must …* can express a strong suggestion.
*You **must** see the Monet exhibition. It's wonderful.*
*You **must** give me a call when you're in town again.*

9.1 Past perfect

Form

had + past participle.
The past participle of regular verbs ends in *-ed*. There are many common irregular verbs. See the list on p. 154.

Affirmative and negative

I He/She/It You/We/They	'd (had) hadn't	arrived.

Question

Had	I he/she/it you/we/they	left already?

Short answer
Yes, I **had**.
No, they **hadn't**.

Use

1 We use the Past Perfect to express a past action that happened before another action in the past.
   *When I arrived at the theater, the play **had** already **started**.*

2 We use the Simple Past to express actions in the order they happened. Look at these actions in the Simple Past.

Action 1	Action 2
*The bear **went**.*	*The man **came** down from the tree.*
*John **left** the party.*	*I **arrived**.*
*They **walked** a long way.*	*They **were** tired.*

   Notice how they are expressed using the Past Perfect.

Action 2	Action 1
The man came down from the tree …	*after the bear **had gone**.*
When I arrived at the party …	*John **had left**.*
They were tired …	*because they'**d walked** a long way.*

3 If it is clear that one action was completed before, it isn't necessary to use the Past Perfect.
   *I cleaned up after everyone **went** home.*
   *I cleaned up after everyone **had gone** home.*

 9.2 Conjunctions

We use conjunctions to join sentences.

1 *When, while, as soon as, after, before, as,* and *until,* are conjunctions of time. They can go in two places in the sentence.
   ***When** I arrived home, Tom was making dinner.*
   *Tom was talking to me **while** he was making dinner.*
   ***As soon as** I arrived home, Tom started making dinner.*
   *Tom made dinner **after** I arrived/I'd arrived home.*
   *He had made dinner **before** I arrived home.*
   ***As** he was talking, I was thinking about the last time we'd met.*
   *He didn't start making dinner **until** I arrived home.*

2 *So* is a conjunction of result.
   *He was bored **so** he went for a walk.*
   Because is a conjunction of reason.
   *He went for a walk **because** he was bored.*

3 *But* and *although* are conjunctions that join contrasting ideas.
   *It was raining, **but** we played tennis.*
   ***Although** it was raining, we played tennis.*

 9.3 *so, such (a), so many, so much*

Form

***so* + adjective/adverb**
*I was **so** scared.*
*He always drives **so** slowly.*

***such a* + adjective + singular count noun**
*She's **such a** nice person.*

***such* + adjective + plural/noncount noun**
*The Smiths are **such** friendly neighbors.*

***so many* + plural nouns**
*Some children have **so many** toys.*

***so much* + uncountable nouns**
*Basketball players earn **so much** money these days.*

Use

So and *such* are used for emphasizing an adjective or noun. They are used more in spoken than written English. They are often exclamations, with an exclamation mark (!).
He works so hard! is stronger than *He works very hard.*

UNIT 10

 10.1 The passive

Form

am/is/are was/were has/have been will	past participle

The past participle of regular verbs ends in *-ed*. There are many common **irregular past participles**. See the list on p. 158.

Present
*English **is spoken** all over the world.*
*33 million cell phones **are thrown away** every year.*
*Fiat cars **aren't made** in France.*
*Where **is** coffee **grown**?*

Past
*The first text message **was sent** in 1992.*
*They **weren't injured** in the accident.*
*When **was** television **invented**?*

Present Perfect

*A lot of new features **have been added**.*
*The bank's **been robbed**!*
*We **haven't been invited** to the wedding.*

will

*Many cars **will be produced** next year.*
*The cars **won't be sold** in the US.*

Short answers

Are cars made in your country?   ***Yes**, they **are**./**No**, they **aren't**.*
Has my car been repaired?   ***Yes**, it **has**./**No**, it **hasn't**.*
Will landline phones be replaced   ***Yes**, they **will**./**No**, they **won't**.*
*   by cell phones?*

Note

The passive infinitive (*be* + past participle) is used after modal auxiliary verbs and other verbs that are followed by an infinitive.
*Driving should **be banned** in the downtown areas of cities.*
*The house is going **to be knocked down**.*

Use

1 The rules for tense usage in the passive are the same as in the active.
Simple Present to express habit:
*My car **is serviced** regularly.*

Simple Past to express a finished action in the past:
*America **was discovered** by Christopher Columbus.*

Present Perfect to express an action that began in the past and continues to the present:
*"Smartphones" **have been sold** since 2007.*

2 The object of an active verb becomes the subject of a passive verb. Notice the use of *by* in the passive sentence.

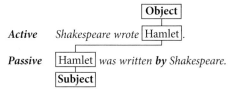

3 The passive is not just another way of expressing the same sentence in a different way. We choose the active or the passive depending on what we are more interested in.
*Hamlet **was written** in 1600.* (We are more interested in *Hamlet*.)
*Shakespeare **wrote** Hamlet in 1600.* (We are more interested in who wrote it.)

Note

The subject of an active sentence is not mentioned in the passive sentence if it is not really important.

Active	*People speak German in parts of Italy.*
Passive	*German is spoken in parts of Italy.*
	NOT ~~*German is spoken in parts of Italy by people.*~~

▶ 11.1 Present Perfect Continuous

Form

has/have + been + -ing (present participle)

Affirmative and negative

I You We They	've (have) haven't	been working.
He She It	's (has) hasn't	

Question

How long	have	I you we they	been working?
	has	he she it	

	Short answer
Have you been running?	***Yes**, I **have**./**No**, I **haven't**.*

Use

The Present Perfect Continuous is used:

1 to express an activity that began in the past and continues to the present.
*He's **been teaching** music for years.*
*It's **been raining** for days.*

2 to refer to an activity with a result in the present.
*I'm hot because I've **been running**.*
*I don't have any money because I've **been shopping**.*

Note

1 Sometimes there is little or no difference in meaning between the Present Perfect and the Present Perfect Continuous.
*How long **have you worked** here?*
*How long **have you been working** here?*

2 Some verbs have the idea of a long time – *wait, work, learn, travel, play*.
These verbs can often be used in the Present Perfect Continuous.
*I've **been waiting** for hours.*
Some verbs don't have the idea of a long time – *find, start, buy, die, lose, break, stop*. It is unusual to find these in the Present Perfect Continuous.
*I've **bought** a new dress.*
*My cat **has died**.*
*My radio's **broken**.*

3 Verbs that express a state – *like, love, know, have* (for possession), are not found in the Present Perfect Continuous.
*We've **known** each other for a few weeks.*
NOT ~~*We've been knowing each other for a few weeks.*~~

4 If the sentence gives a number or a quantity, the Present Perfect is used.
*I've **been writing** emails all morning. I've **written** twenty.*
NOT ~~*I've been writing twenty.*~~

12.1 First conditional

Form

If + Simple Present, *will* + base form

Affirmative and negative

If I work hard, I'll pass my exams.
If we don't hurry up, we'll be late.
If you're late, I won't wait for you.

Question

What will you do if you don't go to college?

	Short answer
Will you go to college if you get good grades?	*Yes, I will.*
	No, I won't.

Notes

1 We use the Simple Present in the condition clause, not a future form.
   If it rains, I'll stay home.   NOT *If it will rain …*
   If I work hard, I'll pass.   NOT *If I'll work hard …*

2 The condition clause (*if*) can come at the beginning of the sentence or at the end. Notice the use of the comma.
   If I work hard, I'll pass my exams. (comma)
   I'll pass my exams if I work hard. (no comma)

Use

The first conditional is used to express a possible condition and a probable result in the future.
If it's sunny, we'll go for a picnic.
You'll get wet if you don't take an umbrella.

If and when

If expresses a possibility that something will happen.
When expresses what the speaker sees as certain to happen.
When I get home, I'll take a shower.   NOT *If I get home*

 12.2 might

Form

might + base form
Might is a modal auxiliary verb. For modal auxiliary verbs, see p. 139.
The forms of *might* are the same for all persons.

Affirmative and negative

I He/She/It You We They	might might not	go to the party. be late. rain tomorrow. go out for dinner tonight.

Note

The negative is often expressed with *I don't think + will*.
I don't think it'll rain tomorrow.

Question

The inverted question *Might you …?* is unusual. Instead, ask *Do you think … + will …?*

Do you think	it'll rain? they'll come to our party?

	Short answer
Do you think it'll rain?	*It might.*

Use

Might is used to express a future possibility. It means *will perhaps*. It contrasts with *will*, which expresses a future certainty.
The Yankees will win the game. (I am sure they will.)
The Yankees might win the game. (It's possible, but I'm not sure.)

 12.3 Second conditional

Form

If + Simple Past, *would* + base form
Would is a modal auxiliary verb. For modal auxiliary verbs, see p. 139.
The forms of *would* are the same for all persons.

Affirmative and negative

If I had more money, I'd (would) buy a new computer.
If she knew the answer, she'd tell us.
If we didn't like you, we wouldn't talk to you.

Question

What would you do if you had a year off?

	Short answer
Would you travel around the world?	*Yes, I would.*
	No, I wouldn't.
If they had the money, would they buy a new car?	*Yes, they would.*
	No, they wouldn't.

Notes

1 As with the first conditional, the condition clause can come at the beginning or the end of the sentence. Again, notice the use of the comma.
   If I had more time, I'd help.
   I'd help if I had more time.

2 *Were* is often used for singular subjects instead of *was* in the condition clause.
   If I were you, I'd go to bed.
   If he were taller, he'd be a police officer.

3 The use of the past tense (*If I had*) and *would* does not refer to past time. It expresses distance from the present because it is not real.
   If I had … (but I actually don't have …)
   I would … (but I actually won't …)

Use

1 The second conditional is used to express an unreal or improbable condition and its result. The use of the past forms show that it is not real.
   If I were the president, I'd stop all wars.
   (But I'm not the president. = reality)
   If I lived in a big house, I'd have a party.
   (But I live in a small apartment.)

2 The phrase, *If I were you, I'd …*, is often used to give advice.
   If I were you, I'd call the doctor.

First and second conditional

The first conditional is possible and probable.
The second conditional is improbable and sometimes impossible.
If I win the tennis match, I'll be so happy. (I think it's possible.)
If I won the tennis match, I'd be so happy. (But I don't think I will.)

Word List

Here is a list of most of the new words in the units of *American Headway* Student Book 2, Third edition.

adj = adjective
adv = adverb
conj = conjunction
coll = colloquial
n = noun
opp = opposite

pl = plural
prep = preposition
pron = pronoun
pp = past participle
v = verb
US = American English

 UNIT 1

aboriginal *adj* /ˌæbəˈrɪdʒənl/
accident *n* /ˈæksədənt/
amazing *adj* /əˈmeɪzɪŋ/
another time /əˈnʌðər taɪm/
apartment *n* /əˈpɑrtmənt/
art gallery *n* /ˈɑrt ˈgæləri/
as many as /əz ˈmɛni əz/
attractive *adj* /əˈtræktɪv/
blind date *n* /ˌblaɪnd ˈdeɪt/
borrow *v* /ˈbɑroʊ/
Bulgaria *n* /bʌlˈgɛriə/
charity *n* /ˈtʃærəti/
check-up *n* /ˈtʃɛk ʌp/
cheek *n* /tʃik/
Cheers! /tʃɪrz/
chopsticks *pl n* /ˈtʃɑpstɪks/
coach *n* /koʊtʃ/
cosmopolitan *adj* /ˌkɑzməˈpɑlətn/
couple *n* /ˈkʌpl/
dates *pl n* /deɪts/
don't worry /doʊnt ˈwəri/
embarrass *v* /ɪmˈbærəs/
exchange *v* /ɪksˈtʃeɪndʒ/
excited *adj* /ɪkˈsaɪtəd/
first impressions *n* /fərst ɪmˈprɛʃnz/
fine thanks /faɪn θæŋks/
gang *n* /gæŋ/
guess *v* /gɛs/
greet *v* /grit/
Have a good weekend! /hæv ə gʊd ˈwikɛnd/
hurry *n* /ˈhəri/
impress *v* /ɪmˈprɛs/
interview *n* /ˈɪntərˌvyu/
mainly *adv* /ˈmeɪnli/
marathon *n* /ˈmærəˌθɑn/
master's degree *n* /ˈmæstərz dɪˈgri/
messenger *n* /ˈmɛsəndʒər/
mistakes *pl n* /mɪˈsteɪks/
more and more /mɔr ənd mɔr/
nervous *adj* /ˈnərvəs/
nice to meet you /ˈnaɪs tə mit yu/
noise *n* /nɔɪz/
Not a great look! /ˈnɑt ə greɪt lʊk/
nothing much /ˈnʌθɪŋ mʌtʃ/
notice *n* /ˈnoʊtəs/
oldest *adj* /ˈoʊldɪst/
opening *n* /ˈoʊpənɪŋ/
percentage *n* /pərˈsɛntɪdʒ/
progress *n* /prəˈgrɛs/
raisins *pl n* /ˈreɪznz/
readers *pl n* /ˈridərz/

reporter *n* /rɪˈpɔrtər/
seat *n* /sit/
shake *v* /ʃeɪk/
shapes *pl n* /ʃeɪps/
show around *v* /ʃoʊ əˈraʊnd/
Shut up! /ʃʌt ˈʌp/
signs *pl n* /saɪnz/
so many things /soʊ ˈmɛni θɪŋz/
successful *adj* /səkˈsɛsfl/
sunshine *n* /ˈsʌnʃaɪn/
survey *n* /ˈsərveɪ/
table manners *pl n* /ˈteɪbl ˈmænərz/
terrible *adj* /ˈtɛrəbl/
that's ok /ðæts oʊˈkeɪ/
theater *n* /ˈθiətər/
to have in common *v* /tə hæv ɪn ˈkɑmən/
train *v* /treɪn/
trip *n* /trɪp/
Turkish *adj* /ˈtərkɪʃ/
wear *v* /wɛr/
wise *adj* /waɪz/
worry *v* /ˈwəri/
Wow! /waʊ/
you're welcome /yɔr ˈwɛlkəm/

 UNIT 2

actually *adv* /ˈæktʃuəli/
afraid *adj* /əˈfreɪd/
architect *n* /ˈɑrkətɛkt/
article *n* /ˈɑrtɪkl/
audience *n* /ˈɔdiəns/
average *n* /ˈævrɪdʒ/
behave *v* /bɪˈheɪv/
bow tie *n* /ˈboʊ taɪ/
Cheer up! /tʃɪr ʌp/
chill out *v* /tʃɪlˈaʊt/
comedy clubs *pl n* /ˈkɑmədi klʌbz/
currently *adv* /ˈkərəntli/
deaf *adj* /dɛf/
depend on *v* /dɪˈpɛnd ɑn/
depressed *adj* /dɪˈprɛst/
download *v* /ˈdaʊnloʊd/
dress up *v* /drɛsˈʌp/
envious *adj* /ˈɛnviəs/
extraordinary *adj* /ɪkˈstrɔrdnɛri/
feel at home /fil ət hoʊm/
fortune *n* /ˈfɔrtʃən/
gig *n* /gɪg/
grateful *adj* /ˈgreɪtfl/
grow *v* /groʊ/

happiness *n* /ˈhæpinəs/
health *n* /hɛlθ/
huge *adj* /hyudʒ/
image *n* /ˈɪmɪdʒ/
inspiration *n* /ˌɪnspəˈreɪʃn/
jealous *adj* /ˈdʒɛləs/
jogging *n* /ˈdʒɑgɪŋ/
jokes *pl n* /dʒoʊks/
marketing *n* /ˈmɑrkətɪŋ/
messy *adj* /ˈmɛsi/
Mind your own business! /ˈmaɪnd yər oʊn ˌbɪznəs/
neighbors *pl n* /ˈneɪbərz/
obviously *adv* /ˈɑbviəsli/
online sales *pl n* /ˌɑnˈlaɪn seɪlz/
on the way /ɑn ðə weɪ/
opportunity *n* /ˌɑpərˈtunəti/
ordinary *adj* /ˈɔrdnɛri/
planning *n* /ˈplænɪŋ/
pleasure *n* /ˈplɛʒər/
reach for your dreams /ritʃ fər yər drimz/
recognize *v* /ˈrɛkəgˌnaɪz/
relationship *n* /rɪˈleɪʃnʃɪp/
remarkable *adj* /rɪˈmɑrkəbl/
satisfaction *n* /ˌsætəsˈfækʃn/
saxophone *n* /ˈsæksəfoʊn/
score *n* /skɔr/
selling *n* /ˈsɛlɪŋ/
sewing tips *pl n* /ˈsoʊɪŋ tɪps/
stand up comic *n* /stændʌp ˈkɑmɪk/
stressed *adj* /strɛst/
suspicious *adj* /səˈspɪʃəs/
take a nap /teɪk ə næp/
tour *v* /tʊr/
unemployed *adj* /ˌʌnɪmˈplɔɪd/
unusual *adj* /ʌnˈyuʒuəl/
young people *pl n* /yʌŋ ˈpipl/

 UNIT 3

activate *v* /ˈæktəˌveɪt/
admire *v* /ədˈmaɪər/
adventure *n* /ədˈvɛntʃər/
adventurer *n* /ədˈvɛntʃərər/
appreciate *v* /əˈpriʃiˌeɪt/
argument *n* /ˈɑrgyəmənt/
beat *v* /bit/
bin *n* /bɪn/
bite *n* /baɪt/
bleed *v* /blid/
cabin crew member *n* /ˈkæbən kru ˈmɛmbər/
chute *n* /ʃut/
coast *n* /koʊst/
companion *n* /kəmˈpænyən/
crime *n* /kraɪm/
damage *v* /ˈdæmɪdʒ/
dangerous *adj* /ˈdeɪndʒərəs/
dearly *adv* /ˈdɪrli/
endanger *v* /ɪnˈdeɪndʒər/
enormous *adj* /ɪˈnɔrməs/
explode *v* /ɪkˈsploʊd/
explosion *n* /ɪkˈsploʊʒn/
fame *n* /feɪm/
fangs *pl n* /fæŋz/
flight attendant *n* /flaɪt əˈtɛndənt/
folk hero *n* /foʊk ˈhɪroʊ/
forest *n* /ˈfɔrəst/
forestry *adj* /ˈfɔrəstri/
fountain *n* /ˈfaʊntn/
furiously *adv* /ˈfyʊriəsli/
guide *n* /gaɪd/
guns *pl n* /gʌnz/
half-time *n* /ˌhæf ˈtaɪm/
hammock *n* /ˈhæmək/
headline *n* /ˈhɛdlaɪn/
hostile *adj* /ˈhɑstl/
injured *adj* /ˈɪndʒərd/
jungle *n* /ˈdʒʌŋgl/
knives *pl n* /naɪvz/
land *v* /lænd/
length *n* /lɛŋkθ/
lost his cool /lɔst hɪz kul/
monkeys *pl n* /ˈmʌŋkiz/
overhead *adj* /ˈoʊvərˌhɛd/
PA system *n* /pi ˈeɪ sɪstəm/
permission *n* /pərˈmɪʃn/
quit *v* /kwɪt/
react *v* /riˈækt/
record *v* /rɪˈkɔrd/
refuse *v* /rɪˈfyuz/
robbery *n* /ˈrɑbəri/
runway *n* /ˈrʌnweɪ/
sleeping pill *n* /ˈslipɪŋ pɪl/

snake *n* /sneɪk/
source *n* /sɔrs/
star *v* /star/
strike *n* /straɪk/
sympathy *n* /'sɪmpəθi/
taxiing *v* /'tæksiɪŋ/
temper *n* /'tɛmpər/
terrified *adj* /'tɛrə,faɪd/
theft *n* /θɛft/
thieves *pl n* /θivz/
tribe *n* /traɪb/
trip *n* /trɪp/
vase *n* /veɪs/
web page *n* /'wɛb peɪdʒ/
worldwide *adj* /'wɔrldwaɪd/

UNIT 4

allergic *adj* /ə'lərdʒɪk/
ambition *n* /æm'bɪʃn/
aspirin *n* /'æsprən/
automated *adj* /'ɔtəmeɪtɪd/
beauty *n* /'byuti/
bottled water *n* /'batld wɔtər/
branches *pl n* /'bræntʃɪz/
breeze *n* /briz/
broccoli *n* /'brakli/
brochure *n* /broʊ'ʃʊr/
calorie *n* /'kæləri/
cans *pl n* /kænz/
clam *n* /klæm/
complain *v* /kəm'pleɪn/
connect *v* /kə'nɛkt/
convenience store *n* /kən'vinyəns stɔr/
coral *n* /'kɔrəl/
courage *n* /'kərɪdʒ/
crane *n* /kreɪn/
crystal-blue *adj* /'krɪstl blu/
dairy *n* /'dɛri/
debit card *n* /'dɛbət kard/
decaffeinated *adj* /,di'kæfə,neɪtəd/
decor *n* /deɪ'kɔr/
delicious *adj* /dɪ'lɪʃəs/
descend *v* /dɪ'sɛnd/
dessert *n* /dɪ'zərt/
diners *pl n* /'daɪnərz/
disappointed *adj* /,dɪsə'pɔɪntəd/
excitement *n* /ɪk'saɪtmənt/
expressions *pl n* /ɪk'sprɛʃnz/
fasten *v* /'fæsn/
fry *v* /fraɪ/
give (someone) a ride *v* /gɪv ə raɪd/
grill *v* /grɪl/
gum *n* /gʌm/
hang *v* /hæŋ/
heights *n* /haɪts/
help yourself /hɛlp yər'sɛlf/
homemade *adj* /,hoʊm'meɪd/
honeymoon *n* /'hʌni,mun/
lend *v* /lɛnd/
limit *n* /'lɪmət/
loaf *n* /loʊf/
loudly *adv* /'laʊdli/
magical *adj* /'mædʒɪkl/

mail carrier *n* /meɪl 'kæriər/
Maldives *n* /'mɔldɪvz/
mangoes *pl n* /'mæŋgoʊz/
meaning *n* /'minɪŋ/
middle *n* /'mɪdl/
nuts *pl n* /nʌts/
patent *n* /'pætnt/
pharmacy *n* /'farməsi/
pick up *v* /pɪk 'ʌp/
platform *n* /'plætfɔrm/
pots *pl n* /pats/
programmer *n* /'proʊgræmər/
raw *adj* /rɔ/
restriction *n* /rɪ'strɪkʃn/
retire *v* /rɪ'taɪər/
roast *v* /roʊst/
robots *pl n* /'roʊbats/
romantic *adj* /roʊ'mæntɪk/
round *adj* /raʊnd/
seat belts *pl n* /'sit bɛlts/
serving *n* /'sərvɪŋ/
sharks *pl n* /ʃarks/
shellfish *n* /'ʃɛlfɪʃ/
sitting *n* /'sɪtɪŋ/
slices *pl n* /slaɪsɪz/
snack bar *n* /'snæk bar/
software *n* /'sɔftwɛr/
spectacular *adj* /spɛk'tækyələr/
speechless *adj* /'spitʃləs/
spiral stairs *pl n* /'spaɪrəl stɛrz/
steam *v* /stim/
sting rays *pl n* /'stɪŋreɪz/
sunken *adj* /'sʌŋkən/
tap water *n* /'tæp wɔtər/
tip *n* /tɪp/
touch-screen *n* /'tʌtʃ skrin/
tropical fish *pl n* /'trapɪkl fɪʃ/
turtles *pl n* /'tərtlz/
underwater *adj* /,ʌndər'wɔtər/
veterinarian *n* /,vɛtərə'nɛriən/
weigh *v* /weɪ/

advertise *v* /'ædvər,taɪz/
amazed *adj* /ə'meɪzd/
apply *v* /ə'plaɪ/
arrange *v* /ə'reɪndʒ/
Belarus *n* /,bɛlə'rus/
bike riding *n* /'baɪk raɪdɪŋ/
billion /'bɪlyən/
biochemistry *n* /,baɪoʊ'kɛməstri/
boomerang *n* /'bumə,ræŋ/
boss *n* /bɔs/
break up *v* /breɪk 'ʌp/
camping *n* /'kæmpɪŋ/
Capricorn *n* /'kæprɪ,kɔrn/
celebrate *v* /'sɛlə,breɪt/
communicate *v* /kə'myunə,keɪt/
contaminate *v* /kən'tæmə,neɪt/
debts *pl n* /dɛts/
dinner *n* /'dɪnər/
disaster *n* /dɪ'zæstər/
divorced *adj* /də'vɔrst/
driver's test *n* /'draɪvərz tɛst/
experts *pl n* /'ɛkspərts/
farmers *pl n* /'farmər/
fed up *adj* /,fɛd 'ʌp/
final exams *pl n* /'faɪnl ɪg'zæmz/
fluent *adj* /'fluənt/
full-time *adj* /,fʊl 'taɪm/
gas *n* /gæs/
get along *v* /gɛt ə'lɔŋ/
grown-up *adj* /,groʊn 'ʌp/
heavy *adj* /'hɛvi/
hope *n* /hoʊp/
immediately *adv* /ɪ'midiətli/
look up *v* /lʊk 'ʌp/
lucky *adj* /'lʌki/
medicine *n* /'mɛdəsn/
miserable *adj* /'mɪzrəbl/
miss *v* /mɪs/
mushrooms *n* /'mʌʃrumz/
nephew *n* /'nɛfyu/
newspaper delivery man *n* /'nuz,peɪpər dɪ'lɪvəri mæn/
nuclear *adj* /'nukliər/
owe *v* /oʊ/
paralegal *n* /,pærə'ligl/
paramedic *n* /,pærə'mɛdɪk/
philosophy *n* /fə'lasəfi/
phrase book *n* /'freɪz bʊk/
pick *v* /pɪk/
pretty good /'prɪti gʊd/
president *n* /'prɛzədənt/
produce *n* /'proʊdus/
run out of *v* /rʌn 'aʊt əv/
regret *v* /rɪ'grɛt/
stressful *adj* /'strɛsfl/
surfing *n* /'sərfɪŋ/
sweater *n* /'swɛtər/
take care of *v* /teɪk 'kɛr ʌv/
test *n* /tɛst/
traffic jams *pl n* /'træfɪk dʒæmz/
warm welcome /wɔrm 'wɛlkəm/

annoyed *adj* /ə'nɔɪd/
blond *adj* /bland/
bug *n* /bʌg/
busier *adj* /'bɪziər/
busiest *adj* /'bɪziɪst/
calm down *v* /kam daʊn/
career *n* /kə'rɪr/
citizen *n* /'sɪtəzn/
climate *n* /'klaɪmət/
culture shock *n* /'kʌltʃər ʃak/
customers *pl n* /'kʌstəmərz/
darker *adj* /'darkər/
democratic *adj* /,dɛmə'krætɪk/
driest *adj* /'draɪɪst/
endangered *adj* /ɪn'deɪndʒərd/
equator *n* /ɪ'kweɪtər/
experience *n* /ɪk'spɪriəns/
extinct *adj* /ɪk'stɪŋkt/
fair *adj* /fɛə(r)/
financial *adj* /fə'nænʃl/
florist shop *n* /'flɔrɪst ʃap/
foreign *adj* /'fɔrən/
friendly *adj* /'frɛndli/
generation *n* /,dʒɛnə'reɪʃn/
hectic *adj* /'hɛktɪk/
herbal *adj* /'ərbl/
honest *adj* /'anəst/
humid *adj* /'hyuməd/
incredible *adj* /ɪn'krɛdəbl/
intelligent *adj* /ɪn'tɛlədʒənt/
investment *n* /ɪn'vɛstmənt/
Kenya *n* /'kɛnyə/
largest *adj* /'lardʒɪst/
messy *adj* /'mɛsi/
mix up *v* /mɪks 'ʌp/
moody *adj* /'mudi/
multicultural *adj* /,mʌlti'kʌltʃərəl/
Philippines *n* /'fɪlə,pinz/
qualities *pl n* /'kwalətiz/
raise *v* /reɪz/
reliable *adj* /rɪ'laɪəbl/
religion *n* /rɪ'lɪdʒən/
rare *adj* /rɛr/
reveal *v* /rɪ'vil/
safe *adj* /seɪf/
salary *n* /'sæləri/
selfish *adj* /'sɛlfɪʃ/
shy *adj* /ʃaɪ/
skies *pl n* /skaɪz/
society *n* /sə'saɪəti/
South American *adj* /saʊθ ə'mɛrikən/
surrounded *adj* /sə'raʊndɪd/
system *n* /'sɪstəm/
temperature *n* /'tɛmprətʃər/
thankful *adj* /'θæŋkfl/
twin *n* /twɪn/
wealthy *adj* /'wɛlθi/
well-behaved *adj* /,wɛl bɪ'heɪvd/
wetter *adj* /'wɛtər/

UNIT 7

accident *n* /'æksədənt/
accountant *n* /ə'kaʊntnt/
acres *pl n* /'eɪkərz/
ancient civilizations *pl n* /'eɪnʃənt
  ˌsɪvələ'zeɪʃnz/
archaeology *n* /ˌɑrki'ɑlədʒi/
charming *adj* /'tʃɑrmɪŋ/
compete *v* /kəm'pit/
correspondent *n*
  /ˌkɔrə'spɑndənt/
decorator *n* /'dɛkəˌreɪtər/
director *n* /də'rɛktər/
discover *v* /dɪ'skʌvər/
electrician *n* /ɪˌlɛk'trɪʃn/
employ *v* /ɪm'plɔɪ/
estate *n* /ɪ'steɪt/
exhibition *n* /ˌɛksə'bɪʃn/
fascinated *adj* /'fæsəˌneɪtəd/
financially *adj* /fə'nænʃəli/
flower shows *pl n* /'flaʊər ʃoʊz/
great-grandmother *n* /greɪt
  'græn,mʌðər/
inherit *v* /ɪn'hɛrət/
interpreter *n* /ɪn'tərprətər/
kindness *n* /'kaɪndnəs/
librarian *n* /laɪ'brɛriən/
movie industry *n* /'muvi
  'ɪndəstri/
musician *n* /myu'zɪʃn/
ninth *adj* /naɪnθ/
novelist *n* /'nɑvəlɪst/
passion *n* /'pæʃn/
politician *n* /ˌpɑlə'tɪʃn/
press photographer *n* /prɛs
  fə'tɑgrəfər/
receptionist *n* /rɪ'sɛpʃənɪst/
running *v* /'rʌnɪŋ/
scientist *n* /'saɪəntɪst/
self-supporting *adj* /sɛlf
  sə'pɔrtɪŋ/
seminars *pl n* /'sɛməˌnɑrz/
several *pron* /'sɛvrəl/
shipyards *pl n* /'ʃɪpyɑrdz/
similarities *pl n* /ˌsɪmə'lærətiz/
situated *adj* /'sɪtʃuˌeɪtəd/
situation *n* /ˌsɪtʃu'eɪʃn/
tourism *n* /'tʊrɪzəm/
wealthy *adj* /'wɛlθi/

UNIT 8

achievement *n* /ə'tʃivmənt/
aftershave *n* /'æftərˌʃeɪv/
aggressive *adj* /ə'grɛsɪv/
allergy *n* /'ælərdʒi/
antibiotic *n* /ˌæntibaɪ'ɑtɪk/
athletic *adj* /æθ'lɛdɪk/
audience *n* /'ɔdiəns/
baseball *n* /'beɪsbɔl/
blouse *n* /blaʊs/
boisterous *adj* /'bɔɪstərəs/
casual wear *n* /'kæʒuəl wɛr/
climbers *pl n* /'klaɪmərz/
competitive *adj* /kəm'pɛtətɪv/
contest *n* /'kɑntɛst/
determined *adj* /dɪ'tərmənd/
diagnosis *n* /ˌdaɪəg'noʊsɪs/
diarrhea *n* /ˌdaɪə'riə/
dive *v* /daɪv/
endlessly *adv* /'ɛndləsli/
exhausting *adj* /ɪg'zɔstɪŋ/
fever *n* /'fivər/
figure *n* /'fɪgyər/
flu *n* /flu/
food poisoning *n* /'fud pɔɪzənɪŋ/
gentle *adj* /'dʒɛntl/
glands *pl n* /glændz/
go-karting *n* /'goʊ kɑrtɪŋ/
gold medal *n* /ˌgoʊld 'mɛdl/
gymnastics *n* /dʒɪm'næstɪks/
heat *n* /hit/
heptathlon *n* /hɛp'tæθlən/
high jump *n* /'haɪ dʒʌmp/
hold on *v* /hoʊld ɑn/
hopeless *adj* /'hoʊpləs/
horseback riding *n* /'hɔrsbæk
  raɪdɪŋ/
infection *n* /ɪn'fɛkʃn/
in shape *adj* /ɪn ʃeɪp/
javelin throw *n* /'dʒævlən θroʊ/
Labrador *n* /'læbrəˌdɔr/
liquids *pl n* /'lɪkwədz/
long jump *n* /'lɔŋ dʒʌmp/
nerves *pl n* /nərvz/
patient *n* /'peɪʃnt/
penicillin *n* /ˌpɛnə'sɪlən/
physical therapist *n*
  /ˌfɪzɪkl 'θɛrəpɪst/
polite *adj* /pə'laɪt/
pouring *adj* /'pɔrɪŋ/
prescription *n* /prɪ'skrɪpʃn/
racing *n* /'reɪsɪŋ/
recover *v* /rɪ'kʌvər/
rock climbing *n* /'rɑk klaɪmɪŋ/
sailing *n* /'seɪlɪŋ/
sensitive *adj* /'sɛnsətɪv/
shot put *n* /'ʃɑt pʊt/
sickness *n* /'sɪknəs/
skateboarding *n* /'skeɪtbɔrdɪŋ/
skydiving *n* /'skaɪˌdaɪvɪŋ/
sneeze *v* /sniz/
sore *adj* /sɔr/
suit *n* /sut/
swallow *v* /'swɑloʊ/

swollen *adj* /'swoʊlən/
symptoms *pl n* /'sɪmptəmz/
talkative *adj* /'tɔkətɪv/
thermometer *n* /θər'mɑmətər/
tourist spot *n* /'tʊrɪst spɑt/
twisted *adj* /'twɪstəd/

UNIT 9

absolutely *adv* /'æbsəˌlutli/
address *v* /ə'drɛs/
advice *n* /əd'vaɪs/
anniversary *n* /ˌænɪ'vərsəri/
ashamed *adj* /ə'ʃeɪmd/
attack *v* /ə'tæk/
autobiography *n* /ˌɔtəbaɪ'ɑgrəfi/
badly-behaved *adj* /'bædli
  bɪ'heɪvd/
battle *n* /'bætl/
behavior *n* /bɪ'heɪvyər/
bend down *v* /bɛnd 'daʊn/
best-known *adj* /bɛst 'noʊn/
best-seller *adj* /ˌbɛst'sɛlər/
break down *v* /breɪk 'daʊn/
burn *v* /bərn/
case *n* /keɪs/
check *n* /tʃɛk/
childhood *n* /'tʃaɪldhʊd/
compliment *n* /'kɑmpləmənt/
cruel *adj* /'kruəl/
disgusting *adj* /dɪs'gʌstɪŋ/
escape *v* /ɪ'skeɪp/
evil *adj* /'ivl/
fables *pl n* /'feɪblz/
fact *n* /fækt/
familiar *adj* /fə'mɪlyər/
fascinating *adj* /'fæsəˌneɪtɪŋ/
fiction *n* /'fɪkʃn/
get rid of *v* /gɛt 'rɪd əv/
homesick *adj* /'hoʊmsɪk/
immediate *adj* /ɪ'midiət/
innocent *adj* /'ɪnəsnt/
lend *v* /lɛnd/
lie *v* /laɪ/
literature *n* /'lɪtərətʃər/
master *n* /'mæstər/
monster *n* /'mɑnstər/
moonlight *n* /'munlaɪt/
murder *n* /'mərdər/
narrative *n* /'nærətɪv/
novels *pl n* /'nɑvlz/
pale *adj* /peɪl/
personality *n* /ˌpərsə'næləti/
poetry *n* /'poʊətri/
potion *n* /'poʊʃn/
pray *v* /preɪ/
pretend *v* /prɪ'tɛnd/
psychological *adj* /ˌsaɪkə'lɑdʒɪkl/
publish *v* /'pʌblɪʃ/
race *v* /reɪs/
racism *n* /'reɪsɪzm/
romance *n* /'roʊmæns/
run away *v* /rʌn 'əweɪ/
servants *pl n* /'sərvənts/
shepherd *n* /'ʃɛpərd/
sight *n* /saɪt/
sniff *v* /snɪf/

split personality *n* /splɪt
  ˌpərsə'næləti/
strength *n* /strɛŋkθ/
success *n* /sək'sɛs/
suspect *v* /sə'spɛkt/
take pleasure *v* /teɪk 'plɛʒər/
terror *n* /'tɛrər/
tiring *adj* /'taɪərɪŋ/
traveler *n* /'trævələr/
true *adj* /tru/
ugly *adj* /'ʌgli/
upset *adj* /ʌp'sɛt/
villagers *pl n* /'vɪlɪdʒərz/
villains *pl n* /'vɪlənz/
wander away *v* /'wɑndər ə'weɪ/
well-respected *adj* /wɛl
  rɪ'spɛktɪd/
whether *conj* /'wɛðər/
whisper *v* /'wɪspər/
wild *adj* /waɪld/
wolf *n* /wʊlf/

UNIT 10

access *v* /'æksɛs/
badly written *adj* /'bædli 'rɪtn/
ballpoint pen *n* /'bɔlpɔɪnt pen/
basement *n* /'beɪsmənt/
battery *n* /'bætəri/
blogger *n* /'blɑgər/
browsing *v* /'braʊzɪŋ/
commercial *adj* /kə'mərʃl/
complaint *n* /kəm'pleɪnt/
copy *v* /'kɑpi/
database *n* /'deɪtəbeɪs/
decorate *v* /'dɛkəˌreɪt/
directory assistance *n* /də'rɛktəri
  ə'sɪstəns/
easily *adv* /'izəli/
employee *n* /ɪm'plɔɪi/
engineer *n* /ˌɛndʒə'nɪr/
estimate *v* /'ɛstəmeɪt/
evolution *n* /ˌɛvə'luʃn/
fashionable *adj* /'fæʃənəbl/
fears *pl n* /fɪrz/
feature *n* /'fitʃər/
found *v* /faʊnd/
gadget *n* /'gædʒət/
introduce *v* /ˌɪntrə'dus/
keeping up to date /'kipɪŋ ʌp tə
  deɪt/
landline *n* /'lændlaɪn/
last *v* /læst/
latest *adj* /'leɪtəst/
launch *v* /lɔntʃ/
luxury *n* /'lʌkʃəri/
middle-aged *adj* /ˌmɪdl 'eɪdʒd/
minicomputer *n*
  /'mɪnikəmˌpyutər/
multimedia *adj* /ˌmʌlti'midiə/

multitude *n* /'mʌltə,tud/
nightmare *n* /'naɪtmɛr/
operators *pl n* /'apə,reɪtərz/
overcrowded *adj* /,ouvər'kraʊdəd/
oversized *adj* /'ouvər,saɪzd/
own *v* /oʊn/
password *n* /'pæswərd/
plans *pl n* /plænz/
pocket-sized *adj* /'pakət saɪzd/
predict *v* /prɪ'dɪkt/
pretty *adv* /'prɪti/
printing press *n* /'prɪntɪŋ prɛs/
rare *adj* /rɛr/
recorded message *n* /rɪ'kɔrdəd 'mɛsɪdʒ/
reignite *v* /,riɪg'naɪt/
replace *v* /rɪ'pleɪs/
replicate *v* /'rɛplə,keɪt/
roommate *n* /'rummeɪt/
routine *adj* /ru'tin/
search engines *pl n* /'sərtʃ ɛndʒənz/
searchable *adj* /'sərtʃəbl/
skinny latte *n* /skɪni 'lateɪ/
smartphone *n* /'smartfoun/
social networking *n* /souʃl 'nɛt,wərkɪŋ/
store *n* /stɔr/
throw away *v* /θroʊ 'əweɪ/
trillion *n* /'trɪlyən/
turn off *v* /tərn ɔf/
variety *n* /və'raɪəti/

UNIT 11

academy *n* /ə'kædəmi/
antiques *pl n* /æn'tiks/
awards *pl n* /ə'wɔdz/
backache *n* /'bækeɪk/
based in /beɪst ɪn/
blind *adj* /blaɪnd/
boarding school *n* /'bɔrdɪŋ skul/
break up *v* /breɪk ʌp/
bridesmaid *n* /'braɪdzmeɪd/
bury *v* /'bɛri/
buyer *n* /'baɪər/
catch up *v* /kætʃ ʌp/
cave *n* /keɪv/
chance *n* /tʃæns/
cheapness *n* /'tʃipnəs/
choir *n* /'kwaɪər/
choirmaster *n* /'kwaɪər,mæstər/
colleague *n* /'kalig/
coma *n* /'koumə/
coping *v* /'koupɪŋ/
country singer *n* /'kʌntri 'sɪŋər/
covered *adj* /'kʌvərd/
demand *v* /dɪ'mænd/
diamond *n* /'daɪmənd/
digging *v* /'dɪgɪŋ/
drama *n* /'dramə/
elite *adj* /ɪ'lit/
engaged *adj* /ɪn'geɪdʒd/
entertain *v* /,ɛntər'teɪn/
exact *adj* /ɪg'zækt/
expecting a baby /ɪk'spɛktɪŋ ə 'beɪbi/
expel *v* /ɪk'spɛl/
fantastic news /fæn'tæstɪk nuz/
fond of /'fand əv/
generosity *n* /,dʒɛnə'rasəti/
Great to hear from you! /greɪt tə hɪr frəm yu/
great-grandson *n* /greɪt 'grænsʌn/
guy *coll* /gaɪ/
headquarters *n* /'hɛd,kwɔrtərz/
hit series *n* /hɪt 'sɪriz/
host *n* /houst/
install *v* /ɪn'stɔl/
keep in touch *v* /kip ɪn tʌtʃ/
kidnap *v* /'kɪdnæp/
leading role *n* /'lidɪŋ roʊl/
lifestyle *n* /'laɪfstaɪl/
millionaires *pl n* /,mɪlyə'nɛrz/
model *n* /'madl/
modest *adj* /'madəst/
overdose *n* /'ouvər,dous/
paralyzed *adj* /'pærəlaɪzd/
party-loving *adj* /'parti 'lʌvɪŋ/
passionate *adj* /'pæʃənət/
photograph *v* /'foutə,græf/
plague *v* /pleɪg/
plant *v* /plænt/
popular *adj* /'papyələr/
postgraduate *n* /,poust'grædʒuət/
pregnant *adj* /'prɛgnənt/
promises *pl n* /'pramɪsɪz/
pronunciation *n* /prə,nʌnsi'eɪʃn/

proof *n* /pruf/
ransom *n* /'rænsəm/
release *v* /rɪ'lis/
remarry *v* /,ri'mæri/
rush *v* /rʌʃ/
serious *adj* /'sɪriəs/
stroke *n* /stroʊk/
Swedish *adj* /'swidɪʃ/
sweetheart *n* /'swithart/
terribly *adv* /'tɛrəbli/
the arts *pl n* /ði 'arts/
tough *adj* /tʌf/
tragedy *n* /'trædʒədi/
tragic *adj* /'trædʒɪk/
Tudor *adj* /'tudər/
upbringing *n* /'ʌpbrɪŋɪŋ/
wealth *n* /wɛlθ/
What a shame! /wat ə 'ʃeɪm/
widowed *adj* /'wɪdoʊd/

UNIT 12

a snap of the fingers /ə 'snæp əv ðə 'fɪŋgərz/
alien *n* /'eɪliən/
angle *n* /'æŋgl/
atmosphere *n* /'ætməs,fɪr/
axis *n* /'æksɪs/
block *v* /blak/
body parts *pl n* /'badi parts/
burn out *v* /bərn 'aʊt/
collapse *v* /kə'læps/
cool *v* /kul/
crossroads *n* /'krɔsroʊdz/
decrease *v* /dɪ'kris/
dilemmas *pl n* /dɪ'lɛməz/
Earth *n* /ərθ/
earthquake *n* /'ərθkweɪk/
economics *n* /,ɛkə'namɪks/
electric shock *n* /ɪ,lɛktrɪk 'ʃak/
encourage *v* /ɪn'kərɪdʒ/
evaporate *v* /ɪ'væpəreɪt/
expand *v* /ɪk'spænd/
express *v* /ɪk'sprɛs/
extreme *adj* /ɪk'strim/
flash *n* /flæʃ/
fundamentally *adv* /,fʌndə'mɛntli/
galaxy *n* /'gæləksi/
gas *n* /gæs/
global *adj* /'gloʊbl/
good-looking *adj* /,gʊd 'lʊkɪŋ/
government *n* /'gʌvərmənt/
gravity *n* /'grævəti/
harmful *adj* /'harmfl/
healthcare *n* /'hɛlθkɛr/
helium *n* /'hiliəm/
hemisphere *n* /'hɛmə,sfɪr/
hold *v* /hoʊld/
hydrogen *n* /'haɪdrɔdʒən/
improbable *adj* /ɪm'prabəbl/
improvement *n* /ɪm'pruvmənt/
in touch /ɪn 'tʌtʃ/
increasing *adj* /ɪn'krisɪŋ/
infinite *adj* /'ɪnfənət/
junk food *n* /'dʒʌŋk fud/

life expectancy *n* /'laɪf ɪk,spɛktənsi/
Mars *n* /marz/
Mercury *n* /'mərkyəri/
metal *n* /'mɛtl/
microchips *pl n* /'maɪkroʊtʃɪps/
Milky Way *n* /,mɪlki 'weɪ/
miraculous *adj* /mə'rækyələs/
moons *pl n* /munz/
observable *adj* /əb'zərvəbl/
oceans *pl n* /'oʊʃnz/
on purpose /an 'pərpəs/
permanently *adv* /'pərmənəntli/
pessimistic *adj* /,pɛsɪ'mɪstɪk/
picnic *n* /'pɪknɪk/
pills *pl n* /pɪlz/
planet *n* /'plænət/
precious *adj* /'prɛʃəs/
radiation *n* /,reɪdi'eɪʃn/
require *v* /rɪ'kwaɪər/
rotate *v* /'routeɪt/
skyscrapers *pl n* /'skaɪ,skreɪpərz/
solar system *n* /'soʊlər sɪstəm/
starving *adj* /'starvɪŋ/
suitable *adj* /'sutəbl/
support *v* /sə'pɔrt/
threats *pl n* /θrɛts/
timescale *n* /'taɪmskeɪl/
travel team *n* /'trævl tim/
universe *n* /'yunə,vərs/
Venus *n* /'vinəs/
volcano *n* /val'keɪnoʊ/
wage *v* /weɪdʒ/
warm *v* /wɔrm/
warning *n* /'wɔrnɪŋ/
wisdom *n* /'wɪzdəm/
wonders *pl n* /'wʌndərz/

Pairwork Activities Student A

UNIT 2 *p. 12*

PRACTICE

Speaking – exchanging information

3 Work with a partner. Answer questions about Alicia.

Ask questions about Bill and Christina. Complete the chart.

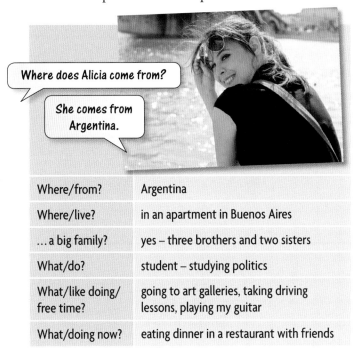

Where/from?	Argentina
Where/live?	in an apartment in Buenos Aires
…a big family?	yes – three brothers and two sisters
What/do?	student – studying politics
What/like doing/ free time?	going to art galleries, taking driving lessons, playing my guitar
What/doing now?	eating dinner in a restaurant with friends

Where/from?	
Where/live?	
…a big family?	
What/do?	
What/like doing/ free time?	
What/doing now?	

UNIT 5 *p. 37*

PRACTICE

When can we meet?

3 Work with a partner. Arrange to meet next week. Look at your calendar.

What are you doing on Monday evening?

I'm meeting Katie in town. Are you doing anything on Monday afternoon?

	morning	afternoon	evening
Monday	study		meet Katie in town
Tuesday	study	visit Uncle Chris	
Wednesday	study		go to the movies with Jenny
Thursday	study		cook meal for Mom and Dad
Friday	study	have piano lesson	

EVERYDAY ENGLISH

Role play

7 Work in pairs. You are going to have three telephone conversations.

PHONE CALL 1	PHONE CALL 2	PHONE CALL 3
Call a friend's cell phone.	You are a receptionist at a marketing company. A client calls to speak to Dave Miller (your manager).	You work at an I.T. company. You are on a business trip and need information from a colleague (Marco). Call the office and ask to speak to Marco.
↓	↓	↓
You can't meet on Tuesday – suggest Thursday instead.	Try to connect them.	You have tried Marco's cell phone, but he didn't answer.
↓	↓	↓
Agree what to do.	Dave is busy.	Decide what to do.
	↓	
	Make a suggestion.	

SPEAKING

Tense review

7 Work with a partner. You have different information about Taylor Swift's life and career. Ask and answer questions to complete the text.

> When was Taylor Swift born?

> She was born in 1989.

Taylor Swift's life and career

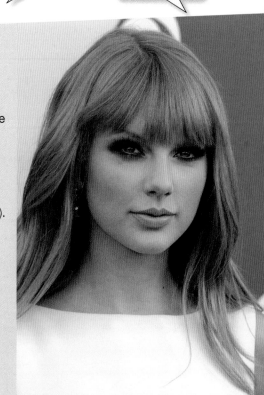

Taylor Swift is an ordinary girl with an extraordinary music career. She was born in _____ (*Where?*) in the US in 1989. She's been singing in public since she was _____ (*How long?*), when she performed in a theater group. When she was 11, she entered a talent show and sang _____ (*What?*). She's been singing and writing songs ever since and has also given concerts at Madison Square Garden and Wembley Arena. She performed at the Grand Ole Opry when she was just _____ (*How old ... when?*).

She has sold over 26 million albums worldwide and has earned _____ (*How much?*). Taylor started her career as a country singer, but she also sings pop and pop rock songs. She has released _____ albums (*How many?*) so far: *Taylor Swift* in 2006, *Fearless* in 2008, *Speak Now* in 2010, *Red* in 2012 and *1989* in 2014.

Taylor is not just a singer. She's recently been acting and she has received good reviews. On TV, she played a rebellious teenager on *CSI: Crime Scene Investigation* and she's been in three movies so far, *Valentine's Day*, *The Lorax*, and *The Giver*.

At 25, Taylor is still single but she has dated several famous (and handsome) men including singer _____ . They dated for several months but broke up in 2013.

Pairwork Activities Student B

PRACTICE

Speaking – exchanging information

3 Work with a partner. Ask questions about Alicia. Complete the chart.

Answer questions about Bill and Christina.

Where does Alicia come from?

She comes from ...

Where/from?	
Where/live?	
...a big family?	
What/do?	
What/like doing/ free time?	
What/doing now?	

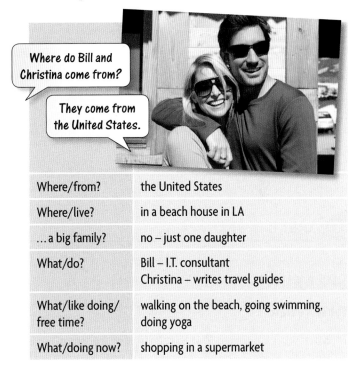

Where do Bill and Christina come from?

They come from the United States.

Where/from?	the United States
Where/live?	in a beach house in LA
...a big family?	no – just one daughter
What/do?	Bill – I.T. consultant Christina – writes travel guides
What/like doing/ free time?	walking on the beach, going swimming, doing yoga
What/doing now?	shopping in a supermarket

PRACTICE

When can we meet?

3 Work with a partner. Arrange to meet next week. Look at your diary.

What are you doing on Monday afternoon?

I'm playing tennis with Joe. Are you doing anything on Tuesday afternoon?

	morning	afternoon	evening
Monday	study	play tennis with Joe	
Tuesday	study		watch football at Dan's house
Wednesday	study	visit Tom in the hospital	
Thursday	study		
Friday	study		

EVERYDAY ENGLISH

Role play

7 Work in pairs. You are going to have three telephone conversations.

PHONE CALL 1	PHONE CALL 2	PHONE CALL 3
A friend will call your cell phone.	You are an important customer for a marketing company. Call the company and ask to speak to Dave Miller.	You work at an I.T. company. A colleague calls to speak to another colleague (Marco).
↓	↓	↓
The connection is bad – ask your friend to repeat what they said.	You need to speak to him as soon as possible.	Marco is not there. He is visiting a customer. He has his cell phone with him.
↓	↓	↓
Agree what to do.	Decide what to do.	Make a suggestion.

SPEAKING

Tense review

7 Work with a partner. You have different information about Taylor Swift's life and career. Ask and answer questions to complete the text.

> Where was Taylor Swift born?

> She was born in Wyomissing, Pennsylvania.

Taylor Swift's life and career

Taylor Swift is an ordinary girl with an extraordinary music career. She was born in Wyomissing, Pennsylvania in the US in _____ (*When?*). She's been singing in public since she was nine, when she performed in a _____ (*Where?*). When she was 11, she entered a talent show and sang *Big Deal*. She's been singing and writing songs ever since and has also given concerts at _____ (*Where?*). She performed at the Grand Ole Opry when she was just 17.

She has sold over _____ (*How many?*) albums worldwide and has earned around $220 million. Taylor started her career as a _____ (*What?*), but she also sings pop and pop rock songs. She has released five albums so far: *Taylor Swift* in 2006, *Fearless* in 2008, *Speak Now* in 2010, *Red* in 2012, and *1989* in 2014.

Taylor is not just a singer. She's recently been acting and she has received good reviews. On TV, she played a rebellious teenager on *CSI: Crime Scene Investigation* and she's been in _____ (*How many?*) so far, *Valentine's Day*, *The Lorax*, and *The Giver*.

At 25, Taylor is still single, but she has dated several famous (and handsome) men including singer Harry Styles. They dated for several months but broke up in _____ (*When?*).

Extra Materials

UNIT 3 *p. 20*

PRACTICE

Talking about the news

7 Choose one of the stories and read it. Make sure you understand all the words.

Work in small groups. Tell your story to the others. Don't read it!
The other students can ask questions.

Texting woman falls into fountain

A woman who fell into a fountain while she was shopping is becoming an international hit on YouTube.

A video of her falling into the water went online last Friday, and since then 1.5 million people have watched it.

The woman was in a shopping mall in Pennsylvania in the US. She was walking along the mall and texting at the same time, so she wasn't looking where she was going. Security cameras filmed her as she fell into a fountain. Fortunately the water wasn't very deep. When she climbed out of the fountain, she finished sending her text, then continued on walking down through the mall.

The app that saved an iPad

A thief who stole an iPad led police straight to his door, because the owner had an app called "Find my iPad."

Ronald Bowe, 59, stole the tablet from Xin Shi's bag while the victim wasn't paying attention.

Mr. Xin reported the theft to the police, and then realized he could use the app to find out where his iPad was. The GPS app gives the location of the computer.

Police followed the app to Bowe's house, where they found a bag containing the iPad, a cell phone, a wallet, and a bank card.

Bowe was found guilty and will be sentenced at a later date.

Chinese vase sells for $69 million

A woman who lives in a suburb of London was clearing out the house of her brother who recently died. She found a vase that her brother kept on a shelf in his dining room.

She said that her brother was very fond of the vase, although she didn't really like it herself.

A local antique shop thought it was worth about $1,300. So she asked an auction house to look at it, and they discovered it was from the Qianlong period, and dated it from the mid 18th century.

Yesterday it sold for $69 million to a Chinese buyer. The woman's son said that his mother was at first surprised, then amazed, and then totally breathless.

UNIT 3 *p. 22*

READING AND SPEAKING

What do you think?

October 20

STEVEN SLATER ADMITS GUILT

The American flight attendant, who received worldwide attention in the summer and became a media and Internet sensation, appeared in court yesterday.

He admitted that he lost his temper, put the lives of passengers in danger, and caused damage to the plane when he activated the emergency chute.

Slater will receive one year of counseling for anger management. If he doesn't complete the treatment, he could go to prison for one to three years.

He also has to pay a fine of $10,000 to JetBlue for damage to the plane.

Slater is currently unemployed.

EVERYDAY ENGLISH

Agree with me

5 Choose two of the conversations and decide where tag questions can be added. Act them out for the class.

1 A The weather is just horrible today.
B Awful!
A The rain makes you miserable.
B And wet!
A Oh, well. We need the rain.
B I guess so.

2 A It's so romantic here!
B Yes, it's beautiful!
A And the ocean looks so inviting!
B I think I'll take a swim before breakfast. I have time.
A Of course you have time! We're on vacation!

3 A You don't like Ann.
B Um … she's all right.
A But you didn't talk to her all night.
B Well … she was talking to Jim.
A Actually, she's very interesting.
B But she never listens! She just talks and talks and talks.

4 A I'd love to buy that car!
B But we don't have any money!
A I thought we had a lot.
B But we spent it all on a new kitchen.
A Oh, yes! That's right. I forgot.
B We can save up.
A Uh … OK.

5 Sally We had an amazing vacation, Dave.
Dave We did. It was very relaxing.
Sally And the weather was fabulous, Dave.
Dave Yup. We were lucky.
Sally And we met some nice people, Dave.
Dave We did. Charming people.

6 A Amanda Seyfried's a fabulous actor.
B Very good.
A And her voice is really good.
B Yes, it's amazing!
A She can hit the highest notes!
B Yeah, I don't know how she does it.

7 A We love each other very much.
B We do.
A And we want to get married one day.
B One day, yeah.
A And we'll have six children.
B Uh … yeah. Six, that's right.

8 A That was a terrible game!
B Awful! What a waste of money.
A Lopez played really badly!
B He was horrible! He didn't do anything right all night.
A We deserved to lose!
B We did. I don't know why I root for them.

LISTENING AND SPEAKING

Discussion

5 Look at the situations. Talk together. What would you do?

Dilemma 1 You've been offered a job in a far country. You would earn a lot of money, but you'd have to leave all your family and friends.

Dilemma 2 Your friend Theo is always in trouble. He says to you one day, "If anyone asks you, tell them I was with you last night. OK?"

Dilemma 3 You go to a party where you meet someone and fall totally and hopelessly in love. At the end of the evening, he/she says to you, "Let's get married tonight!"

Dilemma 4 At work your boss gives you lots of praise and a pay raise for an idea you had. In fact, it was a colleague's idea that you stole.

Dilemma 5 You have neighbors who you really don't get along with. They are on vacation when you see that their house is on fire.

Dilemma 6 A well-known politician is telling the press stories about his/her childhood. In fact, you went to school with this politician and you know that what he/she is saying is all lies.

Dilemma 7 You are shopping in a supermarket. When you come out, you realize that you accidentally put something in your bag and didn't pay for it.

WRITING – Building a story

A fishy tale

Ten days ago businessman, Andrew Cheatle, was walking on the beach near his home, when he lost his cell phone. It fell into the water and unfortunately a wave took it out to sea. One week later fisherman, Glen Kerley, was on his boat catching fish to sell at, the market. The same day, back on land, he was preparing the fish to sell when he noticed something metal inside a cod fish. It was a cell phone. Glen couldn't believe it. The phone was smelly and dirty, but amazingly, it still worked, so Glen called some of the contact numbers. Soon he had a reply.

Andrew was out shopping for a new cell phone with his girlfriend, Rita Smith, when her phone rang. Incredibly, she said, "It's for you! It's a call from your phone." Glen told Andrew the fishy tale of how he found the phone. They met the next day and he returned it to amazed Andrew, who still uses it.

Glen Kerley Andrew Cheatle

Irregular Verbs

Base form	Past form	Past participle
be	was/were	been
become	became	become
begin	began	begun
break	broke	broken
bring	brought	brought
build	built	built
buy	bought	bought
can	could	been able
catch	caught	caught
choose	chose	chosen
come	came	come
cost	cost	cost
cut	cut	cut
do	did	done
drink	drank	drunk
drive	drove	driven
eat	ate	eaten
fall	fell	fallen
feel	felt	felt
fight	fought	fought
find	found	found
fly	flew	flown
forget	forgot	forgotten
get	got	gotten
give	gave	given
go	went	gone/been
grow	grew	grown
have	had	had
hear	heard	heard
hit	hit	hit
keep	kept	kept
know	knew	known
learn	learned	learned
leave	left	left
lose	lost	lost
make	made	made
meet	met	met
pay	paid	paid
put	put	put
read /rɪd/	read /rɛd/	read /rɛd/
ride	rode	ridden
run	ran	run
say	said	said
see	saw	seen
sell	sold	sold
send	sent	sent
shut	shut	shut
sing	sang	sung
sit	sat	sat
sleep	slept	slept
speak	spoke	spoken
spend	spent	spent
stand	stood	stood
steal	stole	stolen
swim	swam	swum
take	took	taken
tell	told	told
think	thought	thought
understand	understood	understood
wake	woke	woken
wear	wore	worn
win	won	won
write	wrote	written

Verb Patterns

Verb + -ing	
like	
love	swimming
enjoy	
hate	
finish	cooking
stop	

Note

We often use the verb *go* + *-ing* for sports and activities.

I **go swimming** every day.
I **go shopping** on Saturday.

Verb + infinitive	
choose	
decide	
forget	
promise	
manage	to go
need	
help	
hope	to work
try	
want	
would like	
would love	

Verb + -ing or infinitive	
begin	
start	raining/to rain

Verb + preposition + -ing	
think of	
look forward to	going

Modal auxiliary verbs	
can	
could	
must	go
had to	
should	arrive
will	
would	

Phonetic Symbols

Consonants			
1	/p/	as in	**pen** /pɛn/
2	/b/	as in	**big** /bɪg/
3	/t/	as in	**tea** /ti/
4	/d/	as in	**do** /du/
5	/k/	as in	**cat** /kæt/
6	/g/	as in	**go** /goʊ/
7	/f/	as in	**four** /fɔr/
8	/v/	as in	**very** /'vɛri/
9	/s/	as in	**son** /sʌn/
10	/z/	as in	**zoo** /zu/
11	/l/	as in	**live** /lɪv/
12	/m/	as in	**my** /maɪ/
13	/n/	as in	**now** /naʊ/
14	/h/	as in	**happy** /'hæpi/
15	/r/	as in	**red** /rɛd/
16	/y/	as in	**yes** /yɛs/
17	/w/	as in	**want** /wɑnt/
18	/θ/	as in	**thanks** /θæŋks/
19	/ð/	as in	**the** /ðə/
20	/ʃ/	as in	**she** /ʃi/
21	/ʒ/	as in	**television** /'tɛlə,vɪʒn/
22	/tʃ/	as in	**child** /tʃaɪld/
23	/dʒ/	as in	**German** /'dʒɜrmən/
24	/ŋ/	as in	**English** /'ɪŋglɪʃ/

Vowels			
25	/i/	as in	**see** /si/
26	/ɪ/	as in	**his** /hɪz/
27	/ɛ/	as in	**ten** /tɛn/
28	/æ/	as in	**bag** /bæg/
29	/ɑ/	as in	**father** /'fɑðər/
30	/ɔ/	as in	**saw** /sɔ/
31	/ʊ/	as in	**book** /bʊk/
32	/u/	as in	**you** /yu/
33	/ʌ/	as in	**sun** /sʌn/
34	/ə/	as in	**about** /ə'baʊt/
35	/eɪ/	as in	**name** /neɪm/
36	/aɪ/	as in	**my** /maɪ/
37	/ɔɪ/	as in	**boy** /bɔɪ/
38	/aʊ/	as in	**how** /haʊ/
39	/oʊ/	as in	**go** /goʊ/
40	/ər/	as in	**bird** /bərd/
41	/ir/	as in	**near** /nir/
42	/ɛr/	as in	**hair** /hɛr/
43	/ɑr/	as in	**car** /kɑr/
44	/ɔr/	as in	**more** /mɔr/
45	/ʊr/	as in	**tour** /tʊr/

OXFORD
UNIVERSITY PRESS

198 Madison Avenue
New York, NY 10016 USA

Great Clarendon Street, Oxford, OX2 6DP,
United Kingdom

Oxford University Press is a department of the
University of Oxford. It furthers the University's
objective of excellence in research, scholarship,
and education by publishing worldwide. Oxford
is a registered trade mark of Oxford University
Press in the UK and in certain other countries

ISBN: 978 0 19 472589 7
STUDENT BOOK (PACK COMPONENT)
ISBN: 978 0 19 472588 0
STUDENT BOOK WITH OXFORD ONLINE SKILLS
PROGRAM (PACK)
ISBN: 978 0 19 472607 8
OXFORD ONLINE SKILLS PROGRAM (PACK
COMPONENT)
ISBN: 978 0 19 472603 0
STUDENT BOOK ACCESS CARD (PACK COMPONENT)

Printed in China

This book is printed on paper from certified
and well-managed sources

ACKNOWLEDGEMENTS

*The authors and publisher are grateful to those who have given permission
to reproduce the following extracts and adaptations of copyright material:*
pp. 66 & 67 From "So what happened when two families
swapped children?" by Tessa Cunningham, *Daily Mail* 11 August
2010. Reproduced by permission; pp. 42 & 43 Interview with
Palina Yanachkina is fictitious and is reproduced by
permission of Palina Yanachkina. Article adapted from "First
person: Palina Yanachkina 'I have two families'" by Danielle
Wrate, 5 May 2008, *The Guardian*. Copyright Guardian News &
Media Ltd 2008. Reproduced by permission; pp. 50 & 51 From
"The British Dream" by Tim Pozzi, 19 July 2008, timesonline.
co.uk. Reproduced by permission of NI Syndication; pp. 65
Interview with Jessica Ennis is fictitious and is based on factual
information from *The Observer*, 15 November 2009. Reproduced
by permission of JCCM Ltd; pp. 82 & 83 Extracts adapted from
"A first time for everything" by Tom Meltzer, 23 October 2009,
The Guardian. Copyright Guardian News & Media Ltd 2009.
Reproduced by permission; p. 87 Information about Gareth
Malone reproduced by permission of Curtis Brown; p. 18
"Money" Words and Music by Berry Gordy JR and William
Robinson JR @ 1958. Reproduced by permission of EMI Music
Publishing (WP) Ltd, London W8 5SW.

Sources: p. 11 "Blind date" Source: www.guardian.co.uk; pp. 26
& 27 "Emergency exit for flight attendant who lost his cool"
Source: *The Evening Standard*; p. 41 "I still can't believe I'm a
grown-up!" Source: *The Times*; pp. 26 & 27 "Steven Slater thanks
public" Source: www.telegraph.co.uk/news

Additional information: p.63 Interview with Tilly Parkins is
fictitious and is based on factual information; CD 2 Track 13
Fictitious interview with Palina Yanachkina reproduced by
permission; CD 2 Track 44 Fictitious interview with Tilly
Parkins is based on factual information. CD 2 Track 49
Fictitious interview with Jessica Ennis is fictitious and is based
on factual information from *The Observer*, 15 November 2009.
Reproduced by permission of JCCM Ltd.

Illustrations by: Ian Baker p.65; Fausto Bianchi/Beehive
Illustration p.68; Gill Button pp.20, 25, 48, 64, 72, 77, 88;
Katriona Chapman/The Bright Agency pp.66, 67; Simon
Cooper/The Organisation pp. 24, 37, 40(throw something away
etc), 84; Tom Croft pp.9, 17(John and Maria), 80, 97; Lucy
Davey/The Artworks p.13; Maxwell Dorsey/Meiklejohn
Illustration Ltd p.12, 40(look after a baby, etc.), 91; Penko
Gelev pp.70, 71; Andy Hammond/Illustration p.102; Martin
Sanders pp.18, 38, 56; Tony Sigley pp.22, 61, 103, 153.

*We would also like to thank the following for permission to reproduce the
following photographs:* Cover- Paul Harizan/Getty Images(2), Ralf
Hiemisch/fstop/Corbis; global- mr_morton/istockphoto; p.2 Zia
Soleil/Getty Images, Fredrik Skold/Getty Images; p.3 VisitBritain/
Getty Images, Ralph A. Clevenger/Corbis, mollypix/istockphoto;
p.4 OUP/Gareth Boden, Mark Bassett/Alamy; p.5 Johner Royalty-
Free/Getty Images, Severin Schweiger/Cultura/Getty Images,
Simon Marcus/Comet/Corbis, Marcy Maloy/Photodisc/Getty
Images, Tim Hale Photography/Comet/Corbis, moodboard/Corbis;
p.6 Courtesy of Ping Pong Ltd www.pingpongdimsum.co.uk,
OUP/Gareth Boden(2); p.7 OUP/Gareth Boden(2), robstyle1/
istockphoto, Floortje/istockphoto; p.8 OUP/CoverBank, Jill
Fromer/Photodisc/Getty Images; p.9 Tom Croft(4); p.10 Trae
Patton/NBCU Photo Bank/Getty Images; p.11 Annabella Charles
Photography, Richard Peterson/shutterstock(2), Madlen/
shutterstock; p.12 Chev Wilkinson/Cultura/Getty Images, Philip
Lee Harvey/cultura/Corbis; p.14 Image Source/Getty Images; p.15
Ben Hupfer/Corbis, Zero Creatives/Getty Images, Martin Barraud/
Getty Images, Erik Isakson/Getty Images, Hans Huber/Westend61/
Corbis, Laurel/Alamy, hsimages/Westend61/Corbis; p.16 OUP/
Gareth Boden; p.17 Tom Croft(2), John Giustina/Iconica/Getty
Images; p.18 Keith Ducatel - www.KeithDucatel.com(2); p.19 Keith
Ducatel - www.KeithDucatel.com(2), Mark Moffett/Minden
Pictures/Getty Images, James P. Blair/National Geographic/Getty
Images; p.21 Fry Design Ltd/Getty Images, Rehan Khan/epa/
Corbis(2), Christopher Pillitz/Reportage/Getty Images, Christian
Liewig/TempSport/Corbis, Imaginechina/Corbis, Yellow Dog
Productions/Getty Images, AFP/Getty Images(3), OUP/Gareth
Boden, Gideon Mendel For Action Aid/In Pictures/Corbis, Peter
Turnley/Corbis, WEDA/epa/Corbis, Neil Marchand/Liewig Media
Sports/Corbis; p.22 sorendls/istockphoto, Myspace/Splash News,
Chromatika Multimedia/istockphoto; p.23 Trevor Hunt/
istockphoto(2), Rick Maiman/AP, AP Photo/Seth Wenig/Press
Association Images, Debbie Egan-Chin/NY Daily News via Getty
Images; p.24 Radius Images/Corbis; p.26 James Robinson/Solo
Syndication; p.27 OUP/Gareth Boden; p.28 Stephen Walls/Getty
Images, H. Armstrong Roberts/ClassicStock/Corbis; p.30 Bill Varie/
Somos Images/Corbis, 13/Noel Hendrickson/Ocean/Corbis,
Westend61/Getty Images, Karoly Arvai/Reuters; p.31 Peter Firus/
istockphoto, Steve Wisbauer/Stockbyte/Getty Images, Jon
Nicholson/Getty Images, Action Press/Rex Features, Daniel
Karmann/epa/Corbis Wire; p.32 Fuse/Getty, Vladimir Maravic/
istockphoto; p.33 Jerry Marks Production/AGE fotostock; p.34
Rick Barrentine/Comet/Corbis, robinimages2013/shutterstock,
Blend Images - JGI/Tom Grill/Getty Images, Ocean/Corbis; p.35
DreamPictures/Riser/Getty, Beau Lark/Corbis; p.36 Hill Street
Studios/Harmik Nazarian/Blend Images/Getty Images, WIN-
Initiative/Getty Images; p.37 B2M Productions/Photodisc/Getty
Images, Hola Images/Getty Images, Dougal Waters/Photodisc/
Getty Images; p.38 Sean Curtin/by kind permission of Palina
Yanachkina and the Quaid family, Ingmar Wesemann/Getty
Images; p.39 Sean Curtin/by kind permission of Palina
Yanachkina and the Quaid family(3), pop_jop/istockphoto, OUP/
Gareth Boden, Burazin/Getty images; p.41 Hill Creek Pictures/
UpperCut Images/Getty Images, Image Source/Getty Images; p.42
OUP/Gareth Boden; p.43 Xiaoyang Liu/Flirt/Corbis, Keith
Mcgregor/Digital Vision/Getty Images, Jose Fuste Raga/Terra/
Corbis; p.44 Andreas Kindler/Getty Images, Simon Wilkinson/
Getty Images, jan kranendonk/istockphoto; p.45 Thomas Fricke/
Design Pics/Corbis, Jon Feingersh/Blend Images/Alamy, maeroris/
istockphoto, Maskot/Corbis, Mark Scoggins/Getty Images,
Juanmonino/istockphoto; p.46 Muir Vidler/The Times/NI
Syndication, Richard Newstead/Getty Images; p.47 Muir Vidler/
The Times/NI Syndication(4); p.49 AP Photo/U.S. Postal Service,
Yuriko Nakao/Reuters/Corbis, Helen Sessions/Alamy, Richard
Cummins/Alamy, Gavin Hellier/Getty Images, Stuart Black/Robert
Harding World Imagery/Corbis, Julie Dermansky/Corbis; p.50
Stephen Simpson/Getty Images, Cory Ziskind; p.51 Historic Map
Works LLC/Getty Images, Bettmann/Corbis; p.52 Vicky Kasal/
Photodisc/Getty Images, Michael Poliza/Getty Images, Martin

Puddy/Asia Images/Getty Images, Patrice Hauser/Getty Images,
TMI/Alamy, Khaled Desouki/AFP/Getty Images; p.54 Fotoluminate
LLC/shutterstock.com, The Biltmore Company; p.55 Remi
BENALI/Gamma-Rapho via Getty Images, Peter Steiner/Alamy;
p.56 Nigel Dobinson/SSPL/Getty Images, Ian Shaw/Alamy, Ocean/
Corbis; p.57 Mika/Comet/Corbis; p.58 Adam Pretty/Stone/Getty
Images; p.59 Adam Pretty/Stone/Getty Images, Stockbyte/Getty
Images, Ryan McVay/Photodisc/Getty Images; p.60 Jupiterimages/
Comstock Images/Getty Images; p.61 Ben Pruchnie/Getty Images,
Jamie Farrant/istockphoto; p.62 Jude Edginton(2); p.63 Jude
Edginton(2), Image Source/Corbis, millionhope/istockphoto; p.65
Chris Whitehead/Digital Vision/Getty Images, Stockbyte/Getty
Images; p.66 Bettmann/Corbis(2), Bazmark Films/The Kobal
Collection, Lebrecht Music and Arts Photo Library/Alamy, DNY59/
istockphoto; p.69 ryan burke/istockphoto, Stephen Shugerman/
Getty Images, Bettmann/Corbis, Ben Molyneux/Alamy, AF archive/
Alamy, Alan Crawford/istockphoto; p.73 altrendo images/Getty
Images, Darryl Leniuk/Getty Images; p.74 Edward Grajeda/
istockphoto, Eric Risberg/AP, SSPL/Getty Images; p.75 Jim Snyder/
Getty Image, Rex/Stuart Hughes; p.76 CCI Archives/SPL, bobo/
Alamy, SSPL/Getty Images, Sheila Terry/SPL, marc Arundale/
Alamy, Klaus Tiedge/Fancy/Corbis, Lawrence Manning/Spirit/
Corbis, TommL/istockphoto; p.78 Blue Jean Images/Collage/
Corbis, PhotoAlto/Michele Constantini/Getty Images, Adrian
Weinbrecht/Cultura/Getty Images, Image_Source/istockphoto,
LWA/Riser/Getty Images, Rex/Patrick Barth, ImageZoo/Corbis;
p.79 OUP/Gareth Boden(2), Philip Barker/istockphoto, David J.
Green - lifestyle 2/Alamy; p.80 Tom Croft(3); p.81 Clerkenwell/the
Agency Collection/Getty Images; p.82 Photographs ©Twenty
Twenty Television 2009(2), red_frog/istockphoto, Joanne Green/
istockphoto; p.83 Photographs ©Twenty Twenty Television 2009;
p.84 Alo Ceballos/GC Images/Getty Images, Steve Vas/Featureflash/
shutterstock.com; p.85 OUP/Gareth Boden; p.86 Gyro
Photography/amanaimagesRF/Getty Images, Hulton Archive/
Getty Images; p.87 Bettmann/Corbis, Bruno Vincent/Getty
Images, Photograph By Brian Aris/Camera Press London, Kevin
Winter/Getty Images; p.88 Andrey Kekyalyaynen/Alamy; p.89
Rosemarie Gearhart/the Agency Collection/Getty Images, John
Slater/StockImage/Getty Images, Peter Dazeley/Photographer's
Choice RF/Getty Images, Jeff Morgan 05/Alamy; p.90 Christine
Schneider/Corbis; p.91 Sigrid Olsson/PhotoAlto/Corbis; p.92
Ruslan Kokarev/istockphoto, Chanyut Sribua-rawd/istockphoto,
Lynn Koenig/Flickr/Getty Images, MM Productions/Corbis, Marcy
Maloy/Photodisc/Getty Images, Sergey Kulikov/istockphoto; p.93
E. Audras/Onoky/Corbis, Ocean/Corbis, scibak/istockphoto;
Cosmonaut Creative Media, LLC/Vetta/Getty Images; p.94 OUP/
Corbis; p.95 Stocktrek Images/Getty Images, Mark Garlick/SPL,
NOAO/AURA/NSF/SPL, Royal Observatory, Edinburgh/AAO/SPL,
Oliver Beatson Wikipedia released on Public Domain licence,
2009; p.96 Floortje/istockphoto; p.97 Tom Croft(6); p.100 Matelly/
Getty Images; p.101 Galiptynutz/shutterstock, Doug Raphael/
shutterstock; p.104 Norbert Schaefer/Corbis; p.105 amana
productions inc/Getty Images, Jill Fromer/Photodisc/Getty Images;
p.106 EdgeOfReason/shutterstock, Corbis, Kevin Ferguson/
Ferguson/Newscom; p.107 Ted Spiegel/Corbis, Rex/Startraks
Photo; p.108 OUP/Goodshoot, Tribalium/shutterstock; p.110 Rex/
Courtesy Everett Collection; p.111 CJG - Lifestyle/Alamy; p.112
Andrew Rich/Getty Images, Doug Armand/Photographer's Choice
RF/Getty Images; p.113 Erik Dreyer/Getty Images; p.147 Chev
Wilkinson/Cultura/Getty Images, Philip Lee Harvey/cultura/
Corbis; p.148 Clerkenwell/the Agency Collection/Getty Images,
Jon Kopaloff/FilmMagic/Getty Images; p.149 Chev Wilkinson/
Cultura/Getty Images, Philip Lee Harvey/cultura/Corbis; p.150
Clerkenwell/the Agency Collection/Getty Images, Jon Kopaloff/
FilmMagic/Getty Images; p.151 Seth Wenig/AP; p.152 Nico
Hermann/Getty Images; p.153 Rex/David McHugh.